# ADVANCE PRAISE FOR *THE NEW BETTER OFF*

"Unabashed, provocative, and deeply soulful, Courtney Martin is the prophet you didn't know you were seeking. In *The New Better Off,* she offers a blueprint for living that's radically different from the one you grew up with. Whether or not you agree with all its details, its spirit will inspire you to examine your life—and if you don't like what you find there, give you the courage to rebuild."

— Susan Cain, co-founder of Quiet Revolution and *New York Times* bestselling author of *Quiet: The Power of Introverts in a World That Can't Stop Talking*

"We all know that money can't buy peace, kindness or honesty—in the Age of Trump, what could be more clear? Courtney Martin is a practical and lyrical explorer in showing us how money as the only measure of "better off" has failed us, and what is needed to create a new American Dream for us and the next generation. Never has there been a more timely and livable book."

— Gloria Steinem

"I've been waiting for someone to articulate what the brilliant Courtney Martin has done in *The New Better Off.* The book poses a question that I believe is critical to our families, our culture, our nation: What does it mean and who gets to determine what a good life, a safe life, a happy life and generous life looks like? And how did we get to this place where to be well-off means to be constantly busy and tired and distracted, disconnected from our families and communities? I hope everyone reads this book and examines what matters most in their lives, and in the life of our society."

— Elizabeth Lesser, author of *Marrow* and *Broken Open,* and cofounder of Omega Institute

"*The New Better Off* is essential to understanding how to have a better life and a new and better you. Too many of us are sick and tired of the 9-5 grind, of having to fall in line, of seeing success as a purely individual pursuit; Martin shows that there is another way."

— Richard Florida, author of *Rise of the Creative Class*

"In times of great disruption we are forced to question everything. Courtney Martin has taken this to heart and challenges us to reassess, rethink and reinvent the very notion of what a 'good life' might be. *The New Better Off* is an invaluable source of insight and inspiration for those wishing to embark on one of post consumer society's most important projects."

— Tim Brown, CEO of IDEO and author of *Change By Design*

"When a moment and a voice align perfectly, you get a book like *The New Better Off.* Courtney Martin reimagines success and purpose in ways counterintuitive and wise. This is our future speaking the language of our ancestors. Listen closely."

—Eric Liu, founder and CEO, Citizen University

"This book encapsulates a huge idea: That our dreams of individual success are in urgent need of an upgrade. Courtney Martin makes the case with extraordinary eloquence anchored in beautiful personal stories. If you're depressed about the current state of America, she offers a powerful antidote."

—Chris Anderson, CEO of TED

"Courtney Martin, who's less than half my age, has been a mentor to me for nearly a decade. In 2008, when her second book came out, I called her 'one of our most insightful culture critics and finest young writers.' With *The New Better Off,* I'm doubling down on that praise. Telling compelling real-life stories backed by carefully researched facts—all of it couched in her beautifully readable prose—Martin reframes what it means to live a good life in ways that offer her generation and mine much-needed inspiration and practical guidance. "

—Parker J. Palmer, author of *Let Your Life Speak,*
*A Hidden Wholeness,* and *Healing the Heart of Democracy*

the new better off

# the new better off

---

## REINVENTING THE AMERICAN DREAM

---

# Courtney E. Martin

SEAL PRESS

Seal Press
An imprint of Perseus Books, a division of PBG Publishing, LLC,
a subsidiary of Hachette Book Group, Inc.
1700 Fourth Street
Berkeley, California
sealpress.com

Library of Congress Cataloging-in-Publication Data

Martin, Courtney E., author.
LCCN 2016006252 | ISBN 9781580055796 (hardback)
    United States—Social conditions—21st century. | United States—Economic conditions—
    21st century. | United States—Civilization—21st century. | BISAC: SOCIAL SCIENCE
    / Popular Culture. | BUSINESS & ECONOMICS / Motivational. | BUSINESS &
    ECONOMICS / Careers / General.
LCC HN59.2 .M377 2016 | DDC 306.0973—dc23

10 9 8 7 6 5 4 3 2 1

Cover design by Faceout Studios, Jeff Miller
Interior design by Domini Dragoone and Tabitha Lahr
Printed in the United States of America
Distributed by Publishers Group West

*To Johnny C., the exuberant architect of my New Better Off. Without you, this book, not to mention my outrageously beautiful life, would not exist.*

# ALSO BY COURTNEY E. MARTIN

*Project Rebirth* with Dr. Robin Stern

*Do It Anyway*

*Click* with J. Courtney Sullivan

*The Naked Truth* with Marvelyn Brown

*Perfect Girls, Starving Daughters*

# contents

# introduction

For the first time in history, nearly two-thirds of Americans do not believe that the next generation will be "better off" than their parents are—an opinion shared by men and women, rich and poor alike.[1]

To some, that may sound sad. To me, it sounds like a provocation. Better off? Based on whose standards?

To be sure, people need jobs. They need housing. They need healthcare. When these basic needs aren't met—and for too many Americans they aren't—we are legitimately *not* better off.

But for many of us, the concept of "better off" is far more abstract than just putting food on the table. Is "better off" a fancy job title, a bank account with more zeros, a manicured lawn? It turns out that none of those things automatically makes you safe or happy, as evidenced by the Great Recession, when the ground underneath so many Americans' feet shifted overnight. And, what's more, some of the things we have historically associated with success actually endanger your health. Underneath the appearance of uplift, a complex story weighs us down. This could play out in any number of ways, like when people decide to erase their ethnic last names; or they set aside authentic—albeit nontraditional—career ambitions in favor of more lucrative paths; or when a father knows his colleagues better than he does his own kids; or a mother leans in so hard she falls flat on her face. Pressure and debt, missed get-togethers, living for the weekends, living someone else's dream. "Better off," left uninterrogated, can be fucking dangerous.

For me, this is not just a societally important matter, but one with personal significance. I was just minding my own business—sweating on subway platforms at 2:00 AM and getting weepy over rejection emails from editors and losing track of time while lying on blankets with dear friends in Brooklyn's Prospect Park and dreaming about the person I would one day be, and then—all of a sudden—I *was* that person. Otherwise known as an adult. I had a husband (something I never thought I'd have). I had a daughter (something I always thought I'd have). I had a job. Well, actually, a lot of jobs. I had a car payment. I had no small amount of frustration when the kid next door played his music too loud on a weeknight (to be fair, it was pretty awful music).

And I had a problem. It wasn't that I didn't want to become a responsible person. I've always been sort of an old soul—watching *Oprah* with a bag of Ruffles potato chips after middle school so I could try on all the grown-up emotions of her guests. Commitment doesn't send me scurrying like it does some people. I like feeling needed. I like being accountable. I believe in sensible shoes.

The problem was that I didn't want to become an adult if it meant falling in line. I didn't want to get golden handcuffs or check my email every two seconds because I was so "important." I didn't want to laugh with my girlfriends over wine at book group about how sexless my marriage was—or stay married for the kids. I didn't want to let myself off the hook because activism is for young people, or utter that familiar, ugly phrase: "Do as I say, not as I do." I didn't want to stop having euphoric experiences or long, wandering philosophical conversations. I didn't want to get a good job, a house with a white picket fence, have 2.5 kids, and then just . . . go . . . to . . . sleep.

And as it turned out, the white picket fence was beyond my reach anyway—as it is beyond the reach of so many people. When the economy plummeted in 2007, it robbed so many Americans, especially the young, of some of the experiences that—up until that point—were widely considered the cornerstones of a successful adult life. Suddenly, owning a home and having a nine-to-five job were stripped of their former glimmer, revealed to be more complicated and maybe even less satisfying than we'd been told. People put off getting married, in part, because they felt like they were supposed to be somebody else when they did it—somebody more financially secure, more established, more sure.

In other words, when the economy crashed, the air was let out of the overinflated ego of the so-called American Dream. I had been scared of what adulthood might do to the state of my soul; I feared chasing symbols of success rather than creating conditions for meaning and joy and justice. But—as fate would have it—the symbols were outrunning everyone.

Since then, so many people continue to reevaluate, turning away from job opportunities that are prestigious but not courageous, making families out of friends and neighbors, buying less, giving away more, sharing and renting rather than owning, reinventing rituals and ritualizing reinvention. So many people are looking compassionately and critically at their own parents' lives and choosing to do things differently, sometimes even reclaiming edifying, abandoned elements of their grandparents' lives.

When I was in my early twenties, my mom gave me a copy of Mary Catherine Bateson's *Composing a Life*. In it Bateson, the daughter of anthropologists Margaret Mead and Gregory Bateson, writes profiles of five diverse women with the goal of turning their lives inside out, showing what it really takes to put a day together when you are a passionate person with only twenty-four hours. I devoured it, writing in the margins and putting sticky notes in places where Bateson took my breath away. And then all of my girlfriends read it, each one passing it on to the next.

As I look back, I realize that it took such hold of us because it was the only book we'd ever encountered that described the nitty-gritty of real, somewhat contemporary lives (at that point, 2002, the portraits were over a decade old). To these women, even structural problems—like the sexist workplace—weren't inevitably crushing, but fodder for subterfuge and rebellion. And *Composing a Life* was written from a place of deep delight in the capacity of ordinary people to pursue meaning and joy in challenging circumstances. In Bateson's telling, we are made even more determined, even more creative by those kinds of circumstances. The book treats "composing a life" as a creative, ongoing opportunity, not a test to be passed. Bateson writes:

> *I believe that our aesthetic sense, whether in works of art or in lives, has overfocused on the stubborn struggle toward a single goal rather than on the fluid, the protean, the improvisatory. We see achievement as purposeful and monolithic, like the sculpting of a massive tree trunk that has first to be brought from the forest and then shaped by long labor to assert the artist's vision, rather than something crafted from odds and ends, like a patchwork quilt, and lovingly used to warm different nights and different bodies.*

The phrase "new better off" is the shorthand I've created for this bourgeoning shift in Americans' ideas about the good life. It's the patchwork quilt version of the American Dream, not the (phallic) sculpture reaching high into the sky. It's about our quest to use our current precariousness as the inspiration to return to some of the most basic, "beginner's mind" questions: *What is enough money? How do we want to spend our finite energy and attention? What makes us feel accountable and witnessed?* It's about creating a life you can be genuinely proud of, an "examined life" (in the words of dead Greek guys), a life that you are challenged by, a life that makes you giddy, that sometimes surprises you, a life that you love.

It's leaving a job that pays well but makes you feel like a cog for a freelance life that makes you feel like a creator—the financial highs and lows be damned. It's sharing a car with a few friends and learning how to repair your favorite pair of jeans. It's moving in with your grandmother because she needs someone to reach the highest shelf in the kitchen and you need someone who helps you keep our turbulent times in perspective. It's putting your cell phone in a drawer on Saturday afternoon and having the best conversation of your life that night. It's starting a group for new dads where you admit how powerful and confusing it is to raise a tiny human.

But lest I fall into the same trap of all those who idealize bootstraps, the New Better Off mentality is not solely about the individual. It's also about the collective. Playwright Tony Kushner writes: "The smallest indivisible human unit is two people, not one; one is a fiction. From such nets of souls societies, the social world, human life springs."[2]

So, yes, this book is about the brave individual choices people are making, but it's also about the movements, formal and informal, that are coalescing around the New Better Off mindset—about how people are reinventing the social safety net, and reforming the laws that have prevented us from sharing and reclaiming communal rituals. A surprising coalition of people—from labor organizers to start-up entrepreneurs to legislators—are coming together to push for portable health benefits. A small but growing group of lawyers are agitating for laws that make it easier to start co-op businesses and create communally owned homes. All over the country groups of young people who are grieving the loss of parents are gathering for dinner, to talk about grief as well as about what is being born in them through their loss. Essentially, this book's message can be conveyed in one phrase: community is everything.

The New Better Off mindset compels you to be wise, to be vulnerable enough to admit that you have limitations, and to surround yourself with people who will take care of you and vice versa. But it's not just about need. It's also about fun—unscripted relationships that evolve over years and years; spontaneous, gut-busting laughter; bread and dogma broken with debates around a dinner table. Communities are joy. There's an almost giddy energy when something as simple as a book club gathers in someone's living room. Sure, wine flows as people are discussing the text, but it's not just that; they're also following the arc of one another's lives. One of the things that has thrilled me to no end while working on this book is meeting so many impatient, innovative people who are actively figuring out how to reclaim community.

We may be artists of our own lives, as Bateson tells it, but we are not self-made men and women. We live in communities, and beyond that, we live in polities. Part of the New Better Off mindset is also about structural transformation. Systems thinkers and agitators and designers are asking: what would an America look like where all people's basic needs are met—where more people have the luxury of making choices about the kind of work they do, the kind of homes they live in, the kinds of families they create?

To be sure, the "creating a beautiful life" portion of the New Better Off mindset is about our personal choices, but it's also about the neighborhood and city and state and nation that we live in, and what their policies say about our rights and responsibilities. One of the sicknesses of privilege is the mistaken belief that we are all islands—when really we are archipelagoes. Technology that makes it easier for young, white guys to order a tuna melt is not an example of living the New Better Off life; it's just a business venture. But technology that makes it easier for everyone to find affordable, high-quality healthcare? *That* is the New Better Off.

We don't create this little life in a finite moment in time. We create our lives informed by our parents and our grandparents and all the decisions they made in the America (or the Mexico or the Iran or the Ethiopia) that *they* came of age in. Or, as author Paul Elie puts it, "We enter the story in the middle."[3] In this manner, while the New Better Off mentality is about the continuous exploration of what is in front of us, it's also fascination and sober reckoning with what lies behind us. Who has lived in these neighborhoods? Who has worshipped in these halls? What worked about the way they built community? Can it be recaptured, maybe even made more effective with modern tools or notions? What was alienating and even discriminatory in these communities? Are there opportunities for reconciliation?

We used to answer these questions within formal institutions—churches, rotary clubs, Junior Leagues, unions—but many of these groups have lost the centrifugal pull they once enjoyed. Many of the authorities we used to rely on to guide us toward the good life no longer exist. Many of the straightforward paths have been bulldozed, or are overgrown with weeds. Many of the institutions have crumbled, destroyed by their own stubborn insistence on doing things as they've always been done. The safety net has been torn—and the ladder to success has fallen down.

The demographic makeup of this country is shifting in profound ways. Women now constitute a full half of the professional workforce. By 2044, whites—the majority source of our most dominant and toxic narratives about achievement—will have become a racial minority.[4] And the percentage of Americans who don't identify with any particular religion has grown sharply in recent years.[5] The demography "rule book" is written in the language of another era.

If you feel like a failure, it might be that you're considering yourself against standards that just don't hold water anymore. Sure, many consider it a sign of success to own a home, but that yardstick got its best traction when the average middle-class *man*'s salary could support an entire family—something we all know no longer applies. The good news is that you might just be a success based on New Better Off standards, which perhaps you've had a hard time articulating but have been bravely grappling toward. Maybe you're a mediocre earner but a masterful father. Or maybe you can't afford your dream home but you throw legendary neighborhood parties.

Starting in 2004 I set out to reinvigorate our language around the concept of "success." I wanted to paint a more accurate picture of the way creative, principled, scrappy people are *actually* living. And the truth is that we're figuring it out as we go along. This book is my attempt to figure it out next to you—along with other kind and generous and interesting people you'd probably really like to have a conversation with. People like Andreina, who described her magic power of getting old people to dance at weddings. Or Brian, who recalled a sleepless night trying to decide whether to take a job that would set him up financially but bankrupt him spiritually. Chris shared the joy of his morning routine with his tiny, beautiful son. Adam showed me how to get a fedora for free. Deanna taught me that getting married isn't the same as being witnessed. Ruthie convinced me that Benjamin Franklin really is the shit.

There's lots of me in here, too. I'm good material—a thirty-five-year-old trying to compose a life with work that I love; a two-year-old daughter, Maya, whom I'm obsessed with; and an ambitious, brave, quirky partner, John, whom I adore. We're luckier than most in some ways: we live in a cohousing community, which you'll hear a lot about, and we're both from white, middle-class backgrounds in the Midwest with plenty of social support and parents who love us bountifully. We're also unlucky in other ways. We don't live near any of those parents. We both have economically volatile freelance careers. We haven't figured out how to live ethically in a gentrifying neighborhood, or to create spiritual structure in our chaotic weeks. I feel too busy most of the time. These days, my daughter frequently stretches her perfect, pudgy hands toward me, looks up, and asks, "Momma, hold you?" She means hold *me*, but I'm grateful for the unintended reminder to take care of myself.

I'm omnivorously interested in anthropology, philosophy, psychology, and sociology, so you'll find lots of that stuff in here, too. I've gotten a lot of inspiration from the podcast series *Invisibilia*, which I think does a beautiful job of taking daunting topics, like fear and computers, and exploring them via little tributaries of interestingness. And just as *Invisibilia* doesn't claim to be comprehensive, nor do I; I couldn't possibly be with a subject this vast. Still, I've made a real attempt to ground the newness that I'm describing in historical context. It's hard to know where we're going, I figure, if we don't know where we've been. I've also attempted to contextualize the individual lives and decisions I profile within larger economic systems.

The book is not prescriptive—composing the New Better Off lifestyle is an improvisatory act, and the elements you're working with are unique to you. But after talking to all of these thoughtful people, and reading all of this interesting research, I've got some ideas about what matters most.

I think the best jobs aren't those with the highest status in the eyes of your snobby aunt but those that light you up. I think men are happier when they take responsibility for and find the nourishment of caretaking. I think that depending on your nuclear family to meet all of your needs is unhealthy, as is living on an airplane, treating your cell phone like an appendage, and neglecting to have big, meaningful parties at moments of profound transition. You'll have to decide if I'm right (spoiler alert: I am), and then figure out how to fit it all together in "your one wild and precious life," as the goddess, badass, and poet Mary Oliver says.

What I'm finding, what you'll find—I hope—is that being mature doesn't mean being numb. To be sure, living in America, at this unequal, messy moment, can break your heart—but it doesn't have to break your spirit. Living in America is so interesting, so fertile, so up-for-grabs. It's also disintegrating and reconstituting and recalibrating. It's up to us to make lives that we can be proud of—and to make communities and systems and policies to cradle those lives. It's up to us to reject tired narratives about success, instead authoring new ones that are less about exceptional heroes and more about creative communities. It's up to us to reclaim the best of what previous generations did that made this country so unique and so beautiful— as well as to own up to the destructive legacies that we're a part of, to expose them to the light, and to figure out how to fix them. It's up to us to be humble, to be brave, to be accountable to our own dreams, no one else. It's up to us to be iconoclastic, to be together, to stay awake.

# *how* do you want to be?

## THINKING DIFFERENTLY
## ABOUT VOCATION

Many of us grew up being told that getting a good job
is about pinpointing a passion and sticking to it. There's a whole
industry devoted to this outdated methodology of "career development"; freaked-out twentysomethings sit in front of glowing screens
and peck away at "career cluster surveys" to try to unlock the mystery
of what they should do with the rest of their lives. In the Old Better
Off mentality, profession is seen as a puzzle to be solved, once and
only once.

Though the old framing—find a secure job that doesn't bore
you to death and do it until you're sixty-five—is well-intentioned, it's
ultimately unhelpful in a time when the "what" of almost everything
is melting down, mixing together, and being reconstituted in newfangled forms.

Sure, there are still lawyers and teachers, but where and how these people work are changing all the time. You might be trained as a lawyer but spend your days advising reproductive-justice organizations on bioethics, or you may be a teacher who coaches other educators on creating emotionally intelligent, culturally aware urban schools. People who work in a variety of fields—called "silo-busters" by anthropologist-turned-business-journalist Gillian Tett—used to be thought of as flighty for jumping around, but now they're described as having "job vitality." They're able to translate between different departments, bring specialized knowledge or practices from one field to the other, and consistently offer the critical perspective of the outsider looking in.[1]

Jobs are dying (RIP travel agents) and being born (hello, digital risk officer) all the time. The latest studies suggest that the average person has been with his or her current job for just 4.6 years.[2] And though the elite media often make it sound like people change jobs more frequently by choice—operating with a "move on" mentality— in fact those decisions are guided by a variety of factors, most of them beyond workers' control, including technological advancements, the declining power of unions, and increased international trade.[3] Anya Kamenetz writes in *Fast Company*: "This decline in average job tenure is bigger than any economic cycle, bigger than any particular industry, bigger than differences in education levels, and bigger than differences in gender."[4]

So if you can't count on one job or one field, what can you count on?

You can count on your own curiosity, about both your gifts and your interests. We need to stop asking kids, "What do you want to be when you grow up?" and start asking them *"How* do you want to be when you grow up?" You're much safer cultivating a healthy sense of detachment from the details of where you work and what you work on, instead pursuing skills that excite you and learning things that interest you. When you're intimately familiar with how you see, solve, organize, empower, communicate, build, tear down, evaluate, and create, you'll know how to be effective no matter what setting you find yourself in.

Sound complicated? It is. It would be way easier to inherit the family business, to do what your mother or father did, to think of your job as a paycheck and retirement security. But we don't live in that world anymore. At least most of us don't. For too long politicians and career counselors have described the professional path to the American Dream as a ladder stretching into the sky, and the only way to succeed is to climb higher than everyone else. Bullshit, I say. It's not bootstraps that we need; it's lie detectors.

It would be way simpler to respond to some pithy questions that pop up on a screen and let the computer calculate the answer on what the hell you're supposed to do with your life. But there is no computer with that kind of intelligence. The knowledge lives inside you. It lights up when you're in that moment of feeling maximally and joyfully used in the world.

## A CALLING FOR CARE

Teresa Hernandez, a Los Angeleno in her early twenties, pulls steaming macaroni and cheese out of the oven and sets it on an oven mitt on the humble kitchen table. Diedre looks expectantly at the steam as it rises; her roommate, Juan, laughs at her childlike exuberance. They're both in their seventies. They're broken. But nothing makes them happier than a visit from their *angelito*.

Teresa is their home healthcare aide (she's listed in the directory provided by the government program In-Home Supportive Services, popularly known as IHSS). Juan had filed an application and been granted a few hours of help a month, and he had selected her from the

---

• Teresa's patient's names have been changed to protect their identities.

directory. The problem was that Teresa was already booked up with other clients. But there was something about his voice when he called—she just couldn't say no over the phone. She decided to go in person.

It was a thirty-minute drive from her home in Riverside, California, to Juan and Dierdre's apartment. When she arrived, she found total disarray. "Here he was—this sweet old man who could barely stand up," she remembers. "He was trying to keep things clean, but it was really obvious that he needed help. Medicine was all over. He was only eating oatmeal because he was unable to cook anything else."

The saddest part was he was actually better off than his roommate, Dierdre, who was bedridden from a back condition. She wasn't even aware that she was eligible for the IHSS program, which is available for people with a disability who have Medi-Cal and are expected to continue longer than a year. So Juan had become her assistant, making her oatmeal alongside his in the microwave. When Teresa told Dierdre about the program, she wept. "I was sitting there thinking, 'How did I end up with a perfect stranger crying in my arms?'" Teresa admits. "But it felt good. It felt amazing, actually. I said, 'Don't cry. You should smile. I'm here. I'm going to help you.'"

There are going to be more and more people like them who need help in the coming years. According to the Administration on Aging, in 2013 there were 44.7 million people sixty-five and older; by 2060, there will be more than twice that number.[5] It is estimated that we will need 1.8 million additional home healthcare workers in the next decade to meet the demand. Caregiving, so long disparaged as "women's work" and often performed for low wages or no pay at all, just might be the boom industry of the twenty-first century.

But most home healthcare workers aren't making a living wage: the average earns about $10 an hour. In California the mean salary for home healthcare attendants, according to the Bureau of Labor Statistics, is $26,140.[6] Ai-jen Poo, labor organizer and MacArthur "genius" grant winner, argues that the "elder boom" is actually a beautiful opportunity for this country to employ millions of the most marginalized Americans, particularly women and immigrants, while caring about our elders. In *The Age of Dignity: Preparing for the Elder Boom in a Changing America*, she writes, "The demographic shift creates a moment when we can set in place a system to affirm the dignity of people at every stage of life and from every walk of life, and create millions of good jobs in the process."

Teresa, in fact, makes nothing from her work with Juan and Dierdre, as she isn't their official aide. She's helped Juan advocate with his social worker to get more than three hours of assistance a month, and has started Dierdre on the process of enrolling in Medi-Cal so she can get assistance as well. When their paperwork comes through, Teresa will introduce them to a home healthcare attendant who has more hours to spare than she does. In the meantime, she makes the drive once a week, bringing a hot dinner to share family-style, and keeping things clean and medications in order.

It's hard for Teresa to say exactly why she does it. She's not religious. "It's sad to say, but I lost my faith when I came back to the U.S.," she says.

Though Teresa was born in Los Angeles, she spent her formative years in Mexico, living with her disabled father and her older brother. In 2009 they returned to California, this time landing farther north. The transition wasn't easy. Teresa was responsible for her father's care while her brother went to school and work. Then she developed hypothyroidism. She was tired all the time, but couldn't sleep at night. Her blood pressure and cholesterol spiked. Her doctor warned that he would have to hospitalize her if she experienced any more stress.

But sometimes stress shows up on your doorstep. One day, a stranger walked right into her living room. She was frightened at first, but quickly realized that the woman was drunk and lost. When she wandered back out intending to drive away, Teresa rushed after her. "We're friends, right?" she said to the woman. "Why don't you come inside and hang out?"

The woman, totally incoherent, followed her back into the house. Teresa called the police. When they arrived, one of them asked, "How do you know this woman?"

"I don't," Teresa replied. "She just wandered in."

"Well, you likely saved this woman's life today," he said. "You're clearly someone who helps people."

Something about the way he looked at her when he said this struck Teresa like lightning. "As weird as it sounds," she explains, "that experience felt like a sign from the universe."

She got her thyroid under control and enrolled in a program to become a home healthcare attendant. And though, given the demographic shifts cited earlier, it's timely that Teresa found work caring for the elderly, the age of her clients and the structure of her work are, in a way, irrelevant. What is valuable is that Teresa realized that she's intrinsically motivated to help people, and she found a job that allows her to do just that, get paid (albeit too little), and gain a sense of satisfaction.

Teresa is not defined by being a home healthcare attendant. She is defined by being a young woman who has realized that what lights her up is the opportunity to ease others' suffering—physically and emotionally (not to mention bureaucratically). In ten years, she might be an occupational therapist or a human resources director or a retirement coach (yup, another one of those newfangled jobs that's popping up). For now, she's a home healthcare attendant with three lucky clients.

Her third client is Arnold, a man in his early seventies she spends two days a week with. They go grocery shopping, go out to eat, and take walks. Sometimes they just sit in front of the television and talk about life. Their conversations are surprisingly wide-ranging. After watching a special about teen pregnancy, for example, they talked all about the pill and the opportunities it's given women to be more in control of their fertility. Arnold tells her about his son, who lives far away, and Teresa tells Arnold about her mother, a seamstress, whom she didn't get to grow up with but now considers a role model.

Some of their conversations are about the hard stuff—losses and regrets—but some are playful and imaginative. "We joke that we're going to travel to Cuba together, now that it opened up, so he can find a wife and I can find a boyfriend," Teresa admits, giggling.

Teresa loves the work because she feels effective at it. She can hear and hold the hard stories, and values watching her clients feel lighter as they share them with her. She gets deep satisfaction from the little things—making sure client medication is in order for the week, or seeing the sunlight on their faces when she coaxes them outside. Mostly, it just feels right. Teresa sums it up: "If you're good to somebody, somebody else is going to be good to you. That's my belief."

## BEYOND COLLARS AND LADDERS

For twentieth-century Americans, the telltale sign that sons or daughters have transcended the status of their parents—i.e., become "better off"—is when blue collars get traded for white ones. But studies show that Americans have a comparably lower chance of social mobility than do people from other middle- to high-income countries.[7] And yet, we have the strongest belief in the magical properties of meritocracy.[8]

The thing is, we're not just delusional about how sticky economic class is from generation to generation; we also have a double consciousness regarding this kind of transcendence. We lionize the kid who is the first in his family to graduate from college and sport a suit to work, and yet we romanticize the seemingly simpler times when a man could count on his job, thanks to unions, and leave work behind when he clocked out.

Think of almost every presidential candidate in the last decade who has proudly spoken of his father's calloused hands and dogged work ethic; the implication is that the candidate is worthy of your vote because he bootstrapped his way up the economic ladder. That he frames his story this way is supposed to be a comfort to the voter, offering reassurance that we live in a country where this can still happen. But what of the father? What did the son escape, exactly? And why is that escape ennobled?

The trusty old collar-color metaphor has some grounding in reality—factory workers preferred darker colors (blue) that better hid the grime of their toil, while office workers, having the luxury of not worrying about such stains, could wear white shirts if they wanted to. But the false dichotomy between intellectual and physical work was always reductive. It fanned the flames of class tension and resulted in a strange and dispiriting state where some people feel looked down on and most people feel misunderstood.

Today, blue-collar—i.e., manual labor—jobs are fewer and farther between, and don't come with the security they used to; many children of elevator repairmen or transportation inspectors would be thrilled to find a job that resembled their parents'—and lucky too. Over the past three decades, the U.S. economy has added just 1 million manufacturing jobs, as compared to 28 million routine service jobs (sometimes called "pink-collar" jobs) and 23 million knowledge, professional, and creative jobs.[9]

White-collar work, long considered the promised land for the American striver, is turning out to be a bit of a mirage. Bigger earnings don't always translate into a better life, as evidenced by the preponderance of miserable lawyers, doctors, sales managers, and investment bankers. Recent studies indicate that the occupations with the highest rates of depression are not correlated with low salaries, but are those that "require frequent or difficult interactions with the public or clients, and have high levels of stress and low levels of physical activity." Top of the list? Public transit, real estate, social work, manufacturing, personal services, legal services, and publishing—jobs with a wide range of earning potential, and many considered white-collar.[10]

Jobs classified as blue-collar have been underrated in terms of their cognitive value. Mike Rose, author of *The Mind at Work: Valuing the Intelligence of the American Worker*, writes: "I grew up a witness to the intelligence of the waitress in motion, the reflective welder, the strategy of the guy on the assembly line. This then is something I know: the thought it takes to do physical work."

In other words, the jobs we've historically described as "skilled or unskilled manual labor" often require strategic and creative thinking. In addition, we're beginning to acknowledge that all people crave a mix of physical and intellectual work. The popularity of "maker culture"—basically, people who are excited to be making things with their hands again—indicates that we're starting to rebalance our ideas about the relationship between thinking and doing. Matthew B. Crawford, think-tanker-turned-motorcycle-repairman and author of *Shop Class as Soulcraft: An Inquiry into the Value of Work*, writes, "Out of the current confusion of ideals and confounding of career hopes, a calm recognition may yet emerge that productive labor is the foundation of all prosperity."[11]

Plus, sitting in front of a computer all day is increasingly equated with health dangers on a par with smoking. Researchers recently found that women who reported significant sedentary time were more likely to die of cardiovascular disease, coronary heart disease, and cancer—even if they exercised regularly.[12]

As the tectonic plates of work shift under our feet, there's a palpable sense of professional insecurity. We can't expect to land a job and keep it for decades, as our parents and grandparents might have. Professions are morphing constantly, so it's unwise to craft your whole identity around just one. Facing today's job market realities, more and more men are bravely evolving beyond traditional ideals of professional masculinity and becoming flight attendants, nurses, and social workers.[13] While that kind of crossover can be daunting, it can also be liberating; in a moment when we don't have as much to lose, we get the opportunity to focus on what really matters: status, or a reliable paycheck?

Most of us want work that demands something of our minds *and* our bodies. We want to avoid unnecessary bureaucracy and long, unpredictable hours. We want to feel that our gifts—whatever weird and wonderful things those might be—are put to good use. We want to wake up in the morning and feel not just that there's a place to direct our energy toward, but also that that place dignifies us, even if it doesn't define us. We want to work alongside other people who see and celebrate our gifts, people who teach us things, people who want to make cool shit with us, people who acknowledge that we're not just workers, but also caretakers and friends, sons and daughters, fathers and mothers, people who are kind and mostly good.

When I was pregnant, my belly just beginning to swell, I decided to try Zumba. Within just a few minutes of shaking my booty in time with the instructor, Andreina Febres-Cordero, I knew I was in the presence of someone doing what she was meant to do. "If it's your first time, don't worry about getting all the moves," she shouted. "Just keep moving." She clearly made all students feel welcome. An old, white guy with a beer belly danced to Shakira un-self-consciously in the back. A woman who looked to be bald from chemotherapy softly stepped near the front. Another woman wearing jazz shoes, her long, black hair coming loose from the bun on her head, leapt and slapped the floor, totally offbeat but somehow freed up to express herself, inspired by Andreina's unconditionally loving presence and patient smile.

I Zumbaed all through my pregnancy, even dancing the day I

went into labor. That class became an oasis for me. From time to time Andreina would look over at me and give a little shake of her head to indicate that a particular move was a no-no for me and my growing belly. When the world seemed heavy with profound unknowns, I would waddle into her class and suddenly feel lighter, freer. Sometimes I would get emotional, tearing up over just the relief of moving my body and getting out of my head, hearing the loud thump of music, being in the safe haven that Andreina had built.

Andreina, a Venezuelan in her late thirties, wasn't always a Zumba instructor. For five years, she'd done the traditional office grind for marketing agencies. Her specialty was advising companies on how to reach the Hispanic market in the U.S. She would recommend what media buys they should make based on her understanding of what television and radio shows were hot—an easy call for someone who keeps her finger on the pulse.

She liked her job, but it was increasingly stressful; she continually got promotions and her workload increased. She really wanted to have a baby and was having a hell of a time getting pregnant and staying pregnant. After multiple miscarriages, she went to her doctor and begged for answers.

"There's nothing wrong with your body," he said. "You're simply too stressed-out."

She was faced with a decision. As a young immigrant from a traditional Venezuelan family, she'd never seen anyone with a freelance lifestyle; her mother had stayed at home with the kids and her father worked a nine-to-five office job. She'd come to the United States in 1999, determined to make something of herself, to prove to her family back home that she could cut it. The idea of things falling apart after so many years of hard work was devastating to her. On the other hand, she knew she wanted a child, and it didn't seem like pregnancy was going to happen if she continued apace. She had two degrees—one in business, the other in photography. She was confident in her capacity to connect with people and find interesting opportunities. There had to be a way. A different way.

She quit in May. By June, she was pregnant. By December, she was getting calls from companies asking her to advise them on the Hispanic market in a consulting capacity.

That first leap of faith became not just an isolated act of courage, but a way of life. When her sister-in-law, a professional dancer was pursuing certification to teach Zumba, she invited Andreina along. Though she'd only taken a couple of classes, she figured, why not? She loved dancing. She loved making other people dance; she'd even drag aunties onto the dance floor at weddings. It sounded fun. In 2009, she became a certified Zumba instructor, and now teaches at Flying Studios in Oakland, California, a few times a week.

Being a Zumba instructor became one more way for Andreina to express her gift; her get-out-and-dance spirit burns brightly in her classes, where she creates community out of whatever motley crew joins in. She could have been a doctor or a janitor or a zoologist. She happened to be a photographer and a Zumba instructor and a marketing consultant. But wherever she landed, she would have shown up with a particular talent for creating community by putting people at ease. When she's in that mode, it's not only evident to those around her—she feels it, too. It's alchemical: "When I'm doing what I love, I sweat," she explains. "It sounds funny to say, but it's true. Whether I'm taking pictures or dancing or helping people in Peru, I'm sweating and I just feel like, I want to stay here forever."

## MOMMAS, DON'T LET YOUR BABIES GROW UP TO BE LAWYERS

So many of the jobs that were once considered bona fide—the careers your parents would brag about to their neighbors and friends—have become impractical. In fact, two of the most popular paths for smart kids (many of whom are really confused about what they want to do)—law school and graduate school, in general—have become canaries in the coal mine.

According to the American Bar Association, in 2014 total enrollment in law school fell to 119,775, down nearly 18.5 percent from its 2010 historic high of 147,525.[14] Why? Because those really smart, really confused kids have caught on to the fact that law degrees are both expensive (the average debt is $122,158 for private school graduates and $84,600 for public school graduates) and don't guarantee meaningful employment. In 2013, 11.2 percent of law school graduates were still unemployed nine months after graduation. That's compared to 10.9 percent of college graduates overall.[15]

Law is a field notorious for "leaky pipeline" issues. For example, women don't make it to leadership positions in significant numbers because the profession is still inhospitable to working parents. And as if that weren't enough to deter you, your parents' bragging might no longer be received so well; according to the latest Pew Research Center survey on professional public esteem, lawyers were rated rock-bottom.[16]

Many people have also soured on going into academia. Once seen as the go-to route for intellectual types, the market is simply too oversaturated, the pay too low, and the path to advancement simultaneously rigid and unpredictable. According to Humanities Indicators, for example, job ads for the majority of the humanities peaked in the 2007–2008 academic year. As of the most recent reports from each society, the number of positions advertised was at least 30 percent lower in just about every discipline.[17]

Patrick Iber, a visiting lecturer in history at the University of California, Berkeley, put a very human face on this statistical drop in a devastating essay he wrote for *Inside Higher Ed*. Even with a PhD from the University of Chicago and a book deal from Harvard University

Press, he struggled to find a secure job as a professor. He writes: "Of all the machines that humanity has created, few seem more precisely calibrated to the destruction of hope than the academic job market. . . . Universities trade on our hopes, and on the fact that we have spent many years developing skills so specialized that few really want them, to offer increasingly insecure careers to young scholars."[18]

This isn't to suggest that specialization is foolhardy, but specialized knowledge must now be coupled with the capacity to translate that knowledge in a wide variety of settings and in the service of a diversity of audiences. My big brother, Chris, is a perfect example: he's an experimental poet, deeply immersed in a relatively small subculture of people who write and read experimental poems. As you might imagine, it doesn't pay the bills. So what does my huge-hearted, big-brained brother do? He starts a company that teaches autistic children how to express themselves through poetry. His wife, also a poet and a graphic designer, designs one-of-a-kind chapbooks of the children's poetry. As a result, parents discover that their kids, often thought of as lacking in empathy and locked in their own minds, are actually deeply emotional and creative. From time to time Chris serves as a visiting professor at universities, including his own alma mater of Carleton College, but he's not waiting around for a tenure track job to fall into his lap; he's making his own money and meaning in the world.

He's unique, but he's not an anomaly. More and more intellectual and artistic people are honing a craft in a wide variety of settings. They're creating consulting practices that allow them to actualize their creative side part-time. They're visionary and practical, thriving in a creative economy that is being technologically remade minute by minute.

Most kids like to pretend and create, of course, but there was something different about how Maureen Towey experienced it. From the time she was a kid her inner boss emerged loud and proud, whether she was creating elaborate obstacle courses sliding down the stairs in a sleeping bag, or raiding her grandmother's closet with the gaggle of girl cousins in her big Irish family. "I would order everyone to strip down to their underpants and then we would take Nana's eight million scarves and turn them into costumes."

That instinct to lead stayed with her, ever present but largely unacknowledged, until one of her high school teachers watched her in action and said: "Maureen, you're a director. That's what you are."

Suddenly Maureen had a name for what she loved doing. This was significant, particularly since she came from a family of civil servants, the kind of people with pensions, not portfolios. She'd never known an artist, much less seriously considered becoming one, but when her teacher said "director," something inside of her clicked.

She went to Northwestern University and majored in theater— an outlandishly impractical choice by some standards, but one that struck her as sensible given what she'd already discovered about herself and about the world. As she says it, "People [with] theater experience [who] go into other fields usually thrive, because they've learned how to collaborate efficiently with diverse groups of people. It's the most useful, transferable skill there is, really."

While Maureen does direct more traditional works (her thesis wove together seven different versions of Euripides' *Bacchae*), she also creates entirely new work out of her own lived experience and the experiences of others—what is called "performance ethnography."

She also spent some of her free time volunteering at the local Planned Parenthood, holding women's hands while they got abortions. (Note that abortions make up only 3 percent of the services the network of clinics provides.) She started interviewing doctors and nurses; she then used those transcripts, along with her own experiences, to create a play about the secret world of abortion clinics.

"When you're doing Shakespeare or Ibsen," she explains, "you're looking at things happening hundreds of years ago. By making art out of what was urgent in my world right then—what was unsolved, what was haunting—I was taking an actual risk. I was scared in the right way."

When she graduated, she moved to New York City and got an entry-level development job at SITI, an experimental theater company. The most significant lessons from that time were about dollars, not directing. "I learned how to be a good fundraiser," Maureen reflects, "which, for the next ten years, allowed me to raise funds for myself. It's proven an essential tool in creating a sustainable and flexible career."

After SITI, Maureen's life took an improbable turn. While she'd been making plays in storefronts and off-off-off Broadway theaters, she'd occasionally let one of her best high school friends, Win Butler, crash on her floor with his band mates. Before long, Arcade Fire—as they were known—was exploding in popularity and heading out on tour.

When Win invited Maureen along for Arcade Fire's Funeral tour, she jumped at the chance to travel all over Europe, Brazil, and Japan. This isn't to say it was glamorous: she did whatever needed to be done, which often meant selling T-shirts and lugging equipment. Even so, it was a magical time—albeit a limited one. In a dingy bar in Germany she learned she'd gotten the Fulbright; she was going to South Africa to study how to create community through performance.

In Cape Town, Maureen interviewed doctors on the front line of the HIV/AIDS epidemic as well as *sangomas*—traditional healers. She recalls how when she visited a sangoma's house she'd quickly realize she was "expected to stay for at least a few days before asking a single question, and then only sparingly and through a Xhosa translator. It was a very involved process," Maureen remembers, "but it was good because learning a place and how time passes there—the rhythm there—really informs what I'm going to make. Hanging out is beautiful."

That material became her first full-fledged show at Sojourn Theatre in Portland, Oregon, called *Throwing Bones*—a reference to one of the typical practices of sangomas, which involves throwing sacred objects, often bones, and divining information from the pattern the thrown pieces form. Ultimately, she found that the same techniques she'd used to uncover the secret world of abortion clinics in Chicago helped her to untangle and examine the knot of traditional approaches and modern medicine in postapartheid South Africa.

Her next gig was trial by fire—serving as Arcade Fire's creative director for the tour promoting the album *The Suburbs*. "Working for rock stars is a great way to learn how to do impossible projects. Win would bring in a marching band last-minute and say, 'Can you do something with them?' They wouldn't let me say, 'I don't know how to do that.' That was really important," she emphasizes, especially since she hailed from the structured world of theater. "This was a great, chaotic answer to that."

Before long, she was back in the theater. One of Maureen's recent projects was *Black Mountain Songs*, a multigenerational, visually and aurally stunning tribute to the utopian spirit of North Carolina's famed Black Mountain. After the show wrapped in London, Maureen dined with one of the dancers in the show—a seventy-eight-year-old man she greatly admired. He said to her: "Artists who survive a whole career make a lot of work. If you keep making the work, eventually you make something great. Not everything is going to be brilliant, but you just keep at it."

Maureen is still figuring out the balance between the commercial work she does for musicians and the experimental work she funds by hobbling together grants and donations. She finds herself in far-flung settings, working with wildly different collaborators, in an astounding variety of mediums. The common thread is the way she works—she likes to immerse herself in a setting, listen and listen and listen, and then create an imaginative world with the people around her based on what she hears. "I wanted to make my career about more than just climbing a ladder in some industry," she says. "I wanted it to be about creating conditions where something unusual and beautiful can happen."

## THE HAPPINESS OF HARD WORK

And why should work and beauty be two distant countries? This is not to romanticize the difficult things we do to pay the bills, each of which is rife with unique frustrations. For home healthcare attendant Teresa, moments spent lugging a piece of equipment or cleaning hardened food from the wrinkles of a client don't exactly enrapture her. Zumba instructor Andreina has days when the last thing she wants to do is try to infuse a group of tired, rhythm-challenged women with a lust for life. And Maureen has felt daunted and humbled by the fundraising process; she's sometimes even wished she could do a job with a clear beginning and end rather than an ever-present one that creeps into her dreams.

But the hard moments—the struggle, the burnout, the rejection, the mess—are a part of work, just as they are a part of love. While we can't expect anything important in life to be easy or entirely enjoyable, we also shouldn't buy the tired public narrative that work is inherently dehumanizing or boring or pointless. Jacob Needleman, author of *Money and the Meaning of Life*, writes: "You should be looking for the joy, the struggle, and the challenge of work. What you bring forth from your own guts and heart. The happiness of hard work. No amount of money can buy that. Those are things of the spirit."

The notion that a job is nothing more than "bringing home the bacon" is a particularly destructive one for American men. Consider the guys who supposedly achieved the American Dream for themselves and their families, but in doing so actually shackled themselves to nine-to-five (or worse, eight-to-nine) jobs that they never really loved. In fact, visualize the basements in all the perfect houses across America filled with the deferred dreams of such men: the unused photo equipment and lonely easels and unchiseled wood. The sense that they could have been great teachers or nurses or poets. Creative energy was boxed up and stored, not unleashed on the world. And the capacity of such family men to take care of and spend time with people they loved was limited by bosses they may not have even respected, for work they may not have even believed in. On the surface, they looked like successes; beneath the surface, they longed to live lives less boring, less safe, less other-directed.

There's a subtlety here: on the other hand, some of us do something for "work" that doesn't feel like a Platonic reflection of our innermost *arête* (our calling, our gift, our purpose). That's fine. That's real. But—if we're taking full advantage of the moment we're living in—we're getting paid to do something we find at least tolerable, maybe even enjoyable; and we're spending oodles of time doing other work, which may be underpaid or even unpaid, but which is priceless in terms of its power to make us feel useful, seen, heard, fulfilled, expressed. How to make this work? The people who have figured this out are attuned to how much money they need to make in order to live a life that makes them feel sane—which usually means having time to take care of and spend time with people they love and do some kind of creative or physical or otherwise meaningful passion project. They may "bring home the bacon" in a way that doesn't thrill them, but they make damn well sure that their time off the clock does.

The silver lining of this disrupted, transitional economy is that there have never been more ways to cobble together a life. That doesn't mean that structural barriers don't remain—they do (more on those later in the book). But it does mean that, if you get curious about yourself, and surround yourself with interesting, generous people, you have more than a slim chance of being a grand success. Not a success measured by your salary, or your job title, or by security—at least not as we've defined such in previous economic eras. But a success that is felt—by you. A success that is reflected in the work you put out into the world, in the way you make other people feel, in the stuff you make.

Psychologist Barry Schwartz, author of *Why We Work*, writes: "Money does not tap into the essence of human motivation so much as transform it. When money is made the measure of all things, it becomes the measure of all things."

If you've settled for the notion that it's perfectly fine, normal even, to spend at minimum eight hours of every weekday of your life doing something you find mind-numbing or even morally wrong, it's time to wake up. In doing so there will be financial realities to contend with, but there are existential realities to consider as well. Don't underestimate the price you could pay if you stay in a job you hate because you've done a calculation that disavows the value of your own soul. And consider these words by Parker J. Palmer, author of *Let Your Life Speak: Listening for the Voice of Vocation*: "Discovering vocation does not mean scrambling toward some prize just beyond my reach, but accepting the treasure of true self I already possess."

Even if we're living close to the bone, we have a chance to live by a multitude of measures. Consider which measures matter the most to you. Choose *how* you work, not just what you do at work. Consider whether you feel seen and heard, not just how much you earn. Consider whether you can afford to sacrifice meaning for safety. Honestly, in our world today, you're likely not all that safe no matter what your job. I say choose challenge. Choose beauty. Choose love.

# working alone, together

## FLEXIBILITY AND FRIENDSHIP
## IN A FREELANCE ERA

"We are not only 'bowling alone,' we are increasingly working alone."

Or so says Jeffrey Pfeffer, a professor at Stanford who was quoted in a much-discussed *New York Times* piece, by economist Adam Grant, that explores new studies indicating that Americans are less likely than people in other countries to be friends with their coworkers.[1] It's more than disheartening to feel lonely in a sea of people—let alone in a sea of cubicles.

But, truth be told, fewer people today actually work in traditional, full-time jobs—the kinds that tend to be organized in cubicles. The U.S. Government Accountability Office recently reported that, in 2010, 40.4 percent of workers were contingent employees,[2] meaning employees who work for an organization in an alternative work arrangement, also known as freelancers, independent professionals, temporary contract workers, independent contractors, or consultants.

Note that not all contingent employees prefer that path. Many of the jobs shed during the downturn economy were the kind of employment that Americans have long idealized—full-time, "permanent" (a misnomer in our turbulent times), with a package of benefits. As businesses have been recovering, many have opted to first add back the nonpermanent employees. While this isn't uncommon in periods of economic recovery, the long-term trajectory is nonetheless historic. "This time around, that process is being drawn out to a much greater degree than in the past," Bernard Weinstein, an economist at Southern Methodist University, told *The Dallas Morning News.* "Normally in the third year of recovery, you'd see businesses shift away from contingent workers and hire full-time. We are looking at a long-term structural shift."[3]

Some people actually prefer contingent employment.[4] Many turn to this kind of work because it can offer flexibility, as well as some control over the social world we spend so many of our waking hours in. When you're a full-time employee, to a large extent your coworkers are predestined, and you're often obliged to collaborate with whoever ends up on your team or project. And while you can try to influence the culture of the company, doing so can feel like shouting into a hurricane—especially at bigger companies.

It's not an accident that some of our country's greatest satire of the last decade has been set in office environments. Shows like *The Office* and movies like *Office Space* make for gut-busting viewing, but only because they speak to the deadening that too many actually endure in real life: bureaucratic bullshit, boneheads running businesses, and office cultures of competition and cattiness.

For some freelancers, especially those just starting out, some of these same downsides endure. But those who have put in enough time and cultivated enough clients get some discretion in choosing where and when they work. This can mean building skills you're genuinely interested in, and working on projects that have meaning for you. You can pursue clients you find interesting, fun, courageous. You can launch projects with your real friends. And you can feel free to say no to lucrative gigs that might create more drama than they're worth. None of that can erase the financial insecurity, but it sure as hell makes it a lot easier to endure.

## TELECOMMUTING GOES GLOBAL

While there's no way to tabulate just how many of the nearly 53 million freelancers in the U.S.[5] feel financially secure enough to pick and choose their projects, clearly many do. One way many young people just launching "portfolio careers" have found to ease the financial burden—and gain new skills in the process—is working abroad for a period of time.

Take graphic designer and North Carolina native Megan Jett. At first it seemed like Megan was destined to fall in line with her parents' expectations that she go to college, find steady employment, and settle down nearby and start a family of her own. She graduated from North Carolina State University in 2007 with degrees in graphic design and Spanish. "Since I heard my first Spanish word at eight years old," Megan says as we chat over Skype, "I fell in love with the language. I knew I wanted to be fluent someday."

But then the economy went south—and so did Megan and her older sister. "My sister had known that I had this secret dream of living and working abroad at some point, so when she lost her job and I had just graduated, she called me up and said, 'Let's do it. Let's go to Chile,'" Megan recounts. "We literally hopped on a plane."

For the first week, they crashed on the couch at their cousins' family's place in Santiago. Soon they found an apartment of their own and began freelancing for clients back in the States—design work for Megan, journalism for her sister. It didn't prove difficult to get one-year professional visas, and the cost of living was far more affordable. As counterintuitive as it sounds, Megan feels that living in Santiago has made it easier for her to get work in the U.S.: "People are always so interested in where I'm living. Rather than seeing it as an obstacle, most clients seem to see it as an intrigue."

One gig has organically led to another. At this point, Megan has designed infographics, event programs, and logos for a wide variety of entities with headquarters strewn throughout the United States, from TED in New York to Make It Right in New Orleans to the Full Frame Documentary Film Festival back in her very own hometown. And though she expects to land back in North Carolina at some point, for now she's thriving in South America. She achieved her dream of being fluent in Spanish; she's also developed a deeper bond with her sister. "It was like getting to know her again for the first time," she said. "It changed our relationship forever."

The definition of the word "telecommuting" has expanded over time. To some the term brings to mind someone who stays at her house in suburban New Jersey one day a week instead of trekking into the city (as she does the other miserable, traffic-filled four days). That kind of flexibility is great, and it's becoming more and more normal. According to analysis by Global Workplace Analytics, which draws on U.S. Census data, half of the U.S. workforce now telecommutes at some point. Among the non-self-employed population, regular working at home grew by 103 percent between 2005 and 2014; in 2014 it grew by an additional 6.5 percent—the largest one-year increase since before the recession. And studies show that employees at Fortune 1000 companies are not at their desks 50–60 percent of the time.[6]

In this kind of climate, more and more people—particularly those who are young and just starting out—are stretching telecommuting to new distances, leaping abroad, where they can build their careers, learn new skills and languages, and have satisfying adventures with less financial strain, all before they get grounded by kids or the caretaking of aging parents.

Samantha McCann, realizing she was spinning her wheels in New York after graduation, moved to Medellín, Colombia, for a year. "I knew I wasn't going to stay in Medellín forever," she explains. "I could deprive myself of good bagels and good friends to save some money and gain knowledge of what I want and don't want from life."

And twenty-four-year-old Juliana Britto Schwartz, a biracial blogger from Marin, California, plans to move to Brazil with her longtime partner. At first she was nervous to tell her employer, online petition platform Change.org, about her plan, as she'd been working there less than a year, but they embraced the idea. Their work is inherently global and virtual, so Juliana being based elsewhere wasn't a fear-inducing prospect for them—which was very meaningful to Juliana. "Moving to Brazil is largely part of my never-ending project to become 'more Brazilian' and feel more comfortable claiming that part of my identity," she explains.

## COWORKING AS THE NEW JOB SECURITY

Wherever you're living, if you work remotely and are looking for community, one of the best things you can do is find the local "coworking" spot and park your laptop there. Coworking is a growing movement of spaces and people, usually independent contractors, who have realized that working together makes for happier, more productive work lives. And they're making it happen: without hierarchy, but not without structure. The spaces vary, but they're generally membership-based and value-driven. People who belong tend to believe in collaboration, openness, accessibility, and sustainability. There are thousands of coworking spaces listed in the Coworking Space Directory (a wiki that's collectively owned and updated). More than

450 of them participate in what they call a coworking visa program, where you can belong to a space in Iowa, for example, but spend a few days working at the one in Italy.

Since this is such a decentralized movement it's hard to come by reliable statistics, but we do have a few figures to work with. Coworking magazine *Deskmag* conducts an annual survey of nearly 3,000 people across the world. In 2014, they found that seven out of ten coworking facilitators reported that the availability of coworking desk space can't keep up with the demand.[7] In order to try to meet that demand, WeWork has built a sort of coworking empire; it has 63 locations in 18 cities around the globe, and was recently valued at $10 billion![8]

Most coworking spaces, however, still have a mom-and-pop mentality—one-off spaces with a highly local, customized spirit. So those living in Oakland might head to Oakstop to work on their small business or write their dissertation; they could also take a break from work to check out the Tupac Birthday Celebration or various exhibits by black artists in the gallery space. In New Orleans, there's The Blue House, where you can learn about community-fueled renovation during a coffee break from your own grind. In Denver, Colorado, there's Green Spaces, which is—true to its name—100 percent solar powered and filled with Patagonia-sporting start-up founders.

These spaces are not just glorified Starbucks. There's some powerful intention behind an environment created by coworkers, starting with the manifesto (collectively created and now signed by people all over the world working in 1,700 different coworking spaces). It begins: "We envision a new economic engine composed of collaboration and community, in contrast to the silos and secrecy of the nineteenth/twentieth century economy."[9]

In a sense, freelancers are scraping away the parts of company life that sucked the life out of them—toxic culture, compulsory collaboration, unnecessary busywork, rigid business hours—and rebuilding the parts that fed them in friendlier, more flexible form. And it's working, as researchers Gretchen Spreitzer, Peter Bacevice, and Lyndon Garrett wrote in *Harvard Business Review*:

> *As researchers who have, for years, studied how employees thrive, we were surprised to discover that people who belong to [coworking spaces] report levels of thriving that approach an average of six on a seven-point scale. This is at least a point higher than the average for employees who do their jobs in regular offices, and something so unheard of that we had to look at the data again.*[10]

So they looked at their data again. It all checked out. They found that, though coworking happiness derived from a wide variety of factors, the most central factor was communities that are characterized by authenticity, autonomy, and diversity. They write: "Unlike a traditional office, coworking spaces consist of members who work for a range of different companies, ventures, and projects. Because there is little direct competition or internal politics, they don't feel they have to put on a work persona to fit in."

The gospel of the new economy is the transformative power of a diverse, genuine network. Many people, understandably, cringe at the term "network." It's been conflated with awkward mixers where people stand around eyeing one another's name badges and making thinly veiled but ultimately transactional conversation. That kind of artificial setting can make even the extroverted among us want to go hide behind a nice, tall plant with our plastic cup of wine rather than brave being reduced to our résumés.

But this isn't how genuine networks get formed. Rather than meeting at mixers, most collaborators bump into one another through shared activities (pickup basketball, improv comedy groups, riffling through old records at a flea market) or while learning (at a CreativeMornings lecture, a welding workshop at the local arts studio, or a coding class at the community center). They meet through friends at a beer garden or a house party. Or they start talking in a shared space, like a coworking kitchen or apartment complex courtyard.

The explosion of coworking spaces is a physical symbol of the renewed belief in the security that comes from having a really broad and diverse network—what sociologist Mark S. Granovetter calls "the strength of weak ties."[11] Particularly for those in the information-based economy, job opportunities—like good ideas, as documented extensively at MIT's Building 20—happen by bumping up against people and seeing where serendipity leads. Genuine friendships, it turns out, are the seeds of a lot of the most fulfilling jobs of the twenty-first century.

Friendship, like love, happens when you least expect it. It happens when you're just going about your already fabulous life, doing fun and interesting things, intersecting with other people doing the same. As the great Margaret Wheatley writes, "There is no power greater than a community discovering what it cares about. . . . Invite in everybody who cares to work on what's possible. . . . Rely on human goodness. Stay together."[12]

These connections, born of serendipity and a little bit of intention, lead to friendship, sure, but also to job opportunities. (I'm a big proponent of sending nerdy emails to people I've met briefly and want to get to know.) Whereas boomers needed a cohort of colleagues big enough to weather the occasional layoff or career transition, their sons and daughters need a network robust enough to support constant flux. Most freelancers have a few gigs going at all times, depending on how absorbing each one is. You need a lot of friends to feed that kind of fire.

Fundraiser Jennifer McCrea and philanthropist Jeffrey C. Walker, authors of *The Generosity Network: New Transformational Tools for*

*Successful Fund-Raising*, believe that "true generosity is rooted in relatedness." They encourage people to create a "jazz band" of supporters and friends with a variety of different gifts and geographies. But, unlike the outdated dogma peddled at some college career counseling offices, they don't profess to have a step-by-step guide to making it happen: "There's no way to script real human connections. And that's a good thing. The outcome is so much more interesting—and potentially rewarding—than what we'd get if we followed a formula."

The thick, black line that once stood between personal and professional connections appears to be fading for many of us. It certainly has for me—my best collaborators are also my best friends. It can be messy, sure, but the benefits of being able to show up as my whole self and spend time with people I love, while making money, far outweigh the extra intention and accountability I have to put into it. We know how to bring out the best in each other. We can more effectively mentor one another through challenges because, unlike a colleague who might be at arm's length, we're aware of one another's history, our idiosyncrasies, our emotional lives. Best of all: when we kick ass, we get to celebrate together.

Even the language we use to describe colleagues these days blends the personal and the professional, such as when people affectionately refer to their "work wives" and "work husbands." In part that vocabulary reveals a critique of how much time some of us spend at work, but it's also an acknowledgment of the intimacy that forms between people who are closely aligned and looking out for one another. If you're going to spend something like eight hours a day interacting with someone, let it be someone you genuinely like, and maybe even love.

Amy Banks, author of *Four Ways to Click: Rewire Your Brain for Stronger, More Rewarding Relationships*, argues that "boundaries are overrated." She doesn't mean that healthy relationships don't have some balance between intimacy and distance, but that we're all better off when we're brave and authentic, even among colleagues. She writes, "Relationships are a dynamic process of experiencing, learning, and integrating your knowledge so that you are able to see both yourself and the other person more deeply and more clearly."

It's as if we used to see people within our professional networks as a bowl full of apples to be sliced and diced in the most efficient, lucrative ways possible. Now we're seeing people as onions with layers to be peeled. What we discover has much more nuanced potential than a bigger paycheck, though that's often a by-product of a more humanized connection. We understand ourselves better through our friends' and collaborators' eyes. We reach for promotions or projects we otherwise might have been too intimidated to attempt. And we have more fun.

What some have called a "psychology of abundance" can be even more critical for people who have historically been deprived of their fair share of opportunities. Journalist Ann Friedman and technologist Aminatou Sow, cohosts of a popular podcast called *Call Your Girlfriend*, call it "shine theory." They believe in the contagion of confidence and the compounding effect that can take place when one individual within a network gets a boost—essentially, that the rising tide lifts all boats.

Friedman writes: "The economy sucks, and awesome jobs are in short supply. In many industries, women are still perceived to be token hires—which means that other women can feel like our chief competition." She continues, "Here's my solution: when you meet a woman who is intimidatingly witty, stylish, beautiful, and professionally accomplished, *befriend her*. Surrounding yourself with the best people doesn't make you look worse by comparison. It makes you better."[13]

It also makes you safer. The more people who have you in mind as job postings show up in their in-boxes, the more likely you are to land on your feet during an unemployment stint. The more people who want to hang out with you—really the most important prerequisite for wanting to hire someone—the more likely you will be to get the offer. And if you decide to go freelance, the more people you know who have already taken the plunge, the more likely you will do so successfully yourself. You know veterans who have already learned how to pay estimated taxes, motivate delinquent clients for overdue payment, and figure out how much work to take on at a given moment. When you run into those hurdles—and you inevitably will—you just ask.

Social media, of course, has helped supercharge our networks, but there's something fundamental to the experience of creating relationships face-to-face. People no doubt benefit professionally from sites like LinkedIn and Twitter, but the "action" on those sites is made exponentially more interesting and productive when the online linkages are grounded in offline relationships. Which means that even if you feel safest behind the warm glow of a familiar screen, you have to venture out and seek human contact. You have to ask good questions of people who work far afield of you. You have to bump into enough people that you eventually latch on to your ideal collaborator.

Which is, once again, why coworking spaces are so well designed for the twenty-first-century worker. We all crave community—both on and off the proverbial clock—but we want community born of bottom-up serendipity, not top-down mandates. We want to collaborate with people who work in fields and mediums totally unlike ours, people with different styles and backgrounds, people who push us to grow—not because they're anticipating that quarterly evaluation, but because they want to do work that impacts the world. That's the sort of social cohesion that a company picnic once a year simply can't create, no matter how good the hot dogs.

Melissa Mesku, the founder of *New Worker Magazine,* has been blown away by the creative, socially engaged spirit of people who work in coworking spaces all over the world. "It's almost like there is a new common language among coworkers," she explains. "You can go almost anywhere in the world, find a coworking space, and immediately be dialed into the most vibrant, entrepreneurial things happening in a given city."

But it's not just a bunch of people bouncing in different directions that gives these places energy; it's also the ways in which they come together. Melissa was part of an accountability group in one of the coworking spaces that she belonged to. They met every Monday morning at 9:00 AM as a way to motivate themselves to start the week off strong. Though they were all working on wildly different projects, and in seemingly unrelated fields, they were effective in problem solving together and encouraging one another, especially around the kinds of short-term hurdles and goals that can often lead to stagnation when you're going it solo. "Sitting around a table with people and exposing what you're working on is, to some extent, exposing your hopes and dreams," Melissa remembers. "Having a crew to hold that and be accountable to was transformative for a lot of us."

## TAKING YOUR FRIENDS SERIOUSLY
## BEFORE THE REST OF THE WORLD DOES

You don't need to belong to a formal coworking space in order to experience the magic of the crew. I experienced the power firsthand early in my own career when I started a writers group. I looked around and realized that I had about a dozen friends—all in our early twenties—trying to make it as writers in various genres. All of us were hungry for feedback, but none of us could at that point dish out tens of thousands of dollars to get it via graduate school.

The structure evolved over time and proved very effective. Two people would send the others their work—everything from long-form journalism to poetry to crime fiction—ahead of time. When we met, which we did every other Tuesday night in someone's cramped Brooklyn apartment, we'd pretty quickly get down to business, starting with a check-in when everyone would say a few words about what they were working on, how they were feeling, etc.

Then the people receiving feedback (who were also charged with bringing wine or beer, because: duh) would give context about the piece they had submitted and specify what type of feedback they were ready for (as in, "Rip it to shreds, I know it's early days and I want as fierce a critique as possible," or, equally valid, "I'm feeling really sensitive about this one, so put your kid gloves on"). Those of us giving feedback would start with what we genuinely loved and work our way toward what we didn't think worked so well—up to the point the author was open for. The author would stay pretty quiet until we'd given a critical mass of feedback. We did it this way because we realized how easy it was for the authors to fritter away time defending their work against the feedback—when really receiving the feedback was the most valuable use of time.

All those Tuesday nights. All those wine stains on coffee tables salvaged from the unceasingly prolific streets of Park Slope. All those slices of ridiculously good New York pizza. All that throat-clearing preceding a friend trying to say something hard and necessary. All those pages on top of pages on top of pages. And yes, all those tears.

What it added up to was this: we took each other seriously before the rest of the world did.

And it mattered. It changed all of our lives in ways that were measurable externally—book deals, job offers, even TV shows—as well as immeasurable internally—processing personal loss of epic proportions. We made each other feel less alone in a notoriously lonely city at a notoriously lonely stage of life. We also kept at it: the writing and the supporting.

Part of why it worked was the structure: we were unapologetically earnest about why we gathered and we stuck to that. We weren't narcissistic millennials who wanted big praise for little work; we sweat hard in pursuit of our creative dreams. We knew that our writing was only going to get better if we did a lot of it—and got critical, compassionate feedback along the way. And it helped that we felt accountable to the crew. Before fancy editors were waiting on our emails, much less knew our names, we would be disappointing our *friends* if we signed up to present and then didn't submit any work. One of our members, Kimmi Auerbach Berlin, sums it up: "If it had just been a group of talented people, but they had all been dicks, it wouldn't have helped, even if the feedback was killer. And if everyone had just been kind and not talented, it wouldn't have pushed me to the next level in my writing."

Another part of why it worked was that, though we shared a passion for writing, we all channeled it into different genres, thus avoiding a whole lot of direct competition. And for those of us who technically were in direct competition, we rejected that paradigm and adopted a "rising tide" mentality instead. Kate Torgovnick May, another group member, explains: "With the group, if one of us made an editor contact, all of us had an editor contact. If one of us made an agent contact, all of us had that agent contact."

And part of why it worked was that we were vulnerable and talked about the unsexy stuff—the frustrating exchanges with editors, the even more frustrating experience of never hearing back from editors, the projects that died on the vine (some, in retrospect, thank God). We helped one another create financial sustainability in our lives, even while working as artists, because we didn't shy away from getting real about the side hustles. While it's widely understood that both sex and money are off-limits topics in polite company, we talked about the latter unabashedly—telling one another exactly what we got paid for writing jobs, as well as all the other stuff we did to pay the bills. (Largely, by the way, tutoring rich kids on taking standardized tests. I swear, if the SATs are ever abolished, while we will have a more equal, less anxious nation, people in their twenties will stop making art.)

"One of the most important things for me was just seeing everyone's process—seeing how much work it takes to sell something, but also that it is possible," another member, Joie Jager-Hyman, explains. "It helped expose me to the necessary (and sometimes evil) process of taking work into a public forum, which is a crucial hurdle that many people fail to overcome."

But mostly why it worked was that we were real friends. We hung out before and after the group work. We weathered heartbreak and death together. Sometimes we fought. We made up. We celebrated. We saw one another not just as sources of feedback on the craft we were honing but also as sources of feedback on the people we were becoming. We wanted to develop into people we *liked*, and we helped one another do that by offering each other a million tiny mirrors. As group member Jennifer Gandin Le puts it, "We were all badass goofballs with big hearts and dreams who were willing to listen."

As our twenties wore on, our schedules got more complicated and it got harder and harder to meet every other week. Then it got harder and harder to meet once a month. Then the mass exodus from New York took place.

These days we have a growing herd of books and babies. We live in Bozeman and Minneapolis and Austin and Amherst and, yes, still New York. We still get together in various configurations and sometimes even give feedback like the old days via Google hangs or old-fashioned phone calls. But the group lives on because we knew one another so well that we've internalized the various voices that once filled those sometimes terrifying, always edifying Tuesday nights.

Ethan Todras-Whitehill, one of the founding members, wrote recently in an email chain exchanged among the members: "Essentially, I internalized all of your perspectives into my own editing. Even yesterday, while I was editing a story for the umpteenth time out on my deck looking at the pond, a little piece of me was saying, 'What would Kate say about this line? What would Kimmi say about the character's want and obstacle? What would Courtney say about his soul?' You guys helped me become my own writers group." When you've internalized the feedback and support and love of several close friends, you're never going it alone.

If your best possible work reflects something fundamental about who you are, then your best possible collaborators are those who help you see if you're developing that truth—one loving, fierce critique at a time. We were invested. We showed up, over and over again. We spoke even when it was hard. And listened even when it was hard. And shut up even when it was hard. In aggregate, it felt like unconditional love.

## TAKING OUR CAREERS INTO OUR OWN HANDS

There's been a lot of hand-wringing about what the freelance era means for American workers. Some of the fears are very real: there is more financial risk inherent in not having a guaranteed yearly salary. And yet, even the instability may be overstated; according to the 2014 national Freelancing in America survey, nearly 8 in 10 freelancers said they earned as much on their own as they did when they were working for a company, and 4 in 10 said they earned more.[14] Let's be real: basic benefits—healthcare, disability insurance, retirement savings—are harder to come by (more on this in the next chapter) for freelancers. There is undeniable risk in breaking out on your own and being a free agent, unencumbered by hierarchy but also unsupported by a safety net. But as Sara Horowitz, founder of the Freelancers Union, sees it, it's also a matter of perspective: "You can think of freelancing as volatile and risky, or as flexible and opportunity-rich. Doesn't having multiple sources of income and multiple moneymaking skills sound less risky than putting all of your eggs in one employer's basket? Freelancing lets you shift gears when the world does."

And let's face it: the world really is shifting gears. Not just economically, but socially and culturally too. More and more people are trading punch cards for coworking memberships because they realize they simply can't protect themselves from financial risk by clinging to a full-time job they don't actually like—not to mention that their psyches will be safer without the monotony and bureaucracy inherent in so many traditional work settings. They are choosing grand adventures—like the ones Megan, Samantha, and Juliana embarked on—while still building their careers. A portfolio career knows no geographic boundaries. Rather than depending on debt-accruing specialized degree programs, or elusive curators or patrons, artists are creating their own creative communities—and relying on each other for feedback and support.

For too long, the cultural archetype of the freelancer has been the twenty-two-year-old, still in his boxers at 2:00 PM, eating a slice of pizza in front of the green glow of a computer screen in a filthy apartment. And, yes, 38 percent of millennials are freelancers—but so are 32 percent of those over thirty-five. "I am so much happier in this new stage of my career," said Mikki Morrissette, a single mom with two kids who left corporate publishing to become a freelancer. "I get to choose the projects I work on, and mostly work with other eclectic entrepreneurs like me."

For some, going freelance is not a matter of personal happiness but of survival. Traditional jobs are still built for a "company man" with no caretaking responsibilities. The rest of us—which at this point is basically all of us—have little people to pick up from childcare and aunts who need someone to hold their hand through chemotherapy and friends we'd like to see more than once in a blue moon. The freelance era promises a fluidity that just fits social animals better.

And therein lies the paradox. As the workforce becomes increasingly individualized, we're forced to become more intentional and imaginative about how we come together and support one another. And this takes more energy than showing up at an office every day at the time you're told to, where your cubicle and coworkers are assigned, and the work is obligatory. But the rewards are vast and diverse—not the least of which is that you feel your work and your life are not cleaved in two, but parts of a whole.

# norma rae
# for a new century

## HOW LABOR, POWER, AND
## CARE ARE BEING REMADE

Job security.

What do those two loaded little words mean to you? For some of us, they play like a grainy, black-and-white film of a different time and a different place, when our grandparents could count on "an honest day's pay for an honest day's work." We're privy to all sorts of clichés that suggest life was just more straightforward in the past. And to some extent, it was—if your grandfather or grandmother worked on the line in a car factory in Detroit or as a public school teacher in Dallas, he or she probably went to work every day with coffee jug in hand and the assumption that it very well might always be like that. No big surprises. No sudden amassing of debt from a medical emergency. Just a job and decent benefits that kept a whole family afloat, come what may.

Of course, for many other Americans this sense of job security was a total fiction. As with so many of our favorite stories about "back in the day," this one renders invisible all of the domestic workers and day laborers and farmers—often immigrants and people of color—who had no other choice, for whom huge job insecurity was simply reality. These are the people who never really retired, the people who never had a nest egg in their bank accounts (if they even had them).

As much as we might wax nostalgic about the buoying merits of yesteryear's job security, it has never been an American absolute. This is not to say job security isn't a virtue worth working toward. People deserve some basic legal rights regarding their employment contracts. People deserve to take some time off to care for loved ones or themselves without fearing financial ruin. People deserve to go to a doctor when they need one, and to not have to weigh the cost of medical care against the danger of not getting that care. People deserve to have a voice in their workplace.

If we view those two loaded little words—"job security"—in a modern light and take a good hard look, we see something far different than that old black-and-white film: we see visionary people dreaming of how a portable social safety net or universal basic income might make us all safer. And, no, these are not pipe dreams. Multiemployer plans (available through construction guilds or places like the Freelancers Union) already cover millions of Americans, and the successful $15 minimum-wage campaigns in New York, Seattle, San Francisco, and Los Angeles could be precedents for even more radical actions to come. We see a resurgence of labor organizing that's more about dignifying than about bargaining. A groundswell of people, connected by imaginative organizations like MomsRising and Make It Work, are agitating for better work/family policy through social media campaigns, cultural entrepreneurship, and boots-on-the-ground organizing. Childcare providers are banding with the parents they work for to argue for legal protections and livable wages for those who nurture the nation's future—as well as everyone's future social security. Networks are taking the best of old school union collectivity and modernizing tactics and telling better stories about who workers really are and what they want, which is, essentially, to be treated fairly. We want to be trusted—to know how and when and where we do our best work. We want to be paid enough to live without the specter of an empty bank account or an empty cupboard hanging over our heads. We want to know that when we develop a disability of some kind, and everyone does at one point or another, the bottom won't drop out.

Job security is at base about two of our most fundamental human drives: we want to work, and we want to feel safe. As explored in the previous chapters, the former is a matter of finding out what we are meant to do and doing it—somewhere, somehow, ideally among other kind, talented people. The latter is about what surrounds us as we attempt to put our short life to good use—the structures and expectations that make us feel supported despite our human frailties.

## REIMAGINING LABOR ORGANIZING

Americans are increasingly looking at the ever-widening gaps between what an employer provides and the basic needs of their lives and asking, *If this job isn't going to keep me "safe," and I'm feeling unfulfilled and penned-in by the top-down approach anyway, why would I stick around?* Oppressive authority *without* stability sends people packing, especially when they have families and friends they want and need to spend time with and care for—something the twentieth-century workplace didn't account for.

Another dysfunctional remnant of the twentieth century is the forty-hour workweek. In 1817 Robert Owen, a Welsh social reformer, coined a slogan that would affect millions of lives: "Eight hours of labor, eight hours of recreation, eight hours of rest." The idea was noble; back then it was normal for adults and children to work up to sixteen hours a day, six days a week. The eight-hour day wasn't fully instituted in the U.S. until 1938, as the Fair Labor Standards Act, part of the New Deal.[1] Of course, in an agrarian society the eight-hour workday was nonsensical; in today's society, the explosion of the Internet, the emergence of a truly global economy, and the restructuring of family and gender roles have made the arbitrary eight hours *really* nonsensical, not to mention impractical.

Another thing that no longer makes a lot of sense is the structure of the social safety net. Historically, our healthcare and pensions have been provided voluntarily by our employers. Wartimes have sometimes made employers extra generous; in Vanport City, Oregon, for example, every imaginable amenity was provided by the big shipyards—including twenty-four-hour, seven-day-a-week childcare—to ensure that all wives of men fighting in World War II could contribute to the nation's economy.[2]

Unfortunately, the American taste for Scandinavian-style social welfare was brief. After the war, Vanport City became like most other places: where companies provided the minimum benefits necessary in order to attract workers but not much more. In 1935, Congress mandated basic retirement income protection under the Social Security program; thereafter, employers were incentivized to provide benefits by making the cost of providing them tax-exempt.

Today, employers pay half of their W2 employees' Social Security tax (6.2 percent on wages up to $118,500), plus half of their Medicare rate (1.45 percent). Certain other benefits, including Social Security, unemployment insurance, workers' compensation, and unpaid family and medical leave, are mandatory—in no small part thanks to organizing and agitating by labor unions, which were at their mightiest in the 1950s.

But workers who are classified as independent contractors—characterized by getting a 1099 contract with an employer rather than a W2—are responsible for paying the entirety of their own taxes (Social Security, Medicare, and income); as a result they're left far more vulnerable. Another huge factor in the growth of independent contractors is the so-called gig economy. Fueled by the Internet (think Uber, TaskRabbit, and Airbnb), it provides people with the option to either patchwork together a bunch of different income streams or add a side hustle on top of full-time work. According to one recent study by the American Action Forum, from 2002 to 2014 the number of workers in the gig economy grew from 8.8 to 14.4 percent. Independent contractors are increasing in number as well, growing by 2.1 million workers from 2010 to 2014, and accounting for 28.8 percent of all jobs added during the recovery.[3] It is estimated that by 2020, freelancers will constitute more than 40 percent of the workforce.[4]

As the gig economy matures, critical legal questions are beginning to surface about how to classify the drivers, cleaners, shoppers, hosts, and personal assistants capitalizing on the trend. Are they independent contractors because they decide when and how much they work? Or are they employees because they're increasingly being told *how* to work, given rules and regulations about what to wear and what equipment to use? Note that such is not unlike a traditional employer—it's just less centralized. As Sarah Kessler writes in *Fast Company*, "the very definition of 'employee' in a tech-enabled, service-driven twenty-first-century American economy is at stake."[5] She goes on: "The social contract between gig economy workers and employers is broken. Who will fix it, and how, will determine the fate of thousands of workers and hundreds of millions of dollars."

In another era, unions would have been the obvious fixers, but their power is in a steep decline. Even the labor movement's leading voices are acknowledging that the old tricks just aren't working their magic any longer. Labor has to be reimagined. David Rolf—president of the Service Employees International Union (SEIU) and considered the "virtuoso organizer" and mastermind of Seattle's $15 minimum-wage campaign—told *The American Prospect*:

> *The death of collective bargaining isn't something we should be senti-*
> *mental about. We should understand what about collective bargain-*
> *ing worked, and try to recapture that. What really mattered was we*
> *created, first, the power to change workers' lives economically; second,*
> *we created it on a scale that benefited millions, tens of millions, of*
> *workers; and third, we created a model of sustainability so our*
> *institutions could survive even in bad economies or when our political*
> *allies weren't in power.*[6]

Some labor activists (and a wave of high-profile, class-action lawsuits) are pushing hard to see that Lyft drivers and Handy cleaners, among others, be considered W2 employees so they can accrue the benefits and protection thereof—without losing the critical freedoms of being an independent contractor.

But collective bargaining isn't proving that effective, even for W2 employees, so it seems shortsighted to pretend that it's the magic bullet for an increasingly large group of independent contractors. And as for those who overhype the gig economy as the future solution to all of society's problems, as well as those who argue it's guaranteed to plunge us into a lawless, unequal hell: they're both wrong.

Many are questioning altogether the wisdom of the dichotomy between W2 employees and 1099 employees. It's not as if full-time work is a panacea—so many W2 employees also struggle with eroded benefit packages and abuse from their employers. Allison Schrager of news outlet Quartz writes that forcing independent contractors to become employees is "like trying to shove a square peg into a round hole. It's not clear the contractors even want to be on staff."[7] Could a third category of worker, one that falls between independent contractor and full-fledged employee, serve both workers and employers?

We are in the midst of a huge transition. Though many of the core ideas of what makes work meaningful and life bearable remain constant, we've come to realize that our old frameworks no longer serve us. The questions before us now aren't just technical, as in: *How do we ensure that a profoundly transient workforce has access to fundamental human rights like healthcare, sick days, and family leave? Should we institute a basic income?* They're philosophical as well, as in: *How do we think about flexibility and fairness in a freelance world? Who is responsible for our fundamental well-being? Whom are we accountable to?*

**Michelle Miller, eighteen years old, was dreading going** to film class. Not because she didn't love the teacher. And not because she didn't love the material. In fact, *Harlan County, USA*, a 1976 documentary film about a coalminers' strike in southeast Kentucky, had made her feel right at home. That's what she was worried about.

You see, Michelle grew up poor in West Virginia. The people she'd watched organize for their rights in the Oscar-winning documentary were *her* people; they looked like her neighbors, they talked like her family. Michelle was afraid she was going to show up to class and be forced to listen to a bunch of rich kids make fun of the "hillbillies" in the film. She was afraid she was going to have to make a choice between keeping her mouth shut, avoiding scrutiny but also feeling like chickenshit, and speaking up, thereby marking herself. She slid into her seat with a palpable sense that, either way, this wasn't going to end well.

But then a magical thing happened. Her classmates didn't make fun of the "hillbillies." They didn't even call them that. Instead, the film proved so dignifying and so absorbing, kids whose parents were more likely to be the CEOs of places like the Duke

Power Company (the employer in the film) were actually identifying more with the plight of the workers.

Michelle fell in love twice over that day: she fell in love with labor—the people agitating for their rights, the conversations they were creating—and she fell in love with the potential of media to engage people in those conversations. These twin passions led her to the video department at SEIU—the Service Employees International Union, which represents 1.5 million public service workers, nurses, hospital staff, nursing-home care providers, building services, and security guards—where for the next decade she directed efforts to get union members engaged in meaningful ways.

While she played many roles in her ten years at SEIU, the most fulfilling was getting workers to create photography series, digital documentaries, and other arts about their own life and work experiences. She found this powerful for two reasons: it brought to the surface largely untold stories about real Americans' lives, and it fostered the talents of rank-and-file union members. When Michelle saw how effectively such creative opportunities strengthened the agency of union members, she began to wonder how workers' agency could be made even more central to labor organizing.

While at SEIU, Michelle met Jess Kutch, who did some of the union's earliest work on using digital tools like Facebook and Twitter to help workers find one another, put pressure on employers, and garner media attention for campaigns. She, too, felt she was doing good work without feeling fully satisfied. "We were in this ongoing conversation about the union we were in and trade unions in general and how they were only reaching 6 percent of workers," Michelle remembers. "We kept wondering, how can we engage more people?"

Eventually, convinced that labor organizing needed to be reimagined in some fundamental way, both Michelle and Jess left SEIU. They started tracking the ways that workers leveraged popular technology tools to try to create change in their own workplaces. Online petitions were the most popular, but they were also using Reddit threads, letters to Gawker, even microsites of their own making.

But there was an unfortunate reality to all this. When an initial campaign petered out, the networks seemed to immediately disband. No one was nurturing the leadership and initiative shown by these individuals. No one was connecting the dots between different campaigns. No one was advocating that the tools themselves continue to evolve.

To fill that vacuum, in 2013 Michelle and Jess created Coworker .org, which began as mostly an online platform. They focus on creating what they call "workplace democracy," which they define quite simply as "the principle that employees should have a voice in determining their working conditions and wages." They write:

> *The history of working people taking steps to improve their lives and their working conditions extends back centuries, long before collective bargaining was codified into law in America and elsewhere. At Coworker.org, we're interested in building technology for the labor movement of the future—one that's nimble, responsive, and inclusive of all working people.*[8]

In just two years Michelle and Jess have helped over 250,000 people create and sign petitions designed to change something about their workplace that they see as unfair. In October 2015, they cohosted a town hall with President Barack Obama on "worker voice" at the White House, a pretty fancy indicator that they're on to something.

Interestingly, a lot of the initial campaigns have been about self-expression. For example, twenty-four-year-old barista Kristie Williams wanted Starbucks to overturn its ban on visible tattoos. On long days behind the espresso machine, she liked gazing down at her daughter's name scrawled across her arm. That she was forced to cover it seemed archaic and out of step with Starbucks' reputation. The staff at Coworker.org helped Kristie figure out how to spread the word on social media and put pressure on the company. She launched her campaign in August 2014; within two months over 25,000 people signed her petition, bringing Starbucks to change the policy worldwide on October 20.

Since that time, workers have waged nearly a dozen other dress code campaigns directed at as many other employers. Michelle is struck by the fact that these campaigns, which are often scoffed at by traditional labor organizers, prove vital to the look and feel of the future of collective organizing. "We think workers should be able to run campaigns on whatever they want," she explains. "And what we're seeing is that, if someone experiences a win organizing with their coworkers about beards, they then get interested in what they might be able to advocate for in terms of work hours or fair pay—some of the harder stuff."

In 2015, Coworker.org won policy changes at ten companies. But Michelle and Jess don't use that figure to measure the success of the organization and the changes it catalyzes in the world; they have more complex metrics in mind. "We're in the process of codesigning a future labor movement," Michelle explains. "We want a platform that doesn't just allow workers to start petitions; we want them to stay together over time and create mutual aid networks."

Though "mutual aid networks" is a bit of a wonky term, it means something pretty simple: groups of people who figure out ways to create more stability by pooling their resources (time and money, primarily) rather than being out for only themselves. Think of it as a pack mentality rather than a dog-eat-dog worldview. So that means a group of airline attendants (interestingly, one of Coworker.org's biggest subscriber demographics) could take care of one another's kids by coordinating their time in the air versus on the ground. Or a dozen Lyft drivers could agree they were going to pool their earnings and split them evenly each month to alleviate the fear of needing to work less while taking care of a sick parent for a couple of weeks.

In addition to seeking a whole different way of creating collective security, Coworker.org is excited about changing the public conversation about work. They've noticed that when they send out fairly mundane Google surveys and ask, "Anything else you want to tell us?" people punch whole paragraphs into their phones about everything they're experiencing at work. Workers are eager to testify; they just haven't had the pulpit.

Michelle's interest is beyond piqued. She knows from her work at SEIU that when you put paintbrushes and microphones and cameras in people's hands, they create beautiful stories. Stories that are the connective tissue for communities. Communities that are the foundation for genuine security.

Meanwhile, her parents back in West Virginia, a payroll clerk and a medical delivery driver, are proud if not sometimes weary of what seem like brave-bordering-on-foolhardy choices. "My mother is very excited for me, but also scared. My father thinks I'm a dirty Bolshevik, in some ways, but he also sees shreds of deep self-reliance in the ways that I'm walking away from the existing structures. When he can calm down, he suggests that he actually respects it."

## A TECH INCUBATOR WITH A UNION HEART

Labor rights also aren't an abstraction for Carmen Rojas. She has a huge Latino family (her mother has seventeen siblings and her father has ten), many of whom are or have been childcare and home healthcare workers. As they pass the plates at family gatherings, they talk about their daily struggles, like getting consistent hours and dealing with cruel supervisors. Carmen listens carefully to their stories and concerns; though she has a PhD, she still considers her family members her best teachers.

She brings those lessons to the Oakland, California, Workers Lab, which she cofounded with David Rolf (quoted earlier) in 2014. She's always scouting for potential solutions to just the kinds of problems that her family describes.

Carmen tells me: "We have an opportunity to lead our economy in a new direction through investing in organizing strategies, business models, and platforms that will lift wages and transform the lives of people who work across the U.S." In essence, the Workers Lab is a tech incubator with a union heart. It's taking the things that made unions so powerful in their heyday—a fierce commitment to the leverage that workers have when they come together, and a bias toward financial structures that don't depend on charity or the "goodwill" of CEOs—and applying them to a whole new world of technological tools.

Case in point: Contratados, a Yelp-style online platform where migrant workers can share ratings and reviews of their experiences with different recruiters and employers. Every year, more than 100,000 migrant workers are recruited to travel to the United States on temporary employment visas. (Note that this figure *doesn't* include the huge influx that come unofficially.) It's a highly vulnerable situation in which they've historically had little reliable information—other than the word of mouth of family and friends.

Centro de los Derechos del Migrante, a Mexico City–based nonprofit, created Contratados in 2014; within twelve months, twenty to thirty migrants uploaded reviews every single day. Part of the success of this venture has been the flexibility of the platform itself: workers can share information via voice message, text, or simply pass along a photo.

The Workers Lab's recent Summer Institute brought a group of unusual suspects together—including venture capitalists, civic entrepreneurs, philanthropists, technologists, and community organizers—to offer advice and even consider investing in various platforms. When Contratados was presented, an exciting discussion got going about how the information latent in an app like this could be mined. Indeed, Sarah Farr, a project coordinator with Centro de los Derechos del Migrante, reports that the U.S. Department of Labor has already expressed interest in using the reviews to target inspections and enforcement efforts.[9]

"Contratados now has access to this group of workers who are so hard to understand," Carmen explains. "We don't have data on them. We don't know how to create policy around them. That could all change if we can figure out how to make the most of this."

Workers Lab maintains a portfolio of platforms on the cutting edge of tech and workers' rights. Another early days app focuses on enabling low-wage workers to bundle their childcare credits so they can use them in daycares they trust in more convenient locations. Historically, childcare credits have been notoriously difficult to use, often only accepted in daycare centers with very high child-to-care-provider ratios and sometimes far from where a parent lives or works.

TOP Server is a gaming platform that provides training for restaurant workers to advance into higher-paying jobs in the industry. The Better Builder Program helps workers partner with local governments and businesses to raise wages and safety standards on construction projects in Texas. And WorkAmerica links job-seeking students with employers. Not surprisingly, Coworker.org is part of Workers Lab's portfolio too.

This is where the virtues of silo-busting becomes undeniable. Why shouldn't new immigrants or restaurant workers have the chance to benefit from the unprecedented potential of technology to connect and inform us? They should. But as long as technologists—predominantly white, privileged, and male—talk mostly to one another and, as a result, have only a visceral sense of their own unmet needs, they won't. As George Packer wrote in *The New Yorker*: "The phrase 'change the world' is tossed around Silicon Valley conversations and business plans as freely as talk of 'early-stage investing' and 'beta tests.'"[10]

I call bullshit. You're not changing the world if you're getting rich by meeting the needs of privileged white people. That doesn't mean that Silicon Valley's best and brightest don't have genuine intentions to do real, tangible things to cut inequality. But they need to sit in rooms with visionaries like Carmen, with the staff at Centro de los Derechos del Migrante, with low-wage workers themselves. They need to talk to their own childcare providers, their elderly aunts, the guy who makes their burrito on Wednesdays. In my fantasy life, Steve Jobs and Grace Lee Boggs are sitting up in heaven somewhere having the most unlikely conversation of the last century.

As with all incubators, the proof is in the scaling. This is part of what makes Carmen a little nervous. "In some ways," she says, "I think we overbet on revenue-generating models. It was a vestige of how the labor movement has traditionally had power and been able to sustain movements in the long term. We still believe in that, but in future years, I think we'll focus on being more lab-like and less incubator."

In other words, some of the best ideas for the future of worker power will generate revenue, but some may need to be philanthropically funded or supported through government programs. The Workers Lab is trying to help start-ups like Contratados to navigate not just the technical hurdles—*How do we hire the best developers? What's the most persuasive way to pitch potential investors?*—but also the theoretical questions—*Is this a public good or a private one? Am I an entrepreneur or an organizer?* And even more important, *Must the two be mutually exclusive?*

As the world of work morphs in unrecognizable ways for everybody—CEO and low-wage workers alike—experimentation and cross-sector collaboration are more needed than ever. Power doesn't flow from top to bottom, or stay in separate silos, as predictably as it used to. This is what movement builder Jeremy Heimans and executive director of 92nd Street Y Henry Timms call "new power." In the *Harvard Business Review* they write:

> *Old power works like a currency. It is held by few. Once gained, it is jealously guarded, and the powerful have a substantial store of it to spend. It is closed, inaccessible, and leader-driven. It downloads, and it captures.*
>
> *New power operates differently, like a current. It is made by many. It is open, participatory, and peer-driven. It uploads, and it distributes. Like water or electricity, it's most forceful when it surges. The goal with new power is not to hoard it but to channel it.*[11]

So in a sense, the Workers Lab is in the very unpredictable business of trying to figure out how best to channel workers' power. Carmen is betting that it's not going to happen by doing what we've always done, but that's scary to a lot of people. "Some people think that job training is the magic bullet, but that presupposes that any job is a good job. I don't want to train people to get another bad job."

She continues: "Then we've got labor organizers who are finally admitting that they need to think more like social entrepreneurs if they're going to innovate, and yet their stereotype of entrepreneurs is blood-sucking business types. We've got to change the frame."

It's not about apps; it's about reimagining power in an era when collectivity is easier, faster, and more potent than ever before. It's about abandoning puritanical ideas about how technology and/or investment inevitably leads to moral compromises. It's about supporting people like Carmen's cousins—so many of whom didn't get a PhD, much less graduate high school—so they can take dinner-table conversations and turn them into small businesses. It's about democratizing where the best ideas come from and how they scale to serve. "It's about prosperity," Carmen says. "Plain and simple. We've just got to get there in more imaginative ways."

## A TWENTY-FIRST-CENTURY SOCIAL CONTRACT

This new generation of people—Michelle and Carmen among them—are restructuring the social safety net and authoring a historic chapter in labor organizing. And while they're drawing on all the age-old questions about power and dignity, they're taking fresh forms and using less antagonistic frameworks. At its essence, the aim is to innovate at the intersection of flexibility and security.

In many ways, the Affordable Care Act helped prove that we are capable of this kind of innovation—despite our tragically dysfunctional government. The Act has proven wildly effective by a range of critical measures: fifteen million Americans, predominantly young and poor, have gained insurance, reporting a high degree of satisfaction with their coverage; premiums came in well below expectations; and 240,000 more jobs were added per month on average since the legislation went into effect, the biggest job gains since the 1990s.

The latest U.S. Census report also proves that Obamacare is keeping people out of poverty—8.8 million people to be exact.[12] Economist Paul Krugman writes, "Put all these things together, and what you have is a portrait of policy triumph—a law that, despite everything its opponents have done to undermine it, is achieving its goals, costing less than expected, and making the lives of millions of Americans better and more secure."[13]

Another little-understood precedent for radical economic shifts is found way up north. The Alaska Permanent Fund, created in 1976, is essentially an experiment (derived from oil revenue) in universal basic income. In 2015, every Alaskan received a check for $2,072.[14] Many argue that just this small but universal injection of capital and comfort into the state's economy has helped it perform above others with regard to poverty.

It would cost something like $2.14 trillion to give every working-age American a basic income equal to the poverty line. That sounds steep, but when you add up all the spending on various public assistance programs, many of which are bureaucratically bloated, patronizing of the poor, and ineffective, it doesn't seem as crazy. Factor in the compounding effects that basic income programs seem to have on lowering a lot of related costs—hospital visits go down, high school completion rates go up, etc.—and it's even more appealing.[15] Annie Lowery of *The New York Times* writes that "basic-income schemes are having something of a moment."[16]

She goes on: "Absurd as a minimum income might seem to bootstrapping Americans . . . if our economy is no longer able to improve the lives of the working poor and low-income families, why not tweak our policies to do what we're already doing, but better—more harmoniously?"

In the year I was born, 1979, actor Sally Field played labor heroine Norma Rae in a film of the same name wherein she famously stood on a desk in the middle of a textile factory holding high above her head a sign reading UNION. The various Norma Rae figures of this nascent era don't stand on desks so much as on online platforms. They don't stick it to "the man" so much as stick with their colleagues and seek to expand power within and "between" workplaces—so that it's the institutional leaders who have to evolve.

And it's not just labor organizers who are interested in these innovation challenges. Elected leaders are starting to wake up to the fact that the gig economy isn't a Silicon Valley problem but an American problem. Senator Mark Warner from Virginia, a former tech entrepreneur himself, has called on his colleagues in Congress to create a social safety net to protect the growing number of Americans who are part of the gig economy. He even floated the idea of an "hour bank" where workers receive benefits based on the number of hours they work. But he cautions that, as with most things of any complexity, no quick fix exists. In an interview with *The Wall Street Journal* he says, "I think this is much bigger than a single piece of legislation and really has much greater ramifications than that."[17]

Entrepreneurs, of course, have a lot at stake; if the legal frameworks don't evolve and people don't feel protected, the gig economy could be over before it's really begun. For example, after some particularly high-profile incidents of renters trashing Airbnb-rented homes, the company introduced a liability insurance program that provides up to $1 million worth of protection to Airbnb hosts. Brian Chesky, the CEO, has spoken widely about the fact that he's not interested in "disrupting" anything so much as returning to an older way of life, one where his grandparents preferred person-to-person arrangements over more anonymous hospitality experiences. Speaking at the Aspen Institute, he said: "We do want to be regulated. We do want to play by the rules. But we also think some of the rules . . . were written for the twentieth century, and now we're in a twenty-first century economy where people aren't the same thing as corporations."[18]

We need everybody's good ideas because this is an everybody problem. Even the rich recognize that. In a *Democracy: A Journal of Ideas* piece coauthored with David Rolf, billionaire businessman Nick Hanauer writes: "An economy based on microemployment requires the accrual of microbenefits, and a twenty-first-century sharing economy requires a twenty-first-century social contract that assures shared economic security and broad prosperity."[19]

In other words, we're *all* going to be better off when we shed our outdated and dysfunctional ideas about what both stimulates the economy *and* keeps Americans healthy and fulfilled at work. Workers need ways to safely advocate for themselves and each other, they need flexibility and trust, and they—most importantly—need to be connected. Employers need ways to balance freedom and protection. They need the capacity to create scalable solutions for the services people want (rides, meals, places to lay their weary heads), while also honoring their workers.

As the eight-hour workday and sea of cubicles disintegrate into the past, as people shed their rigid collars and classifications, as they move from job to job faster (in a given day or a given career), as men "come out" as caregivers, as everyone contends with the globalizing, volatile nature of the economy—we simply have to evolve our expectations of how Americans work, collaborate, rest, and care for one another.

We need to acknowledge that our lives have changed dramatically since the 1950s. Our classifications for workers have to catch up to the realities wrought by so many huge economic and social shifts. We don't work like we used to. We need new language. We need new ways of interpreting old language, especially loaded words like "security," "prosperity," and "dignity." We need safety nets made from spider silk rather than climbing rope. We need to tell new stories—which is to say we need to create a new culture.

# the wisdom of enough

## MAKING SOUND FINANCIAL
## DECISIONS IN A CULTURE
## THAT OVERVALUES MONEY

In recent years, there has been an explosion in awareness and debate over the widening wealth gap in this country. Most
of the conversation has been focused on one of two extremes: the
struggles of the working poor, who just can't seem to get ahead, or,
at its most confrontational, the stockpiling of obscene amounts of
wealth by the 1 percent—what journalist-turned-politician Chrystia
Freeland calls "the age of the global plutocracy." Those of us hover-
ing somewhere in the middle get some airtime, but our concerns are
reduced to the catch-all, political football of the so-called middle class.
The anxiety of those who identify in this way continues to soar as we
hear about the shrinking of our ranks, and yet, who are *we* really?

The Pew Charitable Trusts defines households that earn between
67 and 200 percent of a state's median income as middle class. That
definition, however economically viable, doesn't mean much to the

fragile American ego, which is always looking to see what the folks in the next cubicle, car, or condo seem to be earning. Mass media, filled with both bling and blight porn, further distances us. As Anat Shenker-Osorio wrote in *The Atlantic*: "Not finding popular depictions of wealth and poverty similar to our own lived experiences, we determine we must be whatever's left over."[1]

In fact, according to a study by the Pew Research Center, nearly nine out of ten Americans—people teetering on the poverty line all the way up to those bringing in a hundred thousand dollars a year—consider themselves middle-class.[2] Richard V. Reeves, of the Brookings Institution, told *The New York Times*: "There is a very big difference between the psychological self-definition of class and anything approaching a useful economic definition of class."[3]

People find a psychic comfort in claiming middle-class status. If you're poor pretending to be in the middle, you can avoid suffering from the pity and judgment that some people reserve for those with less, maybe even tricking yourself into believing that you're on equal footing so as not to be discouraged by entrenched inequality. If you're rich pretending to be in the middle, you avoid a different kind of social stigma—the lazy trust-fund kid whose success was bought, not earned; in a country that celebrates bootstrapping, you still have a chance at seeming like you're "self-made."

The paradoxes here are plentiful. Many of both the poor and the wealthy—those not of the middle class—tend to *identify* as being middle-class, as the classification can seem more psychologically comfortable: essentially, the poor don't want to be poor, and the rich don't want to appear too big for their britches. In the meantime, those who are officially middle-class can find the identifier—and all that goes with it—anxiety-producing in an age when everyone talks about the disappearance of the middle class. Some of that anxiety is justified: median per capita income, adjusting for inflation, has basically been flat since 2000. The costs of housing, college, and healthcare continue to rise. Economic volatility has increased, meaning that people's fear of losing their shirts is actually quite realistic—depending on the field in which they work and the place they call home.

But the average American family earns *slightly* less than it did in 2000.[4] So it begs the question: many of us may be earning less money, but are we doing *worse*? I don't mean financially worse, but emotionally, physically, spiritually, communally, existentially worse. I mean the kind of worse that matters most when you're lying on your deathbed and looking back. We all see the benefit of building up our savings, but how do you know when your focus on doing so has become overzealous? How do you catch yourself when the pursuit of a bigger paycheck distracts you from the people you love and the activities that give you the most joy or meaning? How do you know when you're simply earning enough?

It's amazing how rarely we've asked these questions, or at least a variation on them. In part, I think people have avoided the question of enough because they don't want to be seen as the out-of-touch asshole—a risk I'm taking here because I think the conversation is so important. Listen, for people who can't afford basic necessities, focusing on money isn't a choice; it's a matter of survival. That bottom-line reality must be acknowledged.

In part, however, I think people haven't had a complex, honest dialogue about the relationship between money and quality of life because we're socialized to believe that it's obvious. No matter who you are, no matter what you already have: earn as much as you can. The more money you have, the better off you'll be. Case closed. In the Old Better Off worldview, living a financially unexamined life was the norm.

And I'm not just talking about an ignorant, furious "affluenza"— a throng of hysterical, sleep-deprived shoppers mowing each other down as they stampede into stores on Black Friday. I'm talking about those of us who are pretty conscious of the ways in which *things* don't reliably lead to happiness.

Even people who aren't particularly interested in money, at least insofar as it affords you stuff and status, have reason to be optimistic about its benefits. Money, in theory, can buy you emotional safety and the chance to be authentic: it means you can tell a cruel boss to take a hike without worrying about your mortgage. Money can buy you the space to heal: it means you can take time off during a health crisis without having a financial crisis as a result. (Note that medical expenses are the primary reason people plunge into personal debt.)[5] And money can buy you creative time: it means you can pursue the writing/painting/dancing/singing that you've always dreamed about.

To some extent, of course, all of this is true. But it's only part of the story. Or, even more likely, a version of the story that could exist— but doesn't. Additional money often brings additional professional pressure. So while a raise can feel like a financial success, it comes with a promise that you will spend more time working—and thus less time nurturing your personal life. And to return to the benefits named earlier: many people have every intention of telling the boss to take a hike, taking time off to heal, or doing that creative project, yet they simply never get off their job's hamster wheel. Numerous studies have shown that it's very difficult to break habits—and making money, in its own weird way, is a habit. What's more, a higher wage might protect you from plunging into medical debt, but stress and overwork are disastrous for your health in the first place. So many of us pursue more earnings as if on autopilot, either because we're convinced a bigger bank account will bring blanket security, or because we've conflated success with the figure on our paychecks.

Of course, not everyone has the luxury of being on autopilot. Some of us, whether born into poverty or plunged there by the Great

Recession and its aftershocks, are just scraping by. (In 2013, 14.5 percent of Americans lived at or below the poverty line, approximately $23,834 for a family of four.)[6] Some of us, on the other hand, are financially wealthy and uninterested in examining the moral or spiritual implications of our privilege. But, just as necessity is the mother of invention, a recession can be the father of consciousness. More and more Americans are stepping off the hamster wheel, either by force or by choice, and examining the value of money with greater scrutiny—in the context of a life well-lived, not just well-earned and well-consumed.

## $100,000 POORER AND ALL THE RICHER FOR IT

Recent hire Beth Foley Barnes was sitting at her desk, staring into that hypnotizing glow of her computer screen, determined to respond to just a few more emails before lunch. In fact, she thought, maybe she would just pull out her sandwich and work through the hour as in old times. She still didn't know her colleagues that well, and that Mississippi summer was sticky hot—whereas the work was absorbing and the air conditioning was soothing.

A coworker leaned his head into her office and said, "Knock knock! Time for lunch!"

"Oh, thanks. I think I might work through. I have a lot of emails to get to," she replied. "New girl and all."

"I'm afraid that's not an option," he said with a broad smile.

Beth assumed he was joking: "It's fine, really."

"I'm not being nice," he explained. "This is company policy. We all leave and lock the doors at lunch. You can't come back for one hour."

Beth's mouth dropped open: "No kidding?"

"No kidding," he answered. "Get moving, girl."

Beth Foley Barnes, a big-city go-getter, had gotten very used to gobbling down her lunch as quickly as possible at her desk. Hard work had been the most heralded value in her family. She'd grown up in Hillsdale, New Jersey, about thirty miles outside New York City. She'd had a paper route, sold the most cookies in her Girl Scout troop, got good grades, and was determined to land a job in a big Manhattan advertising firm one day.

"When I was little," she explains, "I just loved commercials. I just wanted to be a part of it. I was sure that advertising was the place where all my useless knowledge was going to find a home . . . and I was right."

Over the course of a decade Beth worked at a number of big firms. She prided herself on being the one who would stay late and do whatever she had to do to get the job done and done beautifully. She always exceeded clients' expectations.

When she went on maternity leave from McCann Erickson in June 2008, she stayed in frequent touch with her coworkers. Following the news of the economic meltdown while caring for her new baby, Ruby, she grew nervous about what the future held for everyone. She felt relieved that she at least had a steady job with solid health insurance waiting for her. Her husband, Brian, worked in film production; though he earned a good salary, it was unpredictable and didn't include benefits.

Five days before she was supposed to start back at work, she got a call from human resources telling her there was no position for her to come back to. Her job no longer existed.

Beth was shocked. When she pressed for more information, she was told, "We didn't think you were coming back." But that made no sense: all through her leave she'd been in weekly touch with her team and mentored her account executive over the phone. She'd frequently expressed her excitement about getting back to work after so many dirty diapers and wordless afternoons.

McCann Erickson gave her an extra week of paid leave because of the "misunderstanding" and invited her to interview for another position at the company. She wasn't offered the job. "I knew I was being screwed," Beth remembers. "As an account person, your job is to fight the good fight for the creatives. Here I was, I didn't do anything wrong. I knew that I had to fight for myself."

She found a lawyer and they submitted a demand letter. It took three years to resolve; all she ultimately got from McCann Erickson was four weeks of severance.

By that time Beth had relocated her family to Greenwood, Mississippi, for a number of reasons. Brian had grown up there, and his parents were constantly urging him to return and join the family business, a paper supply and janitorial company. After just a little poking around, Beth found a lead at a small advertising firm in town, and she and Brian realized they could afford to buy a three-bedroom home there.

But the decision was more than just practical; in some weird way it seemed destined. Beth reflects: "I had done everything 'right,' you know, by the book, up until that point. I went to the 'right' school. I got the 'right' job. I worked at the 'right' company. And nothing was working for me."

In contrast, as soon as they merely considered moving to Mississippi, everything seemed to fall into place. At first, she told herself it would just be a way station for them—a place to wait out the economic downturn and get Ruby through preschool. But then another daughter arrived, and soon enough all the bedrooms and broom closets filled up. Beth joined the board of the Boys & Girls Club and the Garden Club. Brian became a manager in the family business. In the blink of an eye, six years passed.

But Beth hasn't exactly drunk the small-town Kool-Aid; when you talk to her you don't get the sense that she's done that very adaptive human thing of convincing herself that everything is better where she is now. While she's happy, she's still unresolved about what she's given up and what she's gotten in return. "I came from a very hard-working family," she says. "I defined my success in a very linear way. I still have pangs of sadness. I mourn the loss of my career as defined by my eighteen-year-old self."

Beth earns $100,000 less than she did at her peak in New York City, but she also lives on significantly less in Greenwood. As she puts it, "I feel like I'm living at a foreign exchange rate." (She's calculated it at 6:1—living in Greenwood is six times less expensive than NYC.) Plus, she's in good company. Money is hard to come by in Greenwood, so people make a hobby out of making a dollar stretch. "They call it 'tight' down here, not cheap," Beth explains. "The women are really handy. People on the coasts live two paychecks away from bankruptcy, but people down here make the little money they have work for them."

Her forty-year-old self recognizes that success is far more complex than how big her salary is. For starters, she and Brian calculated that, by cutting out long commutes and adopting the true nine-to-five (with lunch break!) in Greenwood, they spend four more hours a day with their family than they would if they still lived in New York City.

Beth also feels she's grown in ways she never would have if she were still doing the city grind. Her fingernails are often caked with dirt from her garden, and she's rediscovered her knack for organizing charity events and grant writing.

Brian has grown as well. Though he doesn't consider working at the family business his true calling, having that humble security and lots of free time has allowed him to finish the screenplay he always dreamed of writing. And Beth has noticed that, though she once thought New York City was the birthplace of all worthwhile, creative things, she now realizes "that people in New York City love to *talk* about the creative things they're working on, but then they never seem to actually finish them. People in places like Greenwood actually do it."

Beth admits she would love a full-time job in advertising again (while in Greenwood she's mostly worked on a contingent basis), or even just to get a few clients in New York City so she could return more frequently. But she's unsure if she'd ever want to trust her family's fate to a big corporate employer again.

Perhaps even more importantly, she's just not sure she likes the version of herself that made six figures and deprioritized just about everything else: "I don't necessarily like the person I had to be in New York City to be successful. I'm happy that I get to be more me here."

## GENERATIONAL INHERITANCE

Beth traveled from one extreme—a city of eight million people and a six-figure salary at a corporate behemoth—to the other—a city of 15,000 and earnings just under $30,000 as her own boss. But for most of us, the effort to make conscious decisions about our earning and energy capacity is less of a pendulum swing and more of a tuning fork. If we live beyond the bone, we must constantly calibrate. There is a direct relationship between how much money we make and how we spend our time, what kinds of food we eat, what sort of neighborhoods we live in, what kinds of gifts we give to people we love, what sort of education we receive, how much anxiety we tolerate, and so much more.

All of this, while tangible, is a subjective experience; our take on it is deeply influenced by forces long gone and beyond our control. Just as our DNA is composed of microscopic strands of family inheritance that are turned on or off by environmental effects and tiny twists of fate, we all develop our identities around money through a complex combination of factors.

When I was a little kid I noticed that, each December, my dad's brow would get furrowed and his migraines would increase. When I finally probed my parents about the yuletide phenomenon, they told me that my dad had grown up in a Colorado family where holidays, though characterized by abundance, were also foreboding. My dad's parents frequently splurged on Christmas gifts they couldn't afford; by the time the snow started to melt my dad was forced to answer the door for debt collectors, lying about his parents' whereabouts.

Given his background, my dad understandably craved financial security—to the extent that he became a bankruptcy lawyer. And even though my brother and I enjoyed a childhood characterized by comfort and consistency, we nonetheless ended up putting the pieces together about our family history, and both developed a strong streak of financial anxiety. Throughout our twenties we were teased by friends about how we faithfully ate exactly half of our restaurant meal so we could save the other half for the next day. We are both vintage clothes shoppers, cheap beer drinkers, and get thrilled by the prospect of finding furniture left on the sidewalk. In part this is because of the culture of the company we keep, but it's also deeply determined by days that we didn't even live through. The memories of what furrowed our father's brow continue to influence our lives all these years later—in small but important ways.

Part of waking up to the role of money in your life, and of becoming conscious of the choices you make about work, is getting real about the stories you inherit. Consider Hawaiian businessman Robert T. Kiyosaki's best-selling book, *Rich Dad Poor Dad: What the Rich Teach Their Kids About Money That the Poor and Middle Class Do Not!*, which gives financial advice through the parable of his own experience growing up with two fathers: one who managed to accumulate wealth and another who didn't. Even without reading the book, I'm sure you can guess which one Kiyosaki recommends you emulate. And yet, that kind of pop psychology, spoken in the language of dividends and down payments, is dangerously reductive. Those of us who grew up with a proverbial "poor dad" may aspire to earn more than he did, but many of us who grew up with a "rich dad" may actually aspire to earn less.

Take thirty-three-year-old Brian Jones. His father worked at Bell Labs for over two decades in Murray Hill, New Jersey, and raised his three kids to believe, in Brian's words, that "sweat and effort enable upward mobility." He was living proof, after all. His own father had never held a steady job, and left his wife to raise three kids on her own while he put money in the stock market willy-nilly, thinking he could outsmart other investors. He was left broke. Brian's father wasn't going to make the same mistakes; he clawed his way up the economic ladder. He'd created a nice life for his son and two daughters. He raised them with God-fearing, true-blue American values. He desired great things for them, and knew they had it within themselves to produce (and amass) great things themselves.

At first, Brian's path looked linear. He went to Rice University, just like his dad. He majored in engineering, just like his dad. He got a good job right out of school as a credit analyst at Standard & Poor's. And then the credit crisis hit. "Lehman went under and all hell broke loose," Brian remembers. "I didn't make the mess and I didn't fully understand the mess. It became much less fun."

Brian started volunteering at a nonprofit called Charity: Water, which provides clean, safe drinking water to people in developing nations. Before long, the meaning he was finding after hours started to make him question his connection to his nine-to-five. "I realized that someone six levels above me could snap their fingers and everything that I did, in terms of actual production of work, could be unwound. That's where the power was. I was a cog in someone else's wheel—in the wheel of a Fortune 500 management team and public shareholders that I didn't know and didn't have reason to think their motives and my own were aligned. And I started to think, 'That's how I'm putting my labors to work? For God's glory?' It felt unsatisfying."

Brian realized he was running, with his parents' closely held Christian values, straight into uncharted territory. "My dad's idea is that you set yourself up for success, make good money, put it into the market, let it compound, and then—later in life—if you want to do something more rewarding, you have the freedom to take a haircut. He would say, 'You can always do that stuff later.' But I realized, I didn't want to do it later."

Seeking more from his profession, Brian began exploring the microfinance industry as a movement that better aligned his work to his values. He took a leave of absence from S&P, traveling to Bangladesh so he could learn from the economic philosophies of Muhammad Yunus and his Nobel Peace Prize–winning community development bank. From there he went to MIT business school, where he focused on social entrepreneurship and international finance. While his classmates were headed off to their cushy summer internships at Google, he was getting bitten by mosquitoes while assessing due diligence on mango plantations in West Africa. "It was a wake-up call," Brian admits. "That work was meaningful, to be sure, but I realized how far I had to go in order to be effective in the developing world—not just in terms of language skills, but [also] cultural acumen. I was lonely and frustrated."

When he graduated Brian kept his options open. He even interviewed at Standard & Poor's, as they said they wanted him back. When the offer came in—$115,000 base salary, a $45,000 signing bonus, and up to 20 percent annual bonus, all for a position as a first-year associate—Brian was stunned. It was huge. It would allow him to pay off all of his debt. "I basically went two nights without sleeping," he remembers. "I was watching my business school colleagues, a lot of whom were starry-eyed social entrepreneurs like me to begin with, and they were taking McKinsey jobs. I was lying in the dark thinking, 'I know I don't want to go back, but what's the trade-off, really? It would be giving up a year for money, basically.'"

On the third day, he turned the job down. "It was a huge weight off my shoulders when I said no—not like elation; it was like I was resigned. I fought internally with myself. I wrestled. I came out and I was exhausted. I wasn't empowered so much as relieved that I made the right move."

He took a job at Self-Help Federal Credit Union, a nonprofit that provides financial services and advocacy for those left out of the economic mainstream. The pay was exactly half of what he would have been guaranteed at Standard & Poor's, and he would be living in the notoriously expensive San Francisco Bay Area. And yet, the money couldn't talk louder than his excitement over applying his learning about economic development in Bangladesh and Cambodia and West Africa to stateside struggling communities. While Brian's dad is convinced that poverty is often the result of a refusal to work hard, as he has done, Brian believes that many people are poor because they've been historically oppressed; and even today, many have had trouble accessing capital and fair financial services, educational opportunities, adequate housing, and safe communities—all cornerstones of a successful American life.

Brian and his father mostly manage to keep the peace by not talking about politics, but every once in a while they drift into a conversation about money, and it's painful. On a recent visit home, Brian's dad bashed Elizabeth Warren; Brian thinks she's a modern-day heroine. "It's not just theoretical to me," Brian explains. "This is actually how I spend every day of my life, working on this stuff. I wish I could help him see the way I see it."

But he's not losing sleep over his divergence from his father: "I'm at peace about it. It was uncomfortable for a while, when I felt like I was swinging against the natural flow, career-wise, but I was never a fan of résumé building so that I could one day do something that I love. It's just who I am."

## "THAT GRASPY, HUNGRY FEELING"

Beyond our family story about money, the way we interpret our own financial health is also dependent on those around us. We often think about "keeping up with the Joneses" (not to be confused, of course, with Brian's family of origin) but rarely do we consider what it's actually like to *be* the Joneses. Is their perceived comfort actually comfortable? Does their safety net indeed make them feel safe? Are they spending their time with the people they love, doing things that delight them?

And while these may sound like thoroughly modern questions, people have been asking them for over a century. In fact, the very phrase "keeping up with the Joneses" is said to have originated as a reference to the wealthy family of Pulitzer Prize–winning novelist Edith Wharton. The Joneses, her father's side, were a prominent New York family, made rich by their investment in Chemical Bank. The Hudson Valley was dotted with their opulent, enviable estates; other wealthy New Yorkers, eager to demonstrate their comparable wealth, tried to build with similar grandeur, a phenomenon that came to be known as "keeping up with the Joneses."

But Wharton, a keen observer smack in the middle of the spending maelstrom, had no illusions about the lived experience of the elite. When her aunt, Elizabeth Schermerhorn Jones, built a twenty-four-room Gothic villa, others praised it as regal, but Wharton described it as a "gloomy monstrosity." About a decade later, she published *The House of Mirth*, a biting critique of upper-class life and the seemingly unquenchable thirst for more. Lily Bart, the protagonist, is a well-intentioned woman eventually destroyed by the high society that she was born into. Is it any wonder that Wharton also knew F. Scott Fitzgerald, author of the most famous exposé of the rancid curdling that comes from rabid wealth accumulation, *The Great Gatsby*?

Novelists are probably better at estimating people's sense of security or freedom than neighbors are. Financial health isn't something you can assess on the surface. Eight out of ten Americans have debt, the most common liability being a mortgage.[7] The average American in debt owes $16,140 on their credit cards, $155,361 on his mortgage, and $31,946 on student loans.[8] None of that is visible to those peering over the fence at that beautiful Restoration Hardware patio setup or smelling the grass-fed beef on the grill.

In fact, it's not unlikely that your neighbor with that state-of-the-art Weber grill hasn't used it for weeks. According to the latest American Time Use Survey, one-third of us work on weekends, and about one-quarter of us work at night.[9] Americans work more than do people in most industrialized countries, and take less vacation time. As *Slate*'s Jordan Weissmann put it: "Whatever the reasons, Americans structure their workweeks differently than Europeans. We're night owls and weekend MS Office warriors—which, in the eyes of the rest of the world, probably looks pretty nuts."[10]

In August 2015 *The New York Times* ran a cover story on the workaholic culture at Amazon; this triggered a flurry of writing about how unhealthy and surprisingly unproductive overwork really is, particularly in the tech industry. "Getting incredible results from the few who survive such an environment makes for a compelling narrative, but the data make it a hard one to defend," wrote Joe Lazauskas at *Fast Company*. "As an industry, we're telling ourselves a dangerous, self-propagating myth about the power—and perhaps even moral righteousness—of extreme work hours, fueling the worry that we'll fail catastrophically should we choose any other way."[11]

The data he was referring to were study after study that shows that your productivity actually declines after a certain number of hours worked. For example, according to research by economist John Pencavel of Stanford University, employee output drops off after the forty-ninth hour worked in a week; amazingly, an employee who puts in seventy hours per week is unlikely to produce much more than someone who works fifty-five. What's more, longer work hours endanger an employee for burnout, leading to higher rates of absenteeism and employee turnover.[12]

And it's not just the tech industry that's known for this kind of dumb, and potentially even deadly, pursuit of more productivity. Investment banking is notorious for its long, grueling hours, with some associates working as much as one hundred hours a week. A round of unexpected deaths or suicides of young bankers over the last few years has triggered some soul-searching by Wall Street firms about their work policies. In June 2015 Goldman Sachs told its summer interns they had to leave the office before midnight, not to return before 7:00 AM. Senior partners are now the only full-time bankers allowed in the office between Fridays at 9:00 PM and Sundays at 9:00 AM. Barclays forbids analysts from working more than twelve days in a row. Bank of America employees are forced to take off a minimum of four weekend days a month. As William D. Cohan put it in *The New York Times*: "Only on Wall Street, or perhaps in the equally competitive confines of Silicon Valley, could these kinds of guardrails begin to make sense."[13]

Thomas J. Hughes, a twenty-nine-year-old banker at Moelis & Company, was found dead with drugs in his system after falling from a building in Manhattan. His father told the *Daily Mail*: "The only explanation is that I know he's been working very hard and has been under a lot of pressure. His work did not leave much time for enjoyment, but that's the nature of the assignment that he chose."

Choosing a different assignment—especially one that veers away from the expectations and assumptions of your family or your friends—isn't easy. A small-business owner and mother from Lexington, Massachusetts—let's call her Sarah—messaged me on

Facebook after I posted a column on the subject. She grew up in an upper-middle-class family acutely aware of all the hustle it took to keep up; her parents seemed to believe there was never enough money (even though, from her vantage point, there always was). Sarah felt a different lack: a lack of time, of energy, of attention. She rebelled, dropped out of college, and pursued a very different dream. Now a parent herself, she is working hard to stay conscious of the life that she's creating, particularly as it relates to how much she earns and where and how she spends her time. But that's easier said than done. She writes:

> *The specter of the old value system rears its head at times. In the past, when I've spent time with a particular old friend, I noticed insecurities coming up with some frequency. At its heart it's a grasping, hungry feeling. But this last time, I was noticing the envy arise as she spoke about her upcoming kitchen renovation, but something different happened than the usual abnegating self-talk. I paused, breathed, and just let those emotions unravel while I kept paying attention. Within the next hour, her husband mentioned his workweek, and she mentioned hers, and I did some mental math and realized that they work seventy and fifty hours every week.*

It's not that Sarah wouldn't want to make more money, she admits; her and her husband's combined income is around $70,000. The Boston area is expensive and they find it hard to afford karate and summer camp for their five-year-old. Truth be told, she'd love to update her kitchen. But those humble desires can't compete with her bigger values and the calculations they inspire. Sarah and her husband both work part-time and care for their son part-time. Doing the math on her friends' work hours effectively exorcized that "grasping, hungry feeling." She reflects:

*This all hit me in a flash as I realized that I truly wasn't willing to put in the hours necessary to unbalance my life in favor of work instead of family time right now, that I had created this life out of my own values, to serve me and mine, that I had the flexibility built in to change it as needed, and that I was really doing pretty well, all told. It was a very quiet, fundamental shift in perspective, and it felt really, really good.*

## THE OVERVALUING OF MONEY

The inspiring stories of people like Beth, Brian, and Sarah reveal the relative and very personal nature of what it means to have "enough." Finding that sweet spot where you bring home enough money to afford the life you want *and* actually have enough time to enjoy it appears to be more art than science. And yet, is it possible that there's an objective benchmark?

In a widely discussed study from 2010, psychologist Daniel Kahneman and economist Angus Deaton analyzed data from more than 450,000 U.S. residents and found that there is an income plateau after which money has no measurable effect on daily contentment. The magic number? $75,000.[14]

Of course, this depends on which state you live in—Mississippians, like Beth Foley Barnes, need only $64,000 (interestingly, about what she and her husband earn), while those in the Aloha state, like Robert Kiyosaki, author of *Rich Dad Poor Dad*, need a whopping $91,000. Bay staters like Sarah need $92,000.[15] And households, of course, vary greatly in size and need. For example, a single mom living in an expensive city with three kids with special needs probably needs a lot more money.

Setting all those qualifiers aside for a moment, if $75,000 is a somewhat magic number, how many American households already bring in that or more? According to the U.S. Census Bureau, 34.4 percent.[16]

That means that over a third of Americans should not be asking themselves how they can go about increasing their earning potential— our de facto setting in this country. They should be asking themselves a whole different set of questions: *Would my quality of life be better if I earned less? Do I actually want that raise and all the responsibility that comes with it? Should I consider looking for a job that pays less but brings me more satisfaction or fits better with my dream for how I structure my life? What are the effects of my wealth, however humble, on my child's sense of self and worldview? What are the effects of my earnings, in general, on my relationships?*

If those questions seem strange, there's a reason. We simply don't have a public dialogue featuring this kind of inquiry. If you Google "How much money is enough?" you get a slew of hits on something called "FU money," defined by that utmost authority, Urban Dictionary, as "any amount of money allowing infinite perpetuation of wealth necessary to maintain a desired lifestyle without needing employment or assistance from anyone." You read that right—one of the most popular philosophies for thinking through how much money is enough is fundamentally about avoiding work, however meaningful, and disconnecting from others. (I suppose someone could make enough "FU money" to live the life of a passionate artist, for example, but that doesn't seem to be the widely stated goal.) It's the ultimate delusion of autonomy—that, at some definable dollar amount, we become completely independent beings, free of any needs that we can't fulfill all by our own damn selves ("FU," as you might have guessed, stands for "Fuck You").

Most of the myriad books and television shows about money focus on honing people's willpower on a daily basis so they can afford more stuff on a yearly basis—the fewer-lattes-equals-more-Louis-Vuitton equation. It's the gospel of deprivation and aspiration.

To be fair, financial literacy and one of its modern-day gospels—the delay of gratification—are important. Some of those avoided lattes translate into really valuable experiences, educational and otherwise. Even upper-middle-class Americans have reason to worry about how much money they have socked away: the rising price of college, the threat of medical bankruptcy in a country with such a screwed-up healthcare system, the prospect of retirement. But too often financial literacy frameworks focus almost exclusively on what individuals can do to expand their piece of the pie—while ignoring the fact that already rich people are cooking with different ingredients. Mortgage income tax deductions, negligible financial transaction taxes, lower capital gains taxes, and a variety of other federal policies make it easier for rich people to get richer while poor people are patronizingly reproached to demonstrate better financial behavior.

Yes, we must extend the conversation that was started with the Occupy movement about federal policy that privileges the rich. But we must also look at the ways in which the political is personal. The quality of our very lives depends on a more nuanced dialogue—one more focused on how much money we can *afford* to make, when our relationships mean so much to us and we crave work that feels like a true expression of who we are. It's simply unwise to operate on income autopilot no matter how much you make. For 34.4 percent of us, there's scientific evidence that we may be jeopardizing our chance at daily contentment by blindly pursuing more.

A further complication of this research that I find fascinating is this: Kahneman and Deaton determined that $75,000 is the income plateau for what they call "emotional well-being," but not for another kind of happiness: "evaluation of life." Here's how they define the two:

*Emotional well-being (sometimes called "hedonic well-being" or "experienced happiness") refers to the emotional quality of an individual's everyday experience—the frequency and intensity of experiences of joy, fascination, anxiety, sadness, anger, and affection that make one's life pleasant or unpleasant.*

*Life evaluation refers to a person's thoughts about his or her life. Surveys of subjective well-being have traditionally emphasized life evaluation. The most commonly asked question in these surveys is the life satisfaction question: "How satisfied are you with your life as a whole these days?"*

This makes my head spin. *Life evaluation refers to a person's thoughts about his or her life.* That means that what we're experiencing on a daily basis—that first bite of salad plucked from our very own garden, having a surprisingly wonderful conversation with someone on the bus, watching our kid get a math problem after struggling—makes us happy whether we make $75,000 a year or $7,500,000 a year, and yet, our way of evaluating what all those moments add up to is heavily influenced by our salaries. When we make more money, our experience of life isn't better. But, when we make more money, we *think* our lives are better, even if we feel, hour by hour, the same as we did $10 or $20,000 ago.

Is it crazy to postulate that the presence of the mythology—that we'd be happier if we made more money—actually influences us to value that story above our own, visceral, day-to-day experience? Do we give more credence to the American Dream than we do to our lived reality?

Sociologist Pierre Bourdieu argued that our society has what he called "mental maps"—almost like those old transparencies that teachers used to project lessons on the overhead. These mental maps, created by the elite of society, overlay our personal choices in significant ways. They determine what we think is virtuous, desirable, possible. They keep the status quo in place, even if it's unjust or unhealthy. Bourdieu writes, "The most powerful forms of ideological effect are those which need no words, but merely a complicitous silence."

America's mental map about money is potent, and largely so embedded—like subtle product placement in a sitcom—that we barely realize it's there. It tells us that the more money you make, the better off you are, and that to be rich is to be happy. This subliminal messaging is especially strong in men's ears; even for those who consider themselves thoroughly liberated from gender stereotypes, money and masculinity are toxically intertwined. "Bringing home the bacon" may sound old school, but its reverberations rattle the psyches of even young men.

When we pause from the actual experience of enjoying our lives just as they are, that mental map kicks in, and we reply, "Why yes, I guess I would be that much happier if I had that much more." Meanwhile, our internal experience of "enough" is like a quiet, brave little voice, drowned out by the cacophony of how we're told true abundance looks, feels, and tastes.

Kahneman and Deaton's study was not conducted with people staring down the end of life; dying, of course, is the ultimate destroyer of delusion. In *The Top 5 Regrets of the Dying: A Life Transformed by the Dearly Departing*, palliative nurse Bronnie Ware synthesizes the wisdom she gleaned from years of caring for patients in the twilight of their lives. The number one regret: "I wish I'd had the courage to live a life true to myself, not the life others expected of me."

The second: "I wish I hadn't worked so hard." Ware expounds: "All of the men I nursed deeply regretted spending so much of their lives on the treadmill of a work existence." You might not be surprised to learn that no one in Ware's many years of nursing expressed the wish that they'd made more money. Not one.

In our final moments, it is our authenticity, our courage, our connections that matter most to us. Insofar as money becomes a tool to bring us closer to these things, it's invaluable. But when it becomes an obstacle between us and those we love, between who we truly are and what we're spending our days doing, then it's not just less valuable, it's potentially harmful.

We live in a country with a profoundly weakened safety net and severe economic insecurity. That means that, no matter how engaged we are in the questions of money and meaning, we still aren't supported in exploring nuanced answers. Luckily, this isn't just about each of us individually waking up and asking better questions; that approach falls into the same trap of total self-reliance as FU money and so many other Lone Ranger economic philosophies. We must examine our lives, our relationship with money, our alignment, or lack thereof, between our daily reality and our deeply held values—*and* we must fight for a more embracing, wise economic system for everyone.

It would be far easier for each of us to make conscious decisions about money if we had societal support—both financial and informational—about what actually leads to a higher quality of life. But we can't wait for the systems and cultures that we're a part of to get it right. Lynne Twist, author of *The Soul of Money: Reclaiming the Wealth of Our Inner Resources*, writes, "The biggest, most unquestioned answer of our culture is our relationship with money. It is there that we keep alive—at a high cost—the flame and mythology of scarcity."

We must extinguish that flame. We must honor our own experiences above the deeply engrained mythologies about accumulation and safety. We must seek meaningful work, love our people well, and prioritize play and pleasure—now. We must listen to that quiet, brave little voice saying "enough"; we must consider what it has to say about the overvaluing of money and the undervaluing of time.

Without that kind of dogged discernment, the money, in and of itself, has little true value. The true value lies in the quest to find the precise point at which you have enough—which, it would appear, is when you truly have everything.

# fighting to be whole

## HOW MEN ARE FALLING IN
## LOVE WITH FATHERING

John and I lay in bed, the pregnancy support pillow an overstuffed snake slithering out of the sheets. We tried to imagine what it was going to be like to have a baby in just a few short, strange weeks. There is no liminal space more profound than the anticipation of birth or death. There is no way to prepare. You just stand on the edge of that abyss and cling to your loved ones with all your might, hoping you'll muster up the courage to face the leap when nature nudges you over.

"What are you most excited about?" I ask into the dark.

"Taking slow walks, holding hands with her," John replies. I'm shocked. This is a guy who runs marathons at a rapid pace and prides himself on returning emails at lightning speed. John doesn't do slow.

I'm so touched by his response, never mind that our daughter—yet unnamed—won't be able to walk for a year or more. It is as if his anticipated vision comes from somewhere dormant within him, a slower, noticing version of my man that mostly hasn't manifested within his ambition, his efficiency. Walking beside a little one is a chance to wake up a whole different dimension of who you are.

John was just one of many contemporary men looking forward to the transformation that fatherhood can bring. For decades we've operated on the premise that caretaking is both a woman's responsibility and her unique skill—from which men have been missing out. But that's changing.

There is a perfect storm of demographic, economic, and cultural conditions just right for this shift. For one, sex and marriage are getting remixed in revelatory ways; about 40 percent of babies are now born out of wedlock, a nearly fourfold increase since 1970, and well over 100,000 same-sex couples are raising children in America today.[1] The structure of work is eroding: since so many men aren't tied to a traditional workday as they were in decades past, they are able to prioritize parenting alongside their professional lives. And cultural attitudes are catching up—nearly three-quarters of adults under thirty view the ideal marriage as one in which both partners work and share childcare and household duties.[2]

In a rousing speech at the Omega Institute, of which she is cofounder, Elizabeth Lesser declared: "Men in this century are going to have to want to change as much as women wanted to change in the last century. And not to see that change merely as a duty, but also to know it as a benefit that will bring joy and wholeness to their lives."[3]

Men, like so many women before them, are starting to understand that what has historically been dismissed as a burden—the nurturing of children and the elderly, the creation and cultivation of loving homes, the growing of food and cooking of meals—can actually be a gift. As the concept of family is being remade, so too are views of caretaking. And, despite all the megabytes used discussing whether women are "leaning in" or "having it all," men are some of the most vocal proponents of shifting how we think about, approach, measure, and value caretaking.

## THE DAWN OF THE ENGAGED DAD

Tom Stocky, a Facebook executive living in the Bay Area, doesn't want to be your hero. In July 2013 he wrote a brief reflection about his four-month paternity leave—the kind of thing he predicted his friends and family, and perhaps a few people in his extended network, might find interesting. Among other things, he reflected on how much he grew to really enjoy taking care of his baby daughter:

> *It was nice to have her like me so much, to come to me for comfort when she fell, to come and cuddle with me when she got sleepy, to run toward me screaming with excitement after I'd been away for a while. I realized that's just because I spent so much time with her, but I didn't care, it felt really good. Maybe it was also because I got better at childcare. It feels nice to be good at something, and I got much better at the work I was doing at home.*[4]

Before long, the post had been liked over ten thousand times and shared another six thousand. Comments flooded in, as did blog posts and op-eds piggybacking off the sentiment he expressed.

Readers were captivated by Tom's unusually personal admission that, even as a high-earning, dedicated professional, he'd found caretaking both challenging and rewarding. That kind of public reflection happened incredibly rarely among fathers of the past—not just because fewer of them experienced the highs and lows of intensive caretaking (men engage in nearly three times more childcare than they did in 1965),[5] but also because, even when they did, they feared "coming out" about it. Would they be seen as less legitimate professionals if they admitted to loving a morning snuggle with their children? Would their dedication to the job be questioned if they took time off to be with a baby, or an older kid who needed some TLC?

Another thing that particularly struck a nerve was Tom's seeming irritation that outsiders viewed his caring for his daughter as gallantry. He often got what he called "back-handed compliments," like, "Your wife must work so hard. That's great that you're able to pick up the slack."

"Has someone ever said that to a woman?" Stocky asked.

Peter Mountford, another dad flummoxed by the hero worship, writes: "I'm accosted by strangers who want to praise me because I'm with my kids at noon on Tuesday. But when I was working around the clock and Jen was with the kids, people applauded my ambition. I'm a hero either way, which is nice for me."[6]

Peter is a novelist based in Seattle. He worked for six months while his wife took care of their two kids, and then she worked for six months while he stepped in full-time for the diaper changing, grocery shopping, and everything else that fills up a domestic day. He noticed the unfairness of it all—how his wife doesn't get to be the hero in either scenario; she's either neglecting her kids when she's in ambitious career mode or given no special praise when she's doing her duty as a devoted mother.

James Norton, another new dad, weighed in for *The Christian Science Monitor*: "In the three short months since having Josiah, I've met a number of people who regard my contributions to my son's care as somehow wonderful or unusual."[7]

And while these men don't want special credit for being committed fathers, all of them seem to recognize just how special the experience of taking care of their little ones is. They crave the sacred sweetness just as their female partners do. They want to prevail in the crash course that is adjusting to life with a newborn. They love the bonding time. Norton writes:

*Speaking personally, I like changing diapers. Let me restate that: I take satisfaction in changing diapers. Since breastfeeding isn't an option, it's an aspect of childcare where my own limited talents can contribute, if not actually shine. I like the post-diaper smiles. And I like taking my son on walks, and being around to catch all those silly-but-significant little developmental milestones. But most of all, I like knowing that I'm participating actively in raising him—we've been having dude time together since he was born, something that I hope continues for the rest of my life.*

So there you have it: even "dude time" has been transformed by evolving ideals of fatherhood.

These men are embracing what has long been thought of as "women's wisdom"—that there is meaning in the everyday. This generation of young men is hip to the fact that, as exhausting and monotonous as caretaking can be, there is also pleasure to be found in it. There are delight and surprise as you rediscover the world alongside a little one. There is also profound clarity—caretaking is the strongest antidote against bullshit; you simply don't have the time or energy to entertain manufactured concerns or tolerate unnecessary drama. And there is that incomparable esteem that comes from knowing that you're a source of comfort for a vulnerable creature, not to mention that you're an equal partner to a woman (in the case of a heterosexual relationship) whose professional passions you value. It's not the stuff that gets you promoted; it's the stuff that gives you pride on your deathbed. That's true regardless of your sex.

Ultimately, most men don't want to be thought of as heroes just for taking care of their own kids, and women don't want to be thought of as villains just for wanting to nurture their careers. We can all find meaning in both. We can all find pleasure in both. The struggle is to craft a life where that meaning and pleasure can coexist, where we can sometimes be absorbed in the world of our family—the playground sand stuck between baby toes, a teenager's sloppy admission that he's freaked out, a cup of tea with an aging parent—and sometimes be absorbed in the world of our work—the carefully planned strategy, the thoughtfully balanced curricula, the perfectly coordinated presentation.

In short, to craft that life is to struggle for integration.

What thrills me is that finally, *finally*, it's not just women visibly working toward this integration. While women have been fighting to get into the boardroom, men have—albeit under the radar— been fighting to get into the birth room. In historian Judith Walzer Leavitt's book, *Make Room for Daddy: The Journey from Waiting Room to Birthing Room*, she describes the ways in which men have migrated from puffing cigars obliviously in hospital waiting rooms, seeing birth as mostly an abstraction, to holding their wives' hands and coaching them through the entire process. She writes of these pioneering men: "They wanted to support their partners, they wanted to be witnesses to the births of their children, and they found that both motivations helped them to bond with their families in new and mutually beneficial ways."[8]

It's stunning to think about what a dramatic cultural change has taken place in just a couple of generations. My husband's grandmother told us that when she went into labor her husband literally dropped her off at the Oshkosh, Wisconsin, hospital in the morning, went ahead to his job as a furrier, and then drove back at the end of the day to see if his child had, indeed, arrived. Contrast that with John's role: he not only drove me to the hospital, but he barely left the room for the nearly twelve hours I was in labor, save to take a deep breath and eat a sandwich. He went to the childbirth class. He went to the childcare class. He didn't miss a single prenatal checkup, despite the fact that most of them were totally mundane. And further: none of these actions resulted from negotiation. It was an absolute given between us that, though I would be the one actually giving birth, *we* were the ones bringing this kid into the world—and so were mutually terrified, exhilarated, and responsible.

Yes, we gave birth in Berkeley. And yes, we are progressive, feminist, coconut water–drinking, placenta pill–ingesting clichés of ourselves. But, as it happens, even lumberjacks in red states are showing up for their children's births. It's simply the norm these days—though, strangely, no reliable statistics exist on how many births are attended by fathers, or at least not from the American Congress of Obstetricians and Gynecologists or the American Hospital Association.

That birthing is now much more of a two-parent affair is significant for many reasons, which reach far deeper into the lives of parents and children than just those odd first days in the hospital. Men's presence in the birthing room means that they see women's bodies not just as sexual (beautiful, pristine, coifed, in control) but as multidimensional, even miraculous. I won't go too deep into pregnancy and birth, but let's just say that experiencing both, and even being in close proximity to both, reconfigure your understanding of the human body. Clarissa Pinkola Estés tells women: "Having a lover and friends who support the *criatura* in you . . . these are the people you are looking for."[9]

It's also who men should be looking to be. When they stay out of the birthing room, they may protect themselves from the messiness of birth, and even the potential trauma, but they also lose out on the opportunity to witness their partner's power in a once-in-a-lifetime light. They sacrifice the chance for firsthand knowledge of the awesome complexity of how life begins. Their own lives, in a sense, stay safe and small.

## FUMBLING TOWARD FATHERHOOD

In approaching childbirth jointly, traditional gender roles are obliterated right from the start: women are the physical heroes, men are largely there for emotional strength. My labor and delivery nurses admitted they'd never heard a woman curse as much as I did during labor—something I consider a badge of honor. My husband? He was spraying my back with water, repositioning the horrendous lighting, and cheering me on with his eyes pretty much consistently filled with tears. Unlike his grandfather, whose entry into parenthood was technically spent earning money for the family, John's fatherhood was defined from the very first moment by his empathy. *Esquire*'s Stephen Marche, writing on what he calls "the new fatherhood," emphasizes the significance of this most modern dawn: "Witnessing birth was the beginning of a widening intimacy."[10]

The intimacy extends. While women recover, many men today immediately jump into action nurturing their tiny newborns—figuring out how to hold them, swaddle them, soothe them, change their diapers. That baptism by fire is a great leap into the wild unknowns of fatherhood. Too many men, for far too long, have stood on the sidelines while women figured it all out, only to tentatively tip toe into being sparingly "helpful" with their newborns. In generations past, it was easy to drift away while women got busy with what appeared to be instinct but what was actually practice or inherited wisdom from mothers and grandmothers. While the Greatest Generation of men—those who knew the Great Depression and World War II—hardly seemed to register the intimacy they were missing out on in the early days, Boomer men had more consciousness. And yet, many seemed to sort of slink away, convinced they weren't wanted, needed, or equipped to be a critical part of their newborns' spankin' new narratives.

It's no wonder that many Boomer men express regret over missing the chance or the gumption to get involved with their children from the very beginning, in part just so they could build their own caretaking repertoire. The silver lining is a sort of exuberant embrace of the grandfather role among so many men just now aging into their sixties. Case in point: my own father discovered that he has a strange and wonderful way of shushing tiny babies—his own little Jedi mind trick—that puts newborns right to sleep; when my daughter and nephew were tiny, he spent many an hour cradling the little jumbo, fleece-covered burritos, hissing into their tiny ears. (Fist bump, Harvey Karp!) Yet when my brother and I were newborns, it never occurred to my dad to jump in like that. Everything he grew up with, everything he saw around him, sent the message that early days were women's days. But watching his son and son-in-law soothe, swaddle, and shush sparked his own imagination.

So much of what previous generations accepted as the inevitable distinction between men's and women's experiences of parenting is turning out to be false. We're even discovering that fatherhood changes men neurologically and biochemically. Recent studies confirm that men's brains, especially if they are primary care providers for their children, change in many of the same ways that women's do when they become mothers; essentially the parts of your brain that help you tune in to another person emotionally start conspiring the more you interact with your baby, regardless of your sex.[11] It's widely known that new fathers experience an increase in the "cuddle hormone" oxytocin, but new research even suggests that two hormones associated with more aggressive behavior—testosterone and estradiol—lower in men, even *before* their babies are born.[12]

Now don't get me wrong: as a new mom, I'd be a fool to understate how sobering biological reality is throughout pregnancy, birth, and in the months after. I've never felt so essentially female as I did waddling through the redwoods right around my due date, experiencing the animalistic explosion that was birth, and nursing hour after frickin' hour in the months that followed. While John loves to brag about the three hundred diapers he changed in the first month (our midwife, bless her, told him that my job was to nurse and his job was to change diapers and he took it very seriously), there's just no getting around the inescapable physical differences that women and men experience in the early days. But they're over in a flash and what follows is a lifetime of burden and blessing, fit to be shared in a thousand configurations.

And even those inescapable physical differences, I would argue, don't suggest "rank" in the way that previous generations defined it. The transformation that women experience upon becoming mothers, and all that it requires of their lives, have been widely acknowledged and written about by everyone from Anne Lamott to Tina Fey. Barely a day goes by when one doesn't see a headline or a hotly contested debate on the subject on cable television. As Margaret Talbot recently wrote in *The New Yorker*: "What do Papua New Guinea, Oman, and the United States of America have in common? They are the only three countries in the world with no paid-maternity-leave law."[13]

The transformations that men undergo, especially those that embrace fatherhood from its fumbling beginnings, have historically been far less visible; fortunately, they are starting to bravely appear. Their identity shifts and unmet policy needs (such as paternity leave) are separately, but equally, important. And a new generation of men is, in a sense, "coming out" as fathers—writing about their parenting epiphanies online and publicly wrestling with their sometimes conflicting roles as fathers and professionals.

Alexis C. Madrigal, a journalist best known for his coverage of technology, writes of his own bourgeoning parenthood:

*A couple days after we found out my wife was pregnant, I took a*
*twenty-mile hike up in the Oakland hills, thinking. Near the top of*
*the ridge, I was struck by a rock outcropping that I've returned to*
*again and again in my mind as I stare at his perfect little ears. . . .*
*What was once ground is now wall, and time reads from right to left.*
*Atop the rocks, where new soil has become fresh ground, massive euca-*
*lyptus trees have gained purchase, and their roots wind down through*
*the rock, splitting it, and holding it together. Down at the base, I see*
*myself from the perspective of the rocks: biology on this teensy-tiny*
*human time scale, large in self-importance, small in duration. To the*
*rocks, I'm a barely there ghost in a long-exposure photograph. And yet,*
*the asphalt I'm running on marks a more permanent humanity. . . .*
*Eight days in, fatherhood is the most epic thing I've ever experienced.*[14]

"Epic" is an important choice of words here. It's a word that used
to be reserved for adventures of the über-masculine ilk—bearded men
atop massive sailing vessels, charting their way into strange lands by
the stars, or trudging faithfully up snowcapped mountains far above
the clouds, their sights set on reaching the apex of some iconic peak.
More recently, it sounds like the chosen tongue of Silicon Valley—college dropouts rewarded with epic investments from venture capital
firms who get astronomically rich and notorious off their Internet-
styled inventions. These are the symbols that have occupied the imagination of achievement in so many American men for so many years,
prompting them to ask themselves, "What's my adventure? What's
my invention? What's my legacy?"

Meanwhile, a whole new kind of imagination is taking form—
one that casts adventure in emotional terms, where endurance is
not a test of brawn but of heart. One that recognizes the creation
of a new human to be the most commonplace of inventions, but the
one that miraculously keeps the human race trudging courageously

along. One that traces legacy through hard-earned bonding with a newborn son, not by slapping a junior at the end of his name. In this sense, "epic" is the perfect word to reclaim for new fathers. No smaller word encompasses a challenge and gift as vast as truly engaged fatherhood, and no other word can quite describe how uncharted the territory really is.

## PARENTING AS PRESENCE

Dan Pallotta and his husband, Jimmy, spent years trying to become fathers. First, they tried adopting internationally, but they refused to lie about their sexual orientation in order to be eligible. Then they tried to adopt domestically, but it was a strange time in Los Angeles. "The county was trying to get kids back to their birth parents," Dan explains, "and we didn't want that emotional trauma."

Finally, they decided to pursue surrogacy. Their first egg donor had a medical issue. Then their first surrogate had a medical issue. Finally, they found a donor and surrogate healthy enough to go for it. And let's just say they *went for it*.

"You better get a bigger car," their surrogate told them, fresh from her ultrasound at the Mayo Clinic. "They detected three heartbeats."

Jimmy and Dan were ecstatic; it was an instant family—more than they could have dreamed of. Jimmy, a chef, planned to quit his job and stay home with the kids, while Dan would continue his work advocating for reform of the nonprofit sector.

Dan is best known for founding AIDS Ride and other charity sports events that over nine years collectively raised $582 million and engaged 182,000 people. He wrote about the journey in his popular book *Uncharitable: How Restraints on Nonprofits Undermine Their Potential,* and spoke about it in his TED talk, which has been viewed over three and a half million times. Dan is highly ambitious.

"It's true—my thirties were all about my job," Dan explains. "But I lean much more toward family now. When you have kids later in life, you're very aware of how quickly life goes by. I know this is all going to be gone in ten years and I'm not going to miss it."

Dan was forty-seven when the triplets were born. According to the National Center for Family & Marriage Research, the average American man is 27.4 years old when his first child is born, nearly a two-year jump from twenty years ago.[15] More and more men are having kids later in life, which means they've had more time to establish themselves professionally and financially. This is a key factor in the new fatherhood—so many men simply know themselves better by the time they have children. If they really want to prioritize them, they're more likely to have the professional flexibility (because of years spent "paying their dues"), the financial base that can afford a little time off, and/or the wisdom, as Dan points out, to know that nothing lasts forever.

When Dan was born his dad was a twenty-four-year-old construction worker who was always worrying about getting food on the table. He tried to steal time with his kids when he could, but he just didn't have the same communication skills that Dan has honed over years of therapy. "The biggest difference between my dad's and my style of parenting is presence," Dan reflects. "When my kids are talking, I look them in the eyes and I listen to everything they're saying."

Analissa and Sage, both girls, and Rider, a boy, are now seven years old. Each month, Dan takes one of them out for a special one-on-one day. From nine in the morning until seven at night, they venture all over Boston, beginning with their favorite breakfast buffet, where the kids fuel up with a giant hot chocolate and whipped cream. They tie-dye T-shirts, go bowling, watch movies, and then collapse into bed.

Dan is already aware of the ways in which his son doesn't fit the status quo. He's a sensitive kid who loves to build elaborate Lego kits rather than play sports. He also makes his own fairy houses all over their wooded property. When Dan finds one, he takes great pleasure in writing a little note from the fairy, burning the edges of the paper a bit for maximum authenticity, rolling it up, tying a string around it, and hiding it within for Rider to find.

They tried participating in a local father-son group, but it was all about competition. "There are all these forty-year-old men getting super competitive over a pickup soccer game," Dan remembers. "One of them kicked the ball right into Rider's stomach, trying to score a goal. Two dads almost got in a fight on the field. I was like, 'Screw this. This isn't for us.'"

Dan and Jimmy encounter confusion when they each take their kids out. Dan is often mistaken for a divorcé on "dad duty" for the weekend, and Jimmy is asked to join mothers' groups at school. Dan jokes, "We want to get T-shirts for me and Jimmy that say YES, THEY'RE TRIPLETS, and T-shirts for the kids that say, YES, THEY'RE GAY."

There are times when my conversation with Dan leads him to be very nostalgic, waxing poetic about what it was like to grow up within a few miles of his seventeen cousins, how he alternated Sunday night dinners between his two grandparents' houses, how everything felt so much safer (though Steven Pinker would disagree) and everyone was so much more genuinely connected:

> *This whole generation of immigrants, my grandparents included,*
> *came to the United States because they wanted a better life for*
> *their kids—more money, bigger houses, better neighborhoods, less*
> *struggle. The kids of all of these bakers and carpenters and masons*
> *and bricklayers then went off to college to become economists and*
> *politicians and investment bankers. And for what? Now we lead*
> *these busy, busy lives. Sometimes I go into an airport and look*
> *around at everyone and think, "Is it really so important that all*

*these people be in these places at a given time?" I have some very*
*deep questions about all of it. Is it really progress?*

When I remind Dan that his life would be quite different if he was part of the "silent generation" he has so much admiration for, he chuckles: "I guess you're right. I would be this closeted, alcoholic, gay man having dinner with my family on Sunday."

At base, the nostalgia is about cultural norms. Back then it may have been harder to make ends meet, at least in Dan's family, but it was easier to keep your priorities straight. Family above all else. And yet, even Dan admits that his father didn't have the capacity to be present with his kids in the same way he does (there wasn't even language for it back then, at least any that a working-class guy from Boston would have been exposed to). And further, he simply wouldn't have had the opportunity to be a father—at least as an openly gay man, married to his partner, helped along by technology—if he'd been born even a couple of decades earlier.

"There's nothing more satisfying than being with my kids," he says. "I mean, they're seven-year-old kids. They're so beautiful and so innocent and so curious and so friendly. It's like, who wouldn't want to hang out with them all the time?"

## BEYOND BRINGING HOME THE BACON

Thirty-three-year-old Chris Wallace lives in super-ambitious Washington, DC, where the first question people ask when you meet them is usually: "What do you do for a living?"

Chris's answer throws people off: "I change diapers."

"I use it as a hook to open a conversation," he explains. "Some people are shocked that a younger guy would put his career on pause and work at home with a kid."

Chris has noticed that he gets pretty predictable reactions from people depending on their age. If it's younger people, they usually express how awesome they think it is, and talk about how jealous they are if they aren't able to spend as much time with their own little ones. If it's older people, again, regardless of gender, they are mystified, and often have stories of regret about the choices they made around their own children's early years.

Either way, it leaves Chris feeling affirmed in his decision. Over a year ago, he was sitting in his cubicle day after day, feeling uninspired and missing his family. He was back to the daily grind at his job as a real estate tax analyst with Navy Federal Credit Union after the birth of his son a few months earlier. If he'd been unsure about his job before Gavin arrived, it became crystal clear after he came on the scene. "I was constantly texting, asking for pictures of my son," Chris remembers. "My heart just wasn't in the job."

Let's do a thought experiment: read that last paragraph again, and this time, imagine it is the story of a new mother rather than a new father. It feels both more familiar and like grounds for a go-girl pep talk, right? *Come on, sweetie, give it a little time. You're just feeling the postpartum blues. It will get easier. Lean in!* Ever since women have entered the workforce (historically structured for men with no domestic or caretaking responsibilities), they've been made to feel like their incapacity to "have it all" is a personal failure rather than a collective delusion.

When a woman leaves or scales back at her job, it's rarely acknowledged that it's not just because she "can't cut it"; it's often because the policies and culture of her workplace make it impossible for her to do anything but leave. Despite the fact that studies show that flexibility (things like telecommuting, part-time work, and job sharing) improves the bottom line, far too few companies embrace it.[16] And thus, the quarter of women who supposedly "opt out" (that reductive, evil little phrase) after having kids actually struggle mightily between a rock and a hard place until they just can't do it anymore.

Pamela Stone, a sociologist at Hunter College, studied how women made decisions at moments like these and found "that their decisions to quit were reluctant and conflicted. . . . For these women, most of whom never envisioned having to choose between careers and children, the costs of workplace inflexibility are up close and personal—diverted dreams and foregone earnings and independence."[17]

Part of the unfinished revolution here is a fairly straightforward one—we need to remake workplaces for the twenty-first century, where both women *and* men have the responsibility and privilege of being workers and caregivers. That means a long list of innovations, starting with more flexibility and paid family leave. But part of the unfinished revolution is less straightforward; we need to reimagine what leadership looks like in the twenty-first century.

Max Schireson was hailed all over the Internet for his heartfelt resignation as CEO of MongoDB, a database vendor. In a nutshell, he said that he wanted a less demanding job because he wanted to be more present with his wife and three kids. He writes:

> *I recognize that by writing this I may be disqualifying myself from some future CEO role. Will that cost me tens of millions of dollars someday? Maybe. Life is about choices. Right now, I choose to spend more time with my family and am confident that I can continue to have an [sic] meaningful and rewarding work life while doing so. At first, it seemed like a hard choice, but the more I have sat with the choice the more certain I am that it is the right choice.*[18]

While I, too, love his candor and boldness, it got me thinking: why isn't anyone talking about the fact that being a leader, as we've conceived of it in so many sectors, practically requires neglecting everything outside of work? Is it possible to be a CEO (or school principal or nonprofit director or any other overworked, highly visible leader of an organization) *and* prioritize caretaking? And if the answer is no, what does that say about the kinds of leaders we're cultivating?

Public policy expert Anne-Marie Slaughter caused a firestorm of conversation about work/life balance (a term I despise) after her 2012 cover story in *The Atlantic*, "Why Women Still Can't Have It All." But it was actually her husband's take, which appeared three years later, that I found the most riveting. Andrew Moravcsik talked about the highs and lows of being a male caregiver in terms so explicit as to be almost shocking. This sentence knocked the wind out of me: "For years, Anne-Marie has rarely been home for more than a couple of dinners a week, except during holidays."[19]

This line was positioned as insignificant in the context of the piece—just a detail to support his larger point that "Anne-Marie's job duties are incompatible with being a lead parent." And yet, it struck me as central to the larger conversation we need to be having. Slaughter's accomplishments are admirable and varied. I consider her a role model in many ways. But she shouldn't have had to sacrifice that much time with her loved ones in order to do what she's done.

Many people—women and men—are rejecting that paradigm of leadership because they refuse to believe that doing great things in the big, wide world should require missing out on so much great time with children, partners, neighbors, and friends. And there's yet another layer here. When people don't love their jobs, it's much easier to quit them. If you don't have other commitments, like a kid or a sick parent, it can be tolerable to simply collect a paycheck. But when you need to give more of your time to someone—or, why not be perfectly honest—when you just want to spend more time with someone, it's excruciating to tolerate hours spent in a dull cubicle wondering if the bulk of your day invests in something that actually matters. Having a baby, among other profound personal transformations, forces you to get real about your energy, your time, and the ways in which you most want to make your life count. It's no wonder that women have been leaving uninspiring workplaces for years; what's surprising is that it's taken men this long to start leaving too.

To return to Chris Wallace, the self-named diaper-changer in DC: Chris's wife, Latoya, an editor at ESPN, is a journalist and blogger with a substantial following. Around the time when her maternity leave (at a previous employer) was ending, Chris was growing increasingly disillusioned with his job. They needed to decide what to do about childcare. After weighing all their options, they decided it made the most sense for Chris to quit his job and stay home, liberating him from a job he didn't love in order to spend time with a son he was falling madly in love with.

And while this sounds like a no-brainer, Chris surprised even himself with the decision to become a full-time caregiver. Back when he and Latoya were first dating, he remembers a moment when she said, "If we ever have a kid, you should stay home with him for a little bit."

"I was like, naw," said Chris. "But when he actually arrived, it was a completely different feeling."

According to the Pew Research Center, the number of stay-at-home dads has nearly doubled in the last fifteen years, and not, as is often assumed, because of the rise in unemployment, but because men like Chris *choose* to stay at home.[20] As the definition of the ideal man continues to widen and deepen, "bringing home the bacon" just isn't as satisfying as it once was; men are waking up to the joy and sense of deep fulfillment that can live at home.

"I'm the first face he sees in the morning every day," Chris told me, the pride and pleasure audible in his voice. "He wakes up and we get ready and have some breakfast, or a little fruit or something. We watch our *Sesame Street*. Then we take the dog out, maybe go to the playground."

When they first developed that routine, Chris quickly noticed two distinct cliques at the neighborhood playground: the moms and the nannies, neither of which he fits in with, of course. He also noticed that people's reaction to his presence was dependent not just on what he was wearing but on whether Gavin was in a carrier on his chest or in a stroller. He breaks it down: "When I push Gavin in a stroller, especially if I'm not as dressed up, people assume I'm a baby daddy. If I've got him in the carrier, it's suddenly more legit to people."

Part of this, he assumes, is a result of people's stereotypes about black men as absent fathers—yes, he's African American. And yet, according to the National Center for Health Statistics, in 2013, 70 percent of black dads who lived with young children bathed, diapered, or dressed them every day, compared with 60 percent of white dads and 45 percent of Hispanic dads.[21]

When people find out that Chris is a primary caregiver, many say, "I've never seen that. Wow, how did you work it out? You must have saved a lot of money in order to stay home with your child."

Chris responds to this by saying, "Actually, I'm married. I'm in a partnership. This is something that *we* figured out would work for us." As Chris noted to me: "It's like some people just assume that black parents aren't together."

In fact, Chris comes from an incredibly tight-knit family. His grandmother is the youngest of twelve siblings, and many of his great-aunts and -uncles live in the DC area. He and Latoya often pitch in to help them out. When Chris and I spoke, he was at his grandmother's house, caring for her after a recent knee surgery.

"Do you think of yourself as an extraordinarily caring guy?" I asked him, struck by how many people he was supporting in his extended family—in addition to taking care of little Gavin.

"Not particularly," he replied. "I think I just ask different questions. I mean, what does it mean for you to be a man who thinks the only way you can contribute to your family is financial? I want to lend my presence. I want to put in the time and the care. I want to be there physically and emotionally."

## AN EVERYBODY ISSUE

It has been said (apparently not by Voltaire, though that's what everyone thinks): "Judge a man by his questions rather than his answers." By that standard, I'd say that Chris, and so many men like him, are involved in some pretty impressive inquiry. *What does it mean to be an engaged father? What sacrifices am I willing to make, and what are the rewards? What kind of legacy do I want to create—outside in the world* and *in terms of my family?*

And as they ask new questions, they're freeing women to ask different ones. Not the same old delusions and false dichotomies—*Can I have it all? Work or stay home?*—but questions like *Where can I let go and trust my family to meet each other's needs? In what seasons am I biologically bound to prioritize mothering, and in what seasons can I get more independence? How can I take care of* myself *better?*

Women, so often the pioneers when it comes to valuing caretaking, have been making the case for years. It's time—in fact, it's long overdue—that it becomes an everybody issue, not just a women's issue. For too long we've framed family-friendly policy as beneficial for the female half of the population, a stopgap against losing them from the labor force, against seeing them slide into poverty, against the "mommy tax" in all its pernicious forms. And this is all true: women have a lot to lose from outdated work structures and culture.

But so do men. In fact, men probably have more to lose, because they don't have the cultural conditioning that drives them to care no matter what the logistical or emotional complexities. If a mother can lift a car off her child, imagine what she can do to bureaucracy that gets in the way of her and her baby. For men, the policies are a critical symbol of society's acknowledgment of them as caretakers, as workers *and* dedicated fathers and sons, as whole human beings.

In other words, as men wake up to the pleasure and meaning to be found in caretaking, our whole nation's relationship with care changes.

Fortunately, we're seeing that workplaces have the capacity to change—creating more generous family leave and flexible work options, on-site daycares, and cultures where passionate professionals are acknowledged also to be dedicated parents. The rules have been dramatically rewritten at most leading tech companies in the last few years: at Yahoo, new dads get eight weeks of paid leave and new moms get sixteen; at Google it's twelve for dad and twenty-two for mom; and at Facebook, both get seventeen weeks.[22] Part of that is, no doubt, spurred by very visible women in leadership at these companies, namely Sheryl Sandberg and Marissa Mayer. But part of it is also explained by the generation of young men, guys like Tom Stocky, who are unafraid to make known their desire for time off with their new babies. Studies show that, when a male coworker actually takes his federally protected parental leave, the next new-dad coworker is 11 percent more likely to take paternity leave. Interestingly, the *next* new dad after that is 15 percent more likely to take time off.[23]

The above applies to the tech industry; fortunately, more traditional sectors aren't far behind. Bain & Company, one of the leading consultancies worldwide, gives all parents twelve weeks of paid time off, no matter their title, and has a robust part-time program; and 70 percent of Bain's female partners have worked part-time at some point in their careers.[24] At Morningstar, an investment research firm, employees have generous benefits and access to tuition reimbursement. The icing on top? Every four years, they get to take a six-week paid sabbatical.[25]

But before we go declaring victories, let's put this in perspective: only 11 percent of private-sector employees writ large currently have access to paid family leave (up from 2 percent in 1992).[26] Most of those who do are already in positions of privilege—meaning those who would most need to be care providers, those unable to hire someone else to provide it, are the least likely to be able to afford to take a leave of absence. Most fathers, even if they wanted to take time off to take care of their kids or a sick relative, have neither the legal protection nor the cultural permission to do so.

*The Washington Post* reports that nearly three-quarters of likely 2016 voters say that "workplace laws and policies are out of synch with the changing realities of modern families, and with the changing roles of men and women at work and at home."[27]

In some ways, it's so simple: the workday was structured at a time when American families looked and behaved completely differently than they do today. It needs to be restructured in order to match up with the existing reality—that there are fewer two-parent households, and that even the two-parent households that do exist are not necessarily composed of one parent working outside the home and one working within the home. More flexibility within a given workday, more acknowledgment and creativity around the various seasons a career might take, paid leave for caretakers of babies and sick or aging family members—all of it has to be brought to bear in this twenty-first-century update.

Despite the fearmongering of conservative pundits, the disintegration of the "traditional family" is actually proving to coincide with a different kind of relationship stability: gay marriages, like Dan and Jimmy's, are statistically more stable than straight ones. And, counter to many predictions, divorce is actually on the decline.[28]

This is not to say that there isn't significant instability in so many American families; it's just that this is more a result of economic woes than of fatherlessness—as framed by Daniel Patrick Moynihan and his decades of minions. As Nicole Sussner Rodgers, cofounder of an organization called Family Story, writes: "Marriage may be on the decline, but that is not catastrophic by itself. Love and companionship are alive and well. We just need powerful positive visions of thriving families that don't depend on any one family structure, but rather are guided by values such as compassion, acceptance, and evidence about what really matters for children."[29]

We're not "leaning in." We're not "having it all." We're not doing any damn thing that requires quotations and mostly just ends up being a phrase for women to whip themselves with. We—both men and women—are simply trying to show up for the people we live with and among. We're trying to be both tender and driven. We're trying to love well, so that we can look back on our lives and be proud of what we've accomplished—but also so we can look back with pride in who we were in the longest days and shortest years of our obscenely blessed lives.

# harnessing the wind

## DIRECTING ATTENTION WHERE
## IT MATTERS MOST IN AN
## AGE OF DISTRACTION

If you sometimes feel like you're drinking from a fire hydrant of information, it's understandable. These days, we Americans take in every single day five times as much information as we did in 1986—the equivalent of 175 newspapers per person, according to Daniel J. Levitin, author of *The Organized Mind: Thinking Straight in the Age of Information Overload.*[1] With so much more information coming at us, so much more correspondence, so many options for being entertained, what can we do to stay on top of it all?

Many have turned to multitasking. Don't just rub your tummy and pat your head; do both—while getting your nails done and talking to your bestie on the phone. Walk through any café with a Wi-Fi signal and peer over the shoulders of the heavily caffeinated: you'll see how faithfully we believe in our power to do it all, and all at once, particularly online—ten tabs open in a browser, a Google

Chat conversation in the corner of a half-written email, a Twitter stream flowing by with a thousand tributaries threatening to siphon off your attention.

For my grandmother, virtue was tied up with character and piety. To be successful was to have a solid family, a decent job, and a good reputation—all subjective and slowly evolving standards. In my time, success is measured minute to minute, either by increasingly ubiquitous algorithms on the job or the emotional roller coasters of "likes" and "favorites" on social media. Productivity is the holy grail. It drives too many of us to fritter and flail. As cultural critic Virginia Heffernan writes:

> Today's anxiety is something else. It's that our heroes in training— ourselves or our children—won't settle on a path at all. We'll scatter their attention to the four winds, get lost in diversion and frivolity. More than malaise we fear distraction. More than tragedy we fear trivia. On highways we die not in high-speed chases but because we can't stop texting.[2]

Attention has been taken up as a subject of inquiry by a huge diversity of experts in recent years; think of them as the scientist equivalents of George Clinton and the P-Funk All-Stars—philosophers and psychologists, technologists and neuroscientists, all clamoring to understand how we decide what to see and remember.

Americans are often delusional about how our attention works—that it blossoms when concentrated and weakens, if not dies altogether, when refracted. As psychologist William James wrote: "Focalization, concentration of consciousness are of its essence. It implies withdrawal from some things in order to deal effectively with others."[3] This bears repeating: "It implies withdrawal from some things in order to deal effectively with others." James wrote that at a time when the typewriter had been invented but was not yet widespread; telephones were just becoming de rigueur in businesses and elite homes. The things that the average American had to withdraw from in order to focus on what was important/urgent/lovely were far fewer in number and far less insidious in nature than they are today. Consider how much easier it is to ignore a nonurgent letter—the endangered kind, with a stamp and an envelope that you can hold in your hot little hands—than it is a nonurgent email. Even as letters have become exotic, they can still languish on our kitchen counter for a while, while an email can seem long in the tooth if left unread for just a few hours.

At the end of a day spent flitting around the Internet without committing to one task for an extended period of time, I often feel jittery, as if I've been throwing back espressos on an empty stomach. In fact, according to Daniel Levitin, multitasking actually creates a dopamine-addiction feedback loop—"effectively rewarding the brain for losing focus and for constantly searching for external stimulation."[4] It also increases production of the stress hormone cortisol, as well as the fight-or-flight hormone adrenaline. In other words, all bad things: things that make you feel out of control, things that make you anxious, things that make you sick.

Psychiatrist Edward M. Hallowell called multitasking "mythical."[5] Levitin took it a step further, describing multitasking as "a powerful and diabolical illusion." Study after study after study shows that multitasking is not just unhealthy and unsatisfying, it's also ineffective. Attempting to learn while multitasking sends the incoming information to the wrong parts of our brains; as a result the info is harder to recall in the short run—and leaves us altogether in the long run. But you can be degraded by multitasking even if you're not trying to multitask. Levitin reports that Glenn Wilson, former visiting professor of psychology at Gresham College,

London, found that "being in a situation where you are trying to concentrate on a task, and an email is sitting unread in your in-box, can reduce your effective IQ by ten points."[6]

I have to admit that before I learned this I considered multitasking to be, though exhausting, mostly benevolent—like that very-high-energy friend you can't be around all the time but who can be fun in smaller doses. Sure, I feel jittery after too much multitasking, but sometimes, after what I think of as "just the right amount," I feel triumphant, like I've fooled the universe into letting me squeeze it all in.

But you know what? If I'm honest with myself, it's at just those moments of "diabolical illusion" that everything comes crashing down (including my ego). I burn myself while trying to roast cauliflower, text with my cousin, and keep my baby busy all at once. Or I show up at the airport with a terrible dehydration headache and without my phone charger. Or I forget the birthday of someone I love very much. At those times, of which there are many, that under-control in-box doesn't seem so awesome.

In these moments, I feel myself get psychologically and spiritually weak; where I was once a ponderosa pine, resolute about my people and preferences, my gifts and responsibilities, I'm now rotted from the inside after the pine beetle infestation of overcommitment. I'm hollow and brittle, joyless. I'm a martyr, not a mensch—and the wiser part of me knows this.

And yet, the allure of the "diabolical illusion" of multitasking is so damned seductive. It's like a subliminal message coded into commercials, especially those aimed at women; it's also a literal message in an increasing number of the titles in a bookstore business section. It's the whole infuriating basis for the "having it all" debate that just won't die. The shadow of Kali looms large, her arms multiplying every networked moment.

In fact, in the transcendentally named *Mahanirvana Tantra: Tantra of the Great Liberation*, one of the most important texts of Hinduism, it is written: "At the dissolution of things, it is Kāla [time] who will devour all."

And that's it, isn't it? Time will devour all. There's no escape. What you spend your limited attention on becomes your life. People hip to that fact are using apps like the dramatically named BreakFree and RescueTime so they can track where they misspend attention and redirect it. They are creating new rules and rituals for themselves to sever the addiction to technology—or prevent it from taking hold in the first place. They're buying products designed for one elegant function rather than falling prey to the seduction of multipurpose, crazy-making everything. They're gravitating toward experiences that invite them to lay down the burden of being everywhere at once. They're slowing. They're noticing. They're listening. And they're thriving.

## THE ATTENTION GAP

It's important to note that we don't all get to control where and how our precious attention is spent. If you Google the latest research on attention, it's easy to feel you've been transported to some kind of business school breakout session on how to maximize productivity. Let's just say a lot of "experts" make a lot of money telling already rich people how to get even richer by not checking their email twenty times a day. Where there is a lack of impulse control, consultants rush in. But if you dig a little deeper on the subject, it becomes clear that attention is not only a concern for people with MBAs. While fine-tuning where and how your attention is spent may appear to be a luxury, it's actually a fundamental human right. What this comes down to is significant: we don't just have an unprecedented wealth gap in this country; we have a historic attention gap.

Consider this, again from Levitin: "Successful people—or people who can afford it—employ layers of people whose job is to narrow the attentional filter. That is, corporate heads, political leaders, movie stars, and others whose time and attention are especially valuable have a staff of people around them who are effectively extensions of their own brains."[7]

You've likely experienced an encounter with someone who has outsourced the drudgery that demands the average person's attention. She floats a little. She smiles beatifically. She is sometimes unintentionally inconsiderate; after all, she doesn't experience the same costs for being forgetful, late, wrong, off topic. There is always someone to pick up the pieces, pay the late fees, find the Plan B, advocate on her behalf.

The flip side of this lightness, of course, is the heaviness, the leaden heaviness, of knowing that you are single-handedly responsible for getting the sum total of your and your dependents' needs met without enough resources and within dehumanizing, poorly designed, labyrinthine-like systems. If you're someone lucky enough to have never applied for public assistance, imagine what you encounter at the DMV once a decade, and then imagine dealing with some version of that monthly, if not weekly, for various reasons.

This is what behavioral economists call the "cognitive tax of poverty."[8] The first time I read those three words, threaded together in a study, they knocked the wind out of me. Yes. This is what is missing, among much else, in the public conversation about poverty. Forget marriage. Forget mobility. What really makes life a bitch for those who don't have enough is the daily frustration of spending so much energy on just meeting one's basic needs.

Speechwriter and journalist Joshunda Sanders remembers this tax shaping her life as a little girl. She grew up homeless, off and on, in the Bronx. She writes in an email: "I never really enjoyed holidays or summer vacation because it meant that I probably wouldn't eat for a lot of the time that we were off. So instead of letting my brain relax, vacation for me became a time to hone how I would get my basic needs met without free lunch or breakfast."

This "honing in" Sanders describes is dubbed "tunneling" in the powerful book *Scarcity: The New Science of Having Less and How It Defines Our Lives* by Sendhil Mullainathan, a behavioral economist at Harvard, and Eldar Shafir, a behavioral psychologist at Princeton University.[9] Essentially, our view and even our experience of the world narrow as our attention is focused ever more precisely on the urgent needs right in front of us—particularly when we aren't sure we have the capacity to get them met.

Mullainathan and Shafir have found that when people are dealing with scarcity they tunnel; as a result their quality of life suffers, in part because they simply don't have the bandwidth to focus on the things that bring them joy, or to be truly present with those they love. "Even when we try to do something else," they write, "the tunnel of scarcity keeps drawing us in. Scarcity in one walk of life means we have less attention, less mind, in the rest of life."[10]

Aisha Nyandoro runs a community empowerment program called Springboard to Opportunities in the public housing projects of Mississippi. Much of her work is about collaborating with poor parents to help them navigate a way out of the "tunnel of scarcity." She explains: "In the everyday hustle and bustle of trying to survive, parents just don't have the mental bandwidth for some of what pops up."

Aisha recently watched as a mother finally processed the implications of new state reading standards that might mean her little girl would be held back in third grade. The school had been sending letters about it for a few months, but she hadn't been able to focus on them in the chaos of more-immediate priorities. "I witness parents just feeling totally defeated by unanticipated concerns—what I call 'little foxes,' like this," Aisha says. In the "tunnel of scarcity," it can feel like there's always a "little fox" right around the corner, one more thing that you lost track of while you were focused elsewhere.

What Aisha calls "little fox" I often call "stupid tax." If I get a parking ticket because I was too focused on getting to a meeting and forgot to plug the meter, I categorize it as part of my annual "stupid tax" and try to let it go. When my husband recently got into a fender bender on the George Washington Bridge while admiring a glowing, glittery orange paint job on the car next to us, I saw a dark cloud immediately cover his previously awed face. "Stupid tax," I reassured him.

I've always thought of "stupid tax" as a conceptual weapon against perfectionism, but as I learn more about the cognitive tax of poverty, I'm also realizing what a luxury it is. When you have a safety net, the world doesn't come crashing down when you occasionally fuck up. When you don't have an extra $500 in the bank, an attentional mishap can mean you lose your car, job, home, or even your kid. When a person with a small financial cushion screws up it's considered "absentminded"; when a person with no financial cushion screws up it's deemed "irresponsible" or even "neglectful"—and it's used as evidence of her "lack of deservingness."

Aisha believes that our lack of understanding about the cognitive tax that poor people pay has far-reaching consequences: "I think this is why so many of our social programs don't work. In trying to provide assistance, we put systems in place that further [burden] participants' bandwidth—*you must come to so many programs in order to receive a benefit.*"

This is not to say that scarcity is unequivocally negative; Mullainathan and Shafir point out that scarcity is a fantastic focusing mechanism. While someone with a preponderance of choices and resources can wander aimlessly, struggling to find a sense of meaning, those who have to make a way out can often be far more directed and far more effective with the time, energy, and attention they do have.

Scarcity can also inspire you to turn to your community for support—a healthy adaptation for absolutely everyone. Traditional notions of the ideal American family centered on the idea of self-sufficiency. The ideal family's "cognitive load"—as psychologists might put it—is theirs and theirs alone; when they get overwhelmed, they do it in the privacy of their own home. But that kind of pressure has never been good for social, vulnerable animals, and now we've got the research to prove it.

But don't confuse the community building of turning to others for support with paying others for that support. Though the very rich may be surrounded by people, that doesn't mean they have genuine community. The condition that frees their minds to think creatively—those "layers of people whose job is to narrow the attentional filter"—is also the thing that threatens to leave them isolated. When we have to ask for help, we make friends; when we hire people to help us, we make hierarchy. And it's not just hype—it can be lonely at the top.

Mia Birdsong, who spent years working with economically marginalized families through the Oakland-based organization Family Independence Initiative, hears a lot about their struggles to keep track of competing priorities. But she also hears about the communal gifts of scarcity: "We hear from folks all the time: it's hard to plan for the long term when you've got short-term bullshit on your plate. *And* they talk about how much being in a group of friends (the cohorts we ask them to form) helps combat this problem. One participant said it gave her the psychological breathing room necessary to think long-term. Folks also talk about how it helps organize them, support them, hold them accountable—all the stuff a strong social network does."

All roads, or tunnels as it were, really do lead to community.

## RECLAIMING EMPTY MOMENTS

So if our challenge is to direct our attention—our most precious and threatened resource—and community helps us do this wisely, it's not surprising that people are increasingly craving and creating communal experiences. What is surprising, or at least counterintuitive, is that many people are rallying around a common attentional enemy: our cell phones.

The irony, of course, is that our phones are often sold to us as the ultimate tool of connection. WhatsApp and Kik, for example, are billed as apps that let you chat with the people you love, wherever in the world they happen to be. People connect with old college buddies by trash-talking on Fantasy Football apps, or keep up with a beloved aunt while playing a heady game of Scrabble. And to be fair, the ability to "FaceTime" with a grandparent who lives far away or simply text with your brother on the other side of the country can make you feel a little less alone, a little closer to the people who matter most to you.

But there are so many shadows in the way we stare into the addictive, handheld square of light. "Love/hate" doesn't begin to describe the tumultuousness of our relationship with our cell phones. It's as if everything emotionally complicated about being a human has been reduced to something that fits in the palms of our hands. Some of us get itchy fingers at the first blush of boredom, insecurity, or confusion; we want a "like" or a witty text to allow us to instantaneously pivot; And then it becomes automatic. We don't even necessarily want to pivot, we aren't even consciously experiencing discomfort, but we can still find ourselves "coming to"—our eyes fixed on an Instagram feed, thumb compulsively scrolling—while out to lunch with someone we care about. Though we can hate ourselves in those moments, ashamed, we can in the next instant get defensive: *Everybody does it, right?*

Sort of, yes. According to the Pew Research Center's Internet & American Life Project, the cell phone is the most quickly adopted consumer technology in the history of the world—91 percent of American adults have one, though commercial cell phones weren't even available in the U.S. until 1983 (and were outrageously expensive, of course).[11] According to the Kleiner Perkins Caufield & Byers annual "Internet Trends" report, Americans individually check their phones 150 times, and collectively share more than 500 million photos, every single day.[12]

This thing in our needy, fumbling hands, this power, is relatively new; those of us settling into middle age have had little experience watching anyone older and wiser model enlightened habits around cell phone use. If anything, we've had belly laughs at the expense of our parents' technological fumbles. I can still remember my dad's first mobile phone—big as a brick, plugged into the dashboard of our minivan with a cord as thick as fusilli pasta. That thing was positively giant. The keys glowed green in the calming dark as my mom barreled down Interstate 25.

So as I try to develop positive practices around my own use of various newfangled gadgets, it's not my parents I emulate—they have no more experience or wisdom on this front than I do. In fact, many of our parents are like compulsive adolescents themselves when immersed in "the Facebook" or when gifted their very first iPhone by a gaggle of grandchildren eager to send them updates that don't require a postage stamp. Sherry Turkle, MIT professor and expert on the inept intersection of humanity and our gadgets, interviewed 300 young people and 150 older adults for her popular book *Alone Together: Why We Expect More from Technology and Less from Each Other*. She found that adults had the most egregious cell phone behavior while in the presence of (real, breathing) others. But "these are not people who are dysfunctional, who are out of control, who are addicted," she writes. "We've just kind of let things get away from us."[13]

So how do we get them back?

There are lots of creative experiments afoot, and they're united by a core insight: beautiful and unexpected things happen when people break away from their devices and get present with the world around them. At least for a little while, we have absorbing, face-to-face conversations, or notice the intricate structure of the inside of a pomegranate, or recall a fond memory we didn't even know we had.

Probably the most highly publicized of these experiments are parties where people are asked to check their cell phones at the door. In the hopelessly connected Bay Area, these events are called "Device-Free Drinks." Those who show up hand over their devices and enter a tactile carnival of activities—face painting, sing-a-longs, board games, pie-eating contests, and, of course, drinking—designed to help people remember that there is a body connected to their brain. And those who enter are asked not just to leave their phone at the door, but also to temporarily pause the "statusizing" and strategizing that phones symbolize for so many. "Work-talk" is as frowned upon as Wi-Fi.

Levi Felix, who is thirty-one, started the Device-Free Drinks series—weekend retreats, and eventually a full-blown summer camp—after doing similar experiments at a youth hostel in Cambodia. He told *The New York Times*: "I'm a geek, I'm not a Luddite. I love that technology connects us and is taking our civilization to the next level, but we have to learn how to use it, and not have it use us."[14]

Felix isn't the only "geek" spreading the gospel of disconnection. Tiffany Shlain is an Emmy-nominated filmmaker who created the Webby Awards (basically the Oscars for the Internet) and also invented something called "cloud-based filmmaking" whereby people all over the world collaborate on one project. So it may come as a surprise that she's also a huge proponent of what she calls "Technology Shabbats." Every Friday evening, she and her family unplug from their various devices and spend time reconnecting with one another, nature, and their own creative spirits—until Saturday at sundown. They even made a short film about digital addiction, *Yelp: With Apologies to Allen Ginsberg's "Howl"*—a rewriting of Ginsberg's classic poem, this time with "angel-headed hipsters burning for the ultrafast, heavenly connection to the starry dynamo in the machinery of night."[15]

Key to both of these phenomena—the seasonal parties and the weekly Shabbats—is the group agreement involved. If we are to interrupt the potent purr of our cell phones, we'll need the combined pressure and the camaraderie of others. It's simply too hard, at least for most of us, to effect such a shift on our own—just as it would be to try to diet on a cruise ship. (Or so I've heard. Never been.)

These communal efforts have, at their heart, an invitation for us to step away from our screens and look into the eyes of others, to be more fully present with the people and places we love. But they are also designed to reacquaint us with the wild, neglected landscape of our own minds. One of the losses, after all, of having a device always on hand to fill your empty moments is, well, having no empty moments.

What to one person may be a "waste of time" could be to another a moment of invention or a deliciously pleasurable daydream or just a chance to notice the way the clouds move across the sky. WNYC radio show *Note to Self*, formerly *New Tech City*, launched the Bored and Brilliant Project: The Lost Art of Spacing Out to see what serendipity ensues when people choose not to spend their idle moments with their noses pressed against tiny screens. They gave participants a week of challenges—say, delete a favorite app, or refrain from taking a photo for the whole day—and instead encouraged them to do something creative—build a house out of just the contents in your wallet, or come up with as many ideas as possible for how to use a fork and a sponge.

Why? Because boredom is not just the stuff of a summer day in your adolescence, stretching out in front of you endlessly; it's an indication light blinking helpfully about the state of your soul. As researcher Andreas Elpidorou writes: "In the absence of boredom, one would remain trapped in unfulfilling situations, and miss out on many emotionally, cognitively, and socially rewarding experiences." When you're bored, you're forced to reckon with the state of things—which can propel you to pursue what you actually desire. He goes on: "Boredom is both a warning that we are not doing what we want to be doing and a 'push' that motivates us to switch goals and projects."[16]

Neurologically speaking, boredom is also fruitful. When we're bored, our brains can more easily transition into what's called "divergent thinking"—to travel through all the strange rabbit holes of the overgrown gardens that are our brains. We make unusual connections. We marinate in not knowing. In contrast, we spend much of our lives in "convergent" mode—cognitively traveling from point A to point B as efficiently as possible. Convergent thinking is your commute; divergent thinking is that delicious Saturday when you left the house without a plan and came back hours later invigorated and inspired.

Researchers have found that, while convergent thinking serves critical purposes in our lives, divergent thinking is the stuff of creativity. Importantly, boredom is the bridge to divergent thinking; unfortunately, for so many of us, that bridge is rarely traveled these days. We'd rather play Candy Crush than stare off into space as we wait for the train. Boredom researcher Sandi Mann of the University of Central Lancashire in the U.K. told *Note to Self* host Manoush Zomorodi: "You come up with really great stuff when you don't have that easy, lazy junk food diet of the phone to scroll all the time."[17]

Like empty calories, gigabytes of data are pretty seductive. When participants in the Bored and Brilliant Project were challenged to delete apps from their phones, for example, things got pretty dramatic. Shaunacy Ferro of Brooklyn, New York, tweeted about the sense of social isolation: "I deleted Instagram and it felt like a friend was moving away forever."[18] Charlotte Donlin of Birmingham, Alabama, deleted Twitter from her phone and then tweeted (from her laptop, presumably?!): "App is still off my phone. Withdrawals. Eye twitching."[19] And Nate Bennett, also of Brooklyn, made deading apps sound like a religious experience: "I DELETED FACEBOOK *AND* TWITTER FROM MY PHONE FOR #NTCDELETE BECAUSE I WILL BE REBORN ANEW."[20]

While Nate was being facetious, the emotional undertone of so many of the communications that emerged from the simple but stunning Bored and Brilliant Project has grave implications for our quality of life in these distracted times. The pull that people feel toward their cell phones is often stronger than the pull they feel to connect with real, live human beings, to wander and wonder, to take stock of their lives without the constant comparison effect that lurks at social sites like Facebook and Instagram.

Our cell phones and tablets have unlocked so many possibilities in our day-to-day lives; they've transformed how we communicate with our friends, capture fleeting moments, and find out what's happening in the world. That's all good—profound even. But the strong and strange power of our mobile devices must be balanced by an investment in the off-screen opportunities—the random conversation with a stranger at the donut shop, the chance to smell blooming jasmine with a toddler, the brainstorm that gets us closer to that invention. What these experiments teach us is that, like all behavior change, this one is easier to stick to if we aren't going it alone. Set intentions. Create rituals. Share your intentions with others, giving them your blessing to call you out when you get twitchy and reach for just . . . one . . . more . . . ping.

## THE SIMPLICITY ON THE OTHER SIDE

It's easy to become self-hating when we start reflecting on just how precious and misspent our attention is on a daily basis. It's enough to make us feel weak-willed and flimsy, as if the smallest breeze has the power to completely derail our focus.

But what if it's not *all* our fault? Sure, it would be great if we were better at directing our attention, no matter what distractions threaten to deflect them. But what if there were simply fewer distractions? What if the tools we rely on every day (our cars, our phones, our computers) were designed not to do absolutely everything but to do just the exact thing we most need them to do, and nothing else?

Viewed from this perspective, we might consider ourselves to be, indeed, a little bit broken—struggling to close the gap between what we profess to care about most and what we actually spend our time on. But the truth is that our stuff is a little bit broken, too.

This was the unlikely insight of two friends shooting the shit at a coworking space in Detroit, Michigan. Patrick Paul, a twenty-five-year-old software designer, was describing the wide range of software on the market designed to help writers stay on task: iWriter, Freedom, etc. As an avid writer, he understood the appeal, but was amazed at the lengths some of these programs went to in order to keep the user writing: like disabling the backspace key so people couldn't second-guess their first instinct, or even erasing words if the person stopped writing for too long. Adam Leeb, a twenty-nine-year-old designer, hearing about these software interventions, asked one of those obvious, brilliant questions: "What if there was a distraction-free piece of *hardware*?"

Thus was born the Freewrite, originally called the Hemingwrite. Essentially, it's a minimalist digital typewriter—no Internet, no spell-checker, no drop-down menus: it's a tool designed for an old-fashioned free write, just one that's saved to the newfangled cloud. Within a few

weeks of that first conversation, Leeb and Paul had a physical pro-
totype. Their Kickstarter campaign to produce the first run earned
$342,471—nearly $100,000 above their $250,000 goal.

Some people wrote it off as a hipster gimmick (the Freewrite will
retail at a stiff $499), but Leeb insists that they were simply aiming to
invent something that would allow writers to write with, in his words,
"less friction." What a revelatory word for all the pulls and pushes we
experience on a daily basis, right? It's not just our lack of willpower
that has us reading a text message when we mean to listen with our
undivided attention—it's also a preponderance of unhelpful, priority-
eschewing "friction."

"We weren't trying to make a statement," he explains. "This
wasn't the potato salad Kickstarter. We were trying to create a tool
that would be useful to people."

It wasn't the first time that Leeb had thought about attention as
a precious resource. "My whole work life after college, I was focused
on how I could be as lazy as possible and still get things done," he says,
laughing. After graduating in 2007 with a degree in mechanical engineering from MIT, he was an investment banker for four relatively
content, albeit lazy, years. When he decided to move home to Detroit,
his aim was to become an entrepreneur: "After I started working for
myself, the game changed. I was constantly asking, *How can I get the
most amount done in the littlest amount of time?*"

This led Leeb to thinking about the impact of things like "energy
states"—using your most energetic time of day to do your most complex, important work—as well as about the importance of tools. As a
mechanical engineer, Leeb knew how deeply satisfying it could be to
switch from using a tool that's just adequate for a task—say, using a
crescent wrench to loosen a bolt—to using a tool that's perfect for that
task, in this case, a socket and ratchet. You know the feeling: it's like the
sea parts and a task becomes not just possible, but pleasurable too.

Why shouldn't the same logic be applied to the writing life? (Or almost any part of life for that matter?) Leeb reflects: "There's been a move toward overengineering a lot of products. People throw a computer in a toaster just because it seems like a value add, but it actually distracts from the goal of simply making a really great piece of toast."

The beauty of constraints appears once again. In the nineties and aughts, Americans got hyped about bells and whistles. We got excited about showers with radios, cars with televisions, even sneakers with pumps (I can still picture my dad in those monsters while shooting baskets in our alley). And, to be sure, having a cell phone that's also a camera that's also a computer may simplify our lives in certain ways; I certainly wouldn't give mine up. But we're slowly waking up to the fact that we don't want that one-stop-shopping logic applied to everything in our lives. Some of our daily tools are more supportive of who we aspire to be when they just do one thing exactly right.

Lest you think of this resurgence of attention-preserving tools as insignificant, consider this: Leeb and Paul took the Freewrite to Engadget Expand, a tech conference that generally attracts the kind of tech-obsessed people who camp out in front of an Apple store the day before a new product is released. Near the end of the day, a crew of kids—Leeb estimates they were between the ages of seven and twelve—came up to their booth and started messing with the Freewrite. "This is so cool!" one shouted.

"I've never seen anything like this!" another confessed, wide-eyed.

"Wow, so it only lets you write?" asked another. "That's so amazing."

Now, keep in mind, there were flying drones, virtual reality goggles, and all kinds of other devastatingly sexy gadgets at this event. And yet, these kids were geeking out over the Freewrite—a cloud-connected word processor. Leeb was totally confused, but the mom accompanying them broke it down: "They've never seen a single-purpose electronic device before."

And there you have it—what's simple is sexy again. When it comes to a high quality of life—one where you're supported to aim your attention at just the task at hand, to have that satisfying taste of completion, to maybe even revel in the process—bells and whistles are overrated. There are times when a Swiss Army knife is just the thing, but those times are more rare than we think. Instead, we crave, in the words of Oliver Wendell Holmes Sr., "the simplicity on the other side of complexity." We crave the elegant hack. We crave, as mundane as it might sound, the perfect tool.

"Attention is the most essential mental resource for any organism," says Daniel J. Levitin.[21] While our parents and grandparents may have had the luxury of being laissez-faire about attention, we live in different times. The information we swim in, the bureaucracies we face, the devices we hold: all promise to empower us, but they also derail us. Insofar as we have control—and, no doubt, those of us with more money have more say—we have to set intentions about where we spend our attention. We have to say those intentions out loud and ask our communities to hold us accountable. And we have to demand design that aids us rather than overloading us.

It's not uncommon these days to meet people who say they're going off the grid entirely because of extreme burnout and the unignorable health problems that often follow. They quit their jobs, they delete their Facebook profiles, they move to Thailand. For some, this feels like the only way to hack at the tangled overgrowth that sometimes blocks us from our true path. But most of the people who take the off-the-grid approach have some kind of invisible privilege that makes that possible (namely, a financial cushion or no dependents or a partner who can provide for them for a spell). For the rest of us, the way to hone our attention wisely is not to spend a year insulated from that which distracts us, but to daily practice living amidst the distraction without letting it define us.

In *Reclaiming Conversation: The Power of Talk in a Digital Age*, Sherry Turkle argues that our impulse to look at our phones at every turn erodes not only our empathy but also our capacity for meaningful conversations—both with ourselves and others. But she's not without hope. She believes that we're facing a critical crossroads. We've wised up to our cell phones' corrosive effects on our lives, and we can make different choices. She writes: "This is our moment to acknowledge the unintended consequences of the technologies to which we are vulnerable, but also to respect the resilience that has always been ours. We have time to make corrections and remember who we are—creatures of history, of deep psychology, of complex relationships, of conversations, artless, risky, and face-to-face."

So take your own "bored and brilliant" challenge. Take a walk without looking at your cell phone. Notice weird little shit. Have random thoughts. Witness. Lose track of time. Love people the way they deserve to be loved, which is to say, without a cell phone obstructing your adoration. Ultimately, our attention—which is, remember, finite—is spent one small, seemingly mundane choice at a time. Ensure that your tiny choices reflect your grand ambitions for how people experience you and how you experience the world. It's all you've really got.

# the end of "mine"

## HOW OUR RELATIONSHIP TO OWNERSHIP IS CHANGING

My twenty-month-old daughter, Maya, is sitting in the grass of our friends' backyard, painstakingly removing address labels from a sheet and pressing them onto her jeaned knee. Her little face scrunches in concentration. Next to her is our friends' son, Huck, a little bit older and a whole lot blonder. He grabs for Maya's fire truck, an object of zero interest to her just moments earlier but which is now, predictably, her favorite toy on Planet Earth. She screams, "Mine!" And while most other words come out of her mouth as garbled approximations, this one is crisp and clear.

"No, mine!" replies Huck, not to be outselfished by his young friend.

The irony is that Huck's mom, Natalie Foster, is one of the world's foremost experts on the so-called sharing economy. She was also the CEO and cofounder of Rebuild the Dream, a platform for people-driven economic change, and Peers, a member-driven organization to support the sharing economy movement. She's deeply invested in an economic future where we loosen our grip on our own stuff. As Natalie puts it, "When we turn to each other for what we need the possibilities for abundance are endless."

In some ways, "sharing economy" is a fancy term for a very ordinary practice—offering your neighbors and friends a shovel or a shirt when you're not using it. What's changing, and this is not to be underestimated, is whom people are willing to share with and how that sharing actually takes place. Whereas in decades past it wasn't uncommon for people to offer friends or even friends of friends a couch to crash on when passing through town, Airbnb and Couchsurfing have made it possible for people to extend that same courtesy to perfect strangers (and, in the case of Airbnb, make some money in the process). In 2014, Airbnb's website surpassed 800,000 listings worldwide, which means they now offer more lodging than any other hotel chain in the world.[1]

Business author Lisa Gansky calls this new economic paradigm "the mesh," and argues it is defined by an era when "access trumps ownership."[2] It's not so much access to our *own* stuff that we need, but access to the right stuff at the right times in the right places. Ownership becomes irrelevant; proximity and ease become everything. Another departure from the traditional view of consumption—in "mesh business," as Gansky calls it—is that it's no longer just the products that are most important, but the service that comes with those products—and today that service translates to information. How does ZipCar ensure the efficient use of its fleet of cars, as opposed to private cars, which spend about 90 percent of their time parked?[3] They offer customers readily accessible information on *which* car would best serve them, based on location as well as make and cost; the car itself is just the equivalent of a widget.

If you're one of the vast majority of car owners whose vehicles are more parked than driven, possessing the deed on those wheels doesn't make you smart; it just makes you responsible. It so happens that, in this time of overwhelm and financial strain, many people crave having fewer responsibilities. In her 2011 TEDxMotorCity talk, Gansky explains, "The recession has caused us to rethink our relationship with the things in our lives relative to the[ir] value." In other words, we're "starting to align the value with the true cost."[4]

The true cost includes the economic, ethical, and even emotional implications that come with ownership. *Emotional implications?* you might ask. Yes; there is a direct correlation between the volume of stuff we own and how overwhelmed we feel (more on this later). Whereas status symbols may have been the imprimatur of an earlier era, this era is all about energy conservation. So while for some it's possessions that make the grade, we're heading into an era when you'd more likely be praised (or envied) for living in a zone with a high "walk score," great public transportation, and a tool-lending library nearby.

That basic instinct to accumulate and hoard stuff, as is very much on display in the wild kingdom of toddlers, is being rewired by a new economic era. Superpowered by the Internet, we are sharing more, and starting to trust a wider network of people. Indeed, eighty million people in America have shared something online—from a car to a pet cat![5]

It's easy to read the typical wide-eyed business journalism treatment of all this and chalk it up to an overhyped niche: surely it's mostly just coastal hipsters and twenty-five-year-olds who benefit from the sharing economy, right? Think again: according to the global marketing research firm Nielsen, more than two-thirds of people worldwide want to share or rent out personal assets for financial gain.[6]

The detritus of the old American Dream is shuttered in the 51,000 personal storage facilities in the U.S.—inert, unused, largely forgotten.[7] It may make for riveting reality television (oh, *Storage Wars*), but in real life it mostly produces headaches and heartaches. Just as the fire truck that is technically Maya's does no one any good if it's stashed in a toy chest, our stuff can actually spread more love around if we stop thinking of it as ours and ours alone.

Whereas we used to equate ownership with safety and status, we are beginning to understand that ownership comes with significant strings attached—debt, environmental degradation, distraction, overwhelm, even ill health. Sharing is insurance against all of this—as such, it would appear we're all growing up a little.

## I AM WHAT I HAVE

The instinct to scream "Mine!" when another kid picks up your toy is the first expression of a fundamental human trait called "psychological ownership." Amitai Etzioni, an Israeli American sociologist, beautifully describes ownership as "dual creation, part attitude, part object, part in the mind, part 'real.'"[8]

As children, we crave to own because it's a way of feeling a sense of control over a world that is otherwise mostly choreographed by these giant people called adults—or so say the developmental psychologists. Claiming ownership over the stuff around us has particular appeal when we first begin to realize that we are—gasp!—separate and distinct individuals.

Geneticists believe we're hardwired to own, that it is merely a behavior to protect what we think will help us survive. Along these lines, a second grader who hoards a snack and her winter coat at recess is evolutionarily on point. But others, most famously psychologist Dacher Keltner, author of *Born to Be Good: The Science of a Meaningful Life*, argue that we are also hardwired to share. Keltner points out that Charles Darwin, often cast as the "survival of the fittest" mascot, notes the following in his 1871 *Descent of Man*: "Our regard for the approbation and disapprobation of our fellows depends on sympathy, which, as we shall see, forms an essential part of the social instinct, and is indeed its foundation-stone."[9]

One seed of sharing is sympathy. When we recognize that someone else is in need, some of us feel inclined to help if we can. Sociologists and anthropologists believe there is ample evidence of a human predisposition to help, especially within the realm of social norms. And, interestingly, vastly different expressions of ownership can be seen in different cultures. In the Native American Lakota culture, for example, all resources were gathered and shared among the tribe; there was no such thing as hoarding or stealing. The traditional Māori society in New Zealand and Australia likewise did not have a concept of absolute ownership of land. Members of an extended family or tribe had rights to use the same piece of land in various specific ways that were constantly renegotiated. The Maasai tribe of Kenya didn't have a notion of "private" and "public" until British colonizers came and introduced it; when the erosion of communal livestock practices soon followed, the Maasai were left increasingly vulnerable to hunger and violence.[10]

Sociobiologists—the peacemakers in this particular argument, as in so many—say that our attraction to owning lies somewhere between nature and nurture. We want to own both because it's part of our survival instinct and because other people teach us that ownership is good, safe, and pleasurable.[11] Writer Rebecca Solnit argues that context is everything. Contrary to the cinematic depictions of our worst behavior emerging in emergencies, she explores how disasters actually bring out our altruistic instincts, making us wonder where they were all along. In *A Paradise Built in Hell: The Extraordinary Communities That Arise in Disaster*, she writes, "It's tempting to ask why if you fed your neighbors during the time of the earthquake and fire, you didn't do so before or after."

As we get older, particularly in Western cultures, our interest in ownership becomes intertwined with our need for a unique identity. We still want to control, but we also want to author ourselves through our objects. French philosopher Jean-Paul Sartre went so far as to argue that, along with "to do" and "to be," "to have" is one of the three categories of human existence. "The totality of my possessions reflects the totality of my being. I am what I have . . . what is mine is myself."[12]

It might feel a step too far, especially for those of us who pride ourselves on not being materialistic, and yet, when you really step back and look at the role that your stuff plays in your life, it's awfully intimate and definitive. What shoes are you wearing right now? What do you imagine they say about who you are? Just those two questions can send you through a maze of self-examination.

## RETIMING MINE

"So let's say you really need a fedora."

Adam Werbach, cofounder of a sharing app called Yerdle, explains it to me at a conference table in San Francisco's Mission District. He smiles wryly as he scrolls through dozens of fedoras, some of them quite lovely. "You just select the fedora you're into and, as long as you have Yerdle dollars amassed, the sender pops it in the mail and sends it your way."

Yerdle is a platform for people to get rid of stuff they no longer need or want, and get stuff they are hankering for, all without exchanging a penny. Yerdle dollars are an alternative currency that the company invented in order to make it easier for people to give and receive random items; the fedoras range from Y$2 to Y$60. A nice blender is Y$40 and a decent watch is about Y$10. In early iterations, before each item was assigned a currency, users employed a straightforward barter. But the company found that people were less likely to take when they weren't sure what the expectation would be in terms of giving down the line. Would it seem selfish to others if they took a dress when all they'd offered was a tie? The alternative currency has taken the anxiety out of the exchange.

A little blue bar across the bottom of some of the fedoras catches my eye. It reads: MAKE A WISH. "What's that all about?" I ask.

"This is a really cool new feature," he says, eyes getting bright. "We realized that if we really rewrite people's relationship with owner-ship, then one desirable item could be given away over and over again within the Yerdle community."

MAKE A WISH allows people to put things on their "wish list," even if that item has already been given away. Then, if the original recipient of the item no longer wants it, she can see that someone else could use it and puts it back into circulation. The receiver becomes the giver—and a virtuous cycle, rather than a landfill dead end, is created.

It occurs to me: part of why I hold on to things, besides the fact that it's hard to find the time and energy to purge, is that I have a failure of imagination about who might want my old stuff. It sounds silly and narcissistic to admit, but there's a part of me that assumes if I've lost interest in something, the rest of the world has, too. Where my imagination fails, Yerdle steps in. The rub is that people have to be willing to ship their stuff in the mail, which is why the app is mostly good for things that are both under ten pounds and less than $200. Yerdle sends you a prepaid shipping label, so all you have to do is slap it on a box and drop it at your nearest UPS shipping outlet. I'm phobic of mailing things (I've got Post Office PTSD from dealing with bad attitudes and super-long lines in Brooklyn), so this sounds intimidating to me. But in just its first three years the app has incited 500,000 people to Yerdle to their thrifty hearts' content.

The most commonly found items on the app are women's cloth-ing and accessories, but users have given and received everything from juggling balls to vintage lunch bags. One defunded school music program got thirty-seven musical instruments last fall.

Yerdle isn't just a company looking to scale up its user base—they're looking to transform the way we live. According to their mission statement, they want to "redefine the word 'mine.'"

It's not a simple quest. In some ways, what they are hoping to do is *retime* "mine." Instead of defining our psychological ownership along some infinite timeline, they're hoping they can retrain us to think of an object as possessed "rightly" only as long as its pleasure and use are alive for the owner. After that, it's best catapulted back into circulation, ready for a new heir who will—theoretically—get an emotional boost of safety, control, beauty, self-expression, or whatever else we humans can squeeze out of a really hot leather jacket or a hand blender perfect for making your mom's legendary pumpkin soup.

Identity has previously been thought of as immutable. But almost every category of identity has been proven changeable fairly recently, from the rejection of overly simplified racial or sexual categories to the resistance so many have to affiliating with a single political party or religion. With this new fluidity, our identities shape-shift far faster and more dramatically than those of generations past. Objects that we use to signal our identity don't have the same power for the same length of time as they used to. Take fashion: the life cycle of a trend—ostensibly the lingua franca for who you are trying to communicate you are—has completely transformed in the last decade.

Laver's Law—established by British historian James Laver in 1937—was the fashion norm for nearly seven decades. As explained by the British site Business of Fashion, "BoF" for short: "when a trend is in fashion, it is 'smart.' One year before this it is 'daring.' And twenty years later, it becomes 'ridiculous.'"

Sounds positively civilized, doesn't it? I think even I could keep up with a twenty-year life cycle. But, alas, the Internet killed ol' Laver's Law. Now we have an endless string of products with no cycles per se. BoF reports: "Today, trends are born and die within an infinitely faster and more turbulent environment, in which brands, celebrities, magazines, bloggers, and end consumers on social media all jostle for influence over what's 'in' and 'out' of fashion."[13]

The headline is this: when it comes to consumption, we have to use our energy wisely. We can try to make sense of the increasing quantity of symbols coming our way at increasing speeds, further straining our finances, the environment, and our attention, or we can develop new practices that allow us to keep up with the pace of our personalities more sustainably.

Yerdle is hoping we'll shake things up and choose the latter. They are also trying to disentangle our long-standing preferences and practices around newness. Can we get the same pleasure from scrolling through items on the Yerdle app as we do running our fingers along new shirts, hanging in a store? Each person has a different relationship with used stuff, and these relationships can have deep psychological and familial roots.

San Franciscan Jennifer Berger writes: "I hate going through vintage clothes. I grew up with working-class parents and they wanted to feel 'not poor' anymore, so they didn't want to buy used stuff or have me wear used stuff."

Though Xandria Quichocho also grew up working-class, in her case in San Antonio, Texas, she feels differently than Jennifer: "As a student, I don't see the point in spending more than $15 on a piece of clothing. Thrift store shopping is a blessing in disguise. All the savings you get is more money you can save for something better! Like books!"

While our ideas about receiving used stuff are often fraught, there is a growing interest in shedding stuff, as evidenced by the popularity of the best-selling Japanese decluttering manual, *The Life-Changing Magic of Tidying Up,* by Marie Kondo—countless YouTube videos extol the virtues of her method, called the "KonMari way"—and minimalist fashion challenges like Project 333 and the 100 Thing Challenge.

No doubt this development is linked to how maxed-out people are feeling in our "more, better, faster" society. Brigid Schulte, author of *Overwhelmed: How to Work, Love, and Play When No One Has the Time*, beautifully articulates the sense so many people have: "I feel like the Red Queen of *Through the Looking Glass* on speed, running as fast as I can—usually on the fumes of four or five hours of sleep—and getting nowhere."

She goes on: "The overwhelm . . . was about so much more than just getting mom a gift certificate to a spa to calm down. . . . This was about sustainable living, healthy populations, happy families, good business, sound economies, and living a good life."

It's a tall order, and obviously Yerdle is just one small experiment in context, but is it succeeding? Not yet. Half a million users and zero profit to speak of do not a disruption make. But they have lots of ideas they're going to incrementally test out to see what sticks. "The core challenge is the way retail is structured; you have to make something new and sell something new in order for it to count," Adam explains. "The dream is to build a successful business where people are getting exactly what they need without making anything new."

## FREEDOM NO LONGER BUILT BY FORD

There is an image of my parents that is permanently tattooed on my brain: my mom leans into my dad's right side as his long arm stretches around the back of her beautiful shoulders. His left hand is on the metallic mint-green steering wheel, his fingernails squat and clean like always. My mom's burgundy hair is in a haphazard ponytail. The fuzzy dice swing from the rearview mirror. All is right in the world.

My dad got his first car in 1964—a '55 mint-green-and-yellow Chevy convertible for $550. He bagged groceries in Denver, Colorado, in order to afford it. He wanted the car for a lot of reasons. For one, it was cool. My dad was on the bowling team and the newspaper staff—enough said. But there was something even more fundamental about it. "The Chevy was always freedom to me," he told me. His own family was chaotic and fragile. A Chevy convertible was the exact opposite—built like a steel boat and ready to go anywhere, anytime. He fantasized about sailing into the sunset with his high school sweetheart by his side. With a car like that, life would be different.

My dad wasn't the only teenager lusting after steel and wheels back in the sixties. It was a time of suburban entrenchment. After World War II, the creation of Levittown was the symbolic beginning of a vast expansion of "bedroom communities." Being more spread out meant building more highways (in 1956 the Federal Aid Highway Act connected all the major cities in the U.S.). Cars weren't just the way to get from here to there—they were the ultimate status symbol. The Beach Boys, Jan and Dean, and Ronny & the Daytonas all belted out popular hits about the beauty and danger of these quintessentially American machines.

Now, they just don't make 'em like they used to. Or, more accurately, they just don't make us swoon like they used to. Cars today hold a completely different place in the cultural imagination of the American public, and there are real environmental and economic consequences to that. In a piece in *The New York Times* fatalistically titled "The End of Car Culture," Elisabeth Rosenthal writes: "The United States, with its broad expanses and suburban ideals, had long been one of the world's prime car cultures. . . . But America's love affair with its vehicles seems to be cooling."[14]

She goes on to cite a wide range of factors. The rise of the Internet has increased both telecommuting and the number of people who commute via public transportation. (Who wouldn't rather be scrolling through Instagram photos than grinding her teeth in gridlock?) For those who do commute, there are car-sharing apps and company-sponsored buses that shuttle employees from hip city centers to office parks farther afield. Though it's true that Americans drive fewer miles and buy fewer cars in part because of the economic downturn, the trend was on the rise even before 2008.[15] For one thing, in our increasingly interconnected world, we don't need to get into our cars in order to see people face-to-face. Plus, as many of the best-value cars aren't American-made, you can't drape yourself in patriotism while zooming down the highway. And certainly not least, gasoline is tangled up with at least two decades of morally questionable wars.

The embrace of city living, particularly by younger people who crave the cultural experiences and diversity that come with density, has also cut down on car ownership. Those who want access to four wheels are increasingly turning to car-sharing companies like ZipCar, which now has offices in more than thirty American cities. For their 900,000 members, the monthly fee and occasional inconvenience of not having a car available where and when you need it seem to outweigh the costs of owning one yourself—not to mention the frustrations of insurance, break-ins, and parking expenses.

Juliet Blake, a New Yorker, writes: "Totally over it. So liberating not to have one. Our daughter Lily came and drove our Prius to car-obsessed Los Angeles and not a day goes by when we aren't grateful not to have one."

Many see cars not just as a money-suck but as a time-suck, too. Thirty-year-old Stephanie Marie reluctantly bought her first car after moving from New York to California. She writes: "I hate the time spent in the car when commuting—not socializing, not reading, not finishing a project or anything else. It's a waste."

When my husband, John, was a teenager he saved up money working at a country club in Milwaukee, Wisconsin, to buy his first car. He'd set his heart on a vehicle belonging to one of the guys John caddied for that just gathered dust in the garage: a yellow Jeep CJ7 with a white ragtop. He dreamed about the freedom it would afford him—a chance to get away from his five brothers and sisters and all the chaos they created at home. But shortly after getting his license, John got a speeding ticket for driving twenty-two miles over the speed limit in the family minivan. After that his parents forbade him to buy one of his own, so he became a collector of vintage banana seat bicycles instead. In our first shared apartment—just 700 square feet— four of his bikes filled the living room.

Those born between 1977 and 1994 are 29 percent less likely to buy a car than was the previous generation.[16] They are more likely to share rides, ride bikes, and take public transportation where and when it's accessible—whether by economic necessity, personal prefer- ence, or—in John's case—parental kibosh.

All of this is bad news for American car companies. General Motors, Ford, and Chrysler—dubbed "the big three"—were rescued in 2009 from the financial brink with $80 billion in federal funds, a rescue that only 37 percent of Americans favored at the time.[17]

Thirty years ago, nearly half of sixteen-year-olds got a driver's license; by 2008 that figure had dropped to 31 percent. The top reason cited? Young people say they're too busy to jump through the hoops to get a license (that notorious overload creeps up again). Other reasons: it's too expensive to own a car and get insurance; they can hitch rides where they need to go; and they'd rather walk, bike, or take public transportation.[18] And the country's disillusion- ment with cars is a great thing for the planet: transportation is the second largest source of America's greenhouse gas emissions, just behind power plants.

And, as romanticized as driving has often been in our culture, it is nonetheless deadly. Over 30,000 people died in car crashes in 2013. And you don't have to be in a crash to lose your life. Just last year, the high-profile case of twenty-eight-year-old Sandra Bland, a black woman who died in custody in Waller County, Texas, after a routine traffic stop, highlighted the continued risk of "driving while black" in this country. For many people of color, being behind a wheel doesn't feel safe, not because of road hazards, but because of enduring racism.

Cars still hold a very special place in the hearts of a lot of people, particularly those who turn cars into art. The annual Lowrider and Custom Car Show in Española, New Mexico, known as the "lowrider capital of the world," provides ample evidence of how personalizing a car with custom paint jobs and elaborate sound systems can equate to expressing personality, creativity, even spirituality in the form of Catholic iconography.

But for most people in this country, cars aren't art. They're not even that cool. A lot of experts attribute the fact that today's teenagers are less enamored with cars to the fact that they're more enamored with their cell phones. Whereas the car used to be a magical and rare private space for all the embarrassing, titillating conversations and sweaty make-out sessions of yesteryear, today's teens have WhatsApp and sexting. While my own suburban adolescence is so inextricably linked with cars that it's hard to imagine those awkward, searching years without them (as I write this I can hear "Wheelz of Steel" by OutKast pumping out of my high school boyfriend's Jeep Wrangler), the statistics speak for themselves. Kids these days confer status and pursue freedoms that have nothing to do with cars.

For his part, my dad placed a pretty good bet on that '55 Chevy Bel Air. His high school sweetheart became his wife, and then my mom. And though I have vivid memories of her snuggling on the seat next to him, one of their recurring fights is over his boat of a car: either that it occupies the only garage space available or it takes up too much of the driveway. This has been going on for forty-six years. She hates it.

And yet, she loves it. The second she scoots in his direction on that green leather bench seat, she is sixteen again too. My dad, otherwise not a materialistic person in the least, has told me: "The Chevy became part of me. I could never let it go."

That's the thing about ownership, isn't it? If it never takes hold, there's nothing to lose. For my dad, and even for me, freedom was about driving. It imprinted itself on us at an emotionally charged moment in a car-obsessed country. It was tangible, fun, sometimes dangerous, and always expensive, even back then. But for all those seventeen-year-olds sporting throwback overalls with purple streaks in their hair, riding the bus while grammin' their latest weekend adventures, freedom is alive and well; it just happens to be intertwined with an SD card rather than a car. And, as much as I love that yellow and mint-green boat and everything it symbolizes for my dad, we both know the new freedom is better for everyone.

## THE STUFF/EFFORT EQUATION

*If your house were burning, what would you take with you?*

This is the question at the center of a fascinating, participatory art project called The Burning House, in which people post a photograph of the stuff they would take arranged in one telling image. The site reads: "It's a conflict between what's practical, valuable, and sentimental. What you would take reflects your interests, background, and priorities. Think of it as an interview condensed into one question."

Browsing through the entries reveals so much about what we actually hold dear, regardless of where we come from (there are entries from Belgium to Brazil). Almost every one features a childhood object of some kind—a stuffed animal or a beloved toy. Many feature an object, often unusable, from a grandparent—a pair of eyeglasses or an old watch. Unsurprisingly, people usually include a photo or a photo album, and almost without fail a computer or smart phone. Our increasingly digitized lives mean that we can save the analog version of love notes, notebooks, and Rolodex in one fell swoop by rescuing our devices—and even those are becoming antiquated with our increasing dependence on the cloud.

I was inspired by my wanderings through The Burning House to take to Facebook and ask people a simple question: *What is the most valuable thing you own?* The answers took my breath away:

- "My Narnia set or my cello."
- "My former golden retriever's ashes (although they are really just stardust anyway)."
- "My passport."
- "My mother's shirt. Sealed in a plastic bag that still smells like her ten years later. It is the one visceral experience I have left of my mother, who was killed ten years ago."
- "My box of handwritten letters (that have been sent to me) from the past ten years."
- "The giant dictionary I inherited from my grandfather."
- "My laptop, jeans, good shoes to walk in, and a good kitchen knife."
- "My bicycle! It is a source of freedom, fun, and daily transportation."
- "My 1971 Fender Precision Bass guitar."

The answers tell such a simple, instinctual story. People are defined by their people. They are defined by their pleasure. They are defined by their memories. That's about it. All the rest is, well, stuff.

Increasingly, we're not waiting for a house fire to wake us up to this reality. Chelsea Rustrum, who describes herself as an "interdependence consultant" and authored *It's a Shareable Life: A Practical*

*Guide to Sharing*, told me: "Freedom and time are my currencies. When stuff starts impinging on either of those, it's a problem."

There's a growing exasperation with how owning things, especially things we don't need or value deeply, affects our quality of life, and sometimes the stuff/effort equation just doesn't add up. We have to work harder and longer to afford both buying and storing more stuff—and then we have to spend time finding that misplaced stuff we worked so hard to afford. The less durable the stuff, the faster we have to run on the wheel of earning and spending, accumulating and purging.

If we don't do the maintenance (repair a bicycle, mend a torn shirt), we trash our stuff. This trashed stuff is rapidly killing our other most precious resource: the environment. Consumers are rebelling against companies that employ "planned obsolescence"—corporate speak for designing a product that intentionally becomes unusable or passé quickly in order to increase the market potential. Some of these products are proving to be Frankensteinian; John Sylvan—the designer behind K-Cups, the unrecyclable coffee-in-a-pod system that made Keurig Green Mountain $4.7 billion in revenue in 2014—told *The Atlantic*'s, "I feel bad sometimes that I ever did it."[19]

Additionally, our increasingly urban and more compact homes and abodes don't accommodate a lot of stuff. We feel crowded out, overwhelmed, disenchanted. We can't hear ourselves think amidst all the stuff we thought would make us cooler, cuter, more efficient. Graham Hill, a tech-millionaire-turned-tiny-house-advocate and founder of the popular blog LifeEdited, writes: "I like material things as much as anyone. I studied product design in school. I'm into gadgets, clothing, and all kinds of things. But my experiences show that after a certain point, material objects have a tendency to crowd out the emotional needs they are meant to support."[20]

Status symbols just aren't as satisfying when you've sobered up about the stressful side effects of owning a lot. In *Life at Home in the Twenty-First Century: 32 Families Open Their Doors*, researchers from a range of disciplines at UCLA painstakingly cataloged the possessions of thirty-two middle-class Los Angeles families and found that all of the mothers' stress hormones spiked during the time they spent dealing with their belongings. The authors report: "Twenty-first century America is the most materially affluent society in global history," noting that "our possessions organize and define and, in some cases, engulf us."[21]

In just three rooms in one home, for example, there were 2,260 *visible* possessions. The researchers were understandably overwhelmed by the cataloging, but the owners themselves weren't far behind: "For the first time, we can link measurably high density of household objects—which we call 'stressful house environments'—with physiological responses that can markedly compromise homeowner health."[22]

Our stuff is making us sick. Plenty of science now proves that the temporary boost of esteem we get when we acquire something peters out, leaving behind an accumulation hangover.[23] But it's not just academics that are hip to the false promise of purchase; the American consumer is responding in kind. In many categories, consumer spending hasn't returned to its prerecession levels.[24]

Data released by the U.S. Department of Commerce in recent months show that American buyers are putting what little extra money they *do* have into experiences, not things. Since 1987 the share of consumer spending on live experiences and events relative to total U.S. consumer spending has increased 70 percent.[25] James Hamblin writes, "It's the fleetingness of experiential purchases that endears us to them. Either they're not around long enough to become imperfect, or they are imperfect, but our memories and stories of them get sweet with time. Even a bad experience becomes a good story."[26]

And that's just it, isn't it? Our possessions, like our experiences, are only as valuable as the stories we imbue them with. That's why, faced with a fire and thousands of flammable objects, one would scoop up an obsolete dictionary or a bedraggled stuffed bear that only a child could really love properly. Beyond our most functional objects—a toothbrush, say, or a hammer—we only value the things that are irreplaceable, the things that ignite a real pleasure born of beauty in us, or the ones that we can tell a compelling story about.

## THE HYPE OF HOMEOWNERSHIP

Of course, choosing to fill our homes with less stuff in the pursuit of both environmental and emotional conservation is countercultural at the least. But it's downright radical for us to rethink whether we want that home to be, at least technically speaking, *ours* in the first place. Homeownership, that long-standing foundation of success in Americans' minds, is starting to crumble. In his article "The New American Dream: Renting" in *The Wall Street Journal*, Thomas J. Sugrue, professor of history and sociology at New York University, writes: "Every generation has offered its own version of the claim that owner-occupied homes are the nation's saving grace."

During the Cold War, homeownership was conflated with patriotism, protecting those with a deed from any pesky suspicions of being Communist. As those moral dangers faded, family values took their place. National Homeownership Day was founded during the Clinton administration, cast as the antidote to "broken" families. According to Sugrue, "George W. Bush similarly pledged his commitment to 'an ownership society in this country,' where more Americans than ever will be able to open up their door where they live and say, 'welcome to my house, welcome to my piece of property.'"[27]

The political hype, however, never matched the reality on the ground. From 1900—when the U.S. Census Bureau first started gathering data on homeownership—through 1940, fewer than half of all Americans owned their own homes. That changed when the federal government started incentivizing homeownership in a big way. In 1932 Herbert Hoover signed the Federal Home Loan Bank Act to shore up the housing market during the Great Depression, and a host of other interventions followed. Low-interest loans offered to veterans returning from World War II essentially created the suburbs and a boom in homeownership—*among white people.*[28]

In the decades that followed, decision after decision and policy after policy made it easier for white Americans to become kings of the castle—leaving everyone else to remain in rental serfdom. Sociologist Dalton Conley sums it up: "When the government instituted rental housing in inner cities, in the form of public housing projects for poor minorities, and then developed home ownership in low-cost, suburban communities for low-income whites, where you could put almost nothing down, they created this incredible wealth gap."[29]

When the housing bubble burst in 2007, it became painfully obvious that many of the low-income Americans, disproportionately people of color, had been further screwed by the largely unregulated mortgage market. Historically, lower-quality, subprime mortgages accounted for only about 8 percent of the mortgages in America at a given time—since they were risky, most lenders avoided them. But from 2004 to 2006, the evil twinning of lowered lending standards and the proliferation of higher-risk products amassed nearly a quarter of mortgages in the subprime category.[30]

Owning a home occupies a grand place in the American imagination, one that signifies a "you've definitely made it" status. In countries like France, Germany, and Switzerland, on the other hand, renting is more common than purchasing no matter how successful you are. But in America, the Brady Bunch had a house, even with all those kids.

When the dust settled from the financial crash of 2008, a lot of confusion remained over who was to blame for the mortgage market run amuck; the financial institutions, regulators, credit agencies, and government housing policies had all played a role. But the victims weren't hard to identify: people, usually not all that far from the poverty line, who had dreamed of a home-sweet-home to balance out all the bitterness of living in such an unequal country—and who had seen those dreams shattered. Interestingly, even *high-income* people of color were preyed on. In 2006, at the height of the housing boom, black and Hispanic families making more than $200,000 a year were more likely on average to be given a subprime loan than was a white family making less than $30,000 a year.

So many have suffered as a direct result of both our romanticization of homeownership and a market that preyed on vulnerable buyers who were, understandably, seduced. The silver lining is that the mortgage crisis proved that the king had no castle, and now fewer Americans are rushing to pretend otherwise. According to the U.S. Census Housing Vacancy Survey, homeownership dropped to 63.7 percent in the third quarter of 2015, the lowest level since 1995; Americans thirty-five and under are buying the least: 35.8 percent, the lowest on record since the survey began tracking homeownership by age in 1982.[31]

The young people who do buy homes tend to have one thing in common: rich, generous parents. Over half of millennials who have managed to afford a home have received both tuition assistance from their parents (and, therefore, graduated with less debt) and help with a down payment. While these "doubly lucky" kids— as real estate research company Zillow calls them—may represent over half of millennial homeowners, tellingly they represent only 3 percent of millennials overall.[32]

So, in part, most people simply can't afford homes, and without wealthy parents or the wide variety of predatory loans that existed before the bubble burst, they can't be deluded otherwise. (Though subprime mortgages are making a bit of a comeback, fortunately they have far more sober specifications.) Buying a home has lost a bit of its former shine anyway. People are more aware of the risks involved and, especially in volatile or simply reliably high housing markets, they recognize that renting is a smarter, less onerous choice.

For some, not being able to buy a home feels tragic—like they're being stripped of the sense of security and accomplishment they crave. And, despite some legal protections, renting offers less control over how long we live in our homes and under what circumstances. Given that, we're less likely to invest time, energy, and money into making our home feel just right. In addition, since notions of home are still intertwined with dearly held values of family and heritage, we can feel we're missing out on that too.

For people who have been structurally and systematically deprived of the experience, homeownership can feel like an unfulfilled dream that's passed on from generation to generation. It can be incredibly alluring to imagine being the one to make your parents' and grandparents' marginalization feel less definitive, to in fact break the perpetuating cycle. To some, it is as if the deed to a house somehow disproves all the negative stereotypes that have been perpetuated about one's family, even about one's community. On the flip side, that deed indicates, at least to some extent, that a family has bought into the market and the mythology that discriminated against them in the first place.

The public conversation that followed the cacophonous explosion of the housing bubble almost exclusively focused on economics, but it ignored the huge role emotions play in all of this. For Marc Patrick Malone, a twenty-nine-year-old professor living in rural Kansas, homeownership felt like a counterweight to grief: "I recently bought a home after my father passed away. I found myself 'an orphan' (mother died in 2003) without a clear sense of 'home.' I bought specifically to close that emotional gap."

But the economics worry Malone: "I personally feel like I have less control over my financial future because of the house. I am less mobile and less likely to be adaptive to uncertain times at my educational institution."

Even when young people do aspire to buy a home, they're on a totally different timetable than their parents or grandparents were. Because millennials are getting married later in life, they're also considering buying homes later in life; many can't afford to buy with just one income.[33] And given our oft-changing employment and relationships, roots can feel more like tethers.

Laurie Peterson, a thirty-seven-year-old entrepreneur living in San Francisco, California, experienced this firsthand. She writes: "Since owning a home, so much of our free cash goes into it and we have less flexibility financially and with our time, as we are often taking care of domestic responsibilities. Part of the American Dream is the freedom to pursue possibilities. This house is limiting mine."

Thirty-six-year-old Brittney Retherford found that "a place of her own" just wasn't as appealing as adventure:

> *I bought myself the most adorable log cabin in Fairbanks, Alaska. I still own it, but my dream shifted, and now I rent it out to the most wonderful tenant. I couldn't stand the idea of being moored to one place—and that cabin (even though it's just 640 square feet and has no indoor plumbing) made me feel stuck.*
>
> *Now I'm in the market for a sailboat or some kind of vessel that doesn't tie me down. The idea of my own "space" does drive me, but it's less about money or investment than a place that feels safe and warm and big enough to entertain the people I love.*

The kind of space that Brittney craves, that so many of us want, isn't—by definition—one that we need to own. According to a recent survey, 39 percent of all renters expect to purchase a home in the next three years, while 61 percent believe they will continue to rent for the next few years. Of those 61 percent, 39 percent said they expected to continue renting simply because they don't want the responsibilities that come with owning your own home.[34]

No one, it turns out, opens their door to guests saying, as Dubya encouraged, "Welcome to my house. Welcome to my piece of property." That would be profoundly douchey. What we really want to say, what we are saying more and more, is simpler, and has nothing to do with the fluctuating market: "Welcome to my home. It's safe and warm inside, and we're having an amazing conversation."

A deed doesn't make a house a home; the people who gather there do. The best homes I know are not owner-occupied; they are joy-occupied. They are places known for comfortable, engaging dinner parties where people linger so long at the table that they nibble at all the remaining food and refill each other's wine glasses without asking. They are places where you feel safe to be vulnerable, and where you can heal from physical and emotional malaise. They are places that inspire their inhabitants to express their history and personality, perhaps with a clothesline of chapbooks strung across the living room, a shelf lined with beautiful old photographs, a painstakingly arranged train set, a closet door painted with favorite rap lyrics.

These are the sorts of things that make a house a home, that make an existence a life. It is the size of our psyches, not our storage space, that determines the amount of accumulation that's healthiest. What matters is the amount of time we have to appreciate what we possess, time that is inherently limited when we have to work so hard to earn the money to acquire those possessions. We are wise to have less and give away more—to pursue experiences over objects, and memories over status symbols. We are wise to let go of the century-old mythology that would have us believe we haven't "made it" until we've bought it—whether "it" is a designer bag or a suburban home.

The New Better Off mindset is vested in pursuing the most permanent pleasures—which, strangely, turn out to be the fleeting experiences we have and the intangible stories we tell about them.

# tearing down the white picket fence

## RECLAIMING COMMUNITY

If there is one universal symbol of the old American Dream, it is surely the white picket fence. That quintessentially suburban boundary marker has taken up powerful residence in our collective consciousness. Can't you just see it now—smugly snaked through a perfectly coifed green lawn around a two-story home somewhere nondescript and sunny? For many of our parents, and for our grandparents before them, it was an unequivocal indication of success. You got yourself the wife. You got yourself the good stable job. You got yourself the home. You got yourself a couple of kids. And you positioned it all squarely within that lily-white fence.

The fence is the classic American symbol of self-containment and self-possession. It suggests an intimate world with its own mores. Those who dwell within get all their needs met by one another. Their strife is secret; or, if acknowledged at all, it's in a light, convivial language—poking fun at impenetrable boys, dramatic teenage girls, or oblivious hardworking fathers. Within that white picket fence the same stories are told over and over again about unique traditions and funny childhood moments—as if the tellers believe that, if they say these stories often enough, the other ones—the unspoken stories of genuine suffering and misunderstanding—will be forgotten. (But they never are.)

But Kodak moments just aren't what they used to be, are they? As explored in the last chapter, subprime mortgages have undermined the already shaky foundations of our obsession with homeownership. But they've done something else that's remarkable, something that's less about the hunt for real estate and more about the hunger for a modern village.

Our new economic "normal" caused us to turn to one another, no matter how humbling we found the act. We had to ask each other for childcare in a tough spot, career advice, maybe even a loan or a hot meal. And that turning, that sharing, demonstrated that the white picket fence, stripped of its sentimentality, serves mostly to divide. Us from our neighbors. Public space from private. The part of the world that we, the owners, will take responsibility for and the part that is not ours to bother with. But what, truly, is the purpose of these squat, smooth, white picket fences? They don't offer protection—they declare KEEP OFF with a wink and a smile. They just keep people apart.

What's happening instead—for now, among just a creative, rebellious minority, but one that's steadily growing and diversifying—is a rejection of both the white picket fence and the kind of highly privatized life that happened within it. People are becoming less focused on owning, and even when they do, they are buying and living in homes with a distinctively different mentality. No longer the primary norm, the traditional, nuclear family is giving way to many generations living under one roof; from 2007 to 2009, this country experienced its largest recorded increase in multigenerational households: from 46.5 million to 51.5 million (the historic low was in 1980). And while this shift was largely spurred by the downturn economy, it turns out that people actually like living with their relatives; more than three-quarters of those living in such households reported that their relationships had actually improved from the change. And, far from the stereotype peddled in most mainstream publications about dysfunctional "boomerang kids," nearly 50 percent of adult children who return home pay rent or other household expenses; in addition, their parents report being just as satisfied with their family life and housing situation as do the parents whose kids didn't return to the nest. Heck, even the most visible household in the country, the Obama White House, was a multigenerational unit—Michelle's mother, Marian Shields Robinson, lived with the first family.[1]

Sometimes these shared homes are created out of an experiment in what author bell hooks calls "revolutionary parenting": the notion that the ideal living situation isn't inherently the most conventional one but whatever actually promotes the thriving of the human beings involved.[2] The Obamas do it; so do single mothers, many of them on the opposite side of the economic spectrum from the first family. CoAbode, an online matching service for single moms looking to share homes with other single moms, has over 70,000 users.[3]

We're living in shared housing with various configurations, and in a range of styles and sizes—from old farmhouses to Victorian mansions. The organizing principle is that, while people have their own bedrooms, they otherwise live intertwined lives, cooking together, cleaning together, and swapping skills and wisdom. Everyone participates; everyone is enriched.

The demographic of those aged twenty-five through thirty-four has seen the biggest increase in unrelated adults living together. The growing popularity of college co-ops, where students live in a house together, sharing meals and domestic duties, has led many postgraduate wanderers to seek out "householding" arrangements. Some of these arrangements are fleeting; after all, postcollege life tends to be pretty itinerant. But group homes established by older adults often last for years, and sometimes even gain notoriety. Lytheria, a mammoth house on Milwaukee's east side, for example, has been a group home since 1980 and consistently has a waiting list. Qumbya Housing Cooperative, in Hyde Park, a neighborhood of Chicago, describes itself as an "affordable, community-oriented, group-equity housing cooperative." In existence since 1988, they have about fifty members in three houses; they're currently looking for a fourth house to meet the huge demand.[4]

The growing population of aging Boomers is also inspiring a range of radical new living arrangements. One of the most popular is known as Naturally Occurring Retirement Communities (NORCs), whereby a group of aging neighbors collectively benefit from wraparound services. Sometimes a NORC is created in an existing community, where a group of people who want to "age in place" need a bit of help to do so. Sometimes a NORC is created whole cloth, often with state and federal funding to help subsidize everything from classes in nutrition and exercise to financial planning to environmental improvements to transportation assistance. Fredda Vladeck, the creator of New York City's first government-funded NORC program, told *The New York Times*: "There's no question that they can have a profound effect on the quality of life for older people, by helping them stay in their homes for as long as possible, as well as having a positive impact on the overall community. And that's a huge public benefit."[5]

We are now sowing those communal seeds all over America, dismantling the white picket fences and building something more interdependent in their stead. We're techies and teachers, nurses and engineers, architects and accountants. We're owners and renters, subletters and squatters. We're married couples, single parents, aunties, cousins, and siblings. We're less invested in the perfect family than in the imperfect village. We're what Bella DePaulo calls "life space pioneers," people who understand the importance of a balance between the need for solitude and the need for social ties. She writes: "The special twenty-first century adaptation of village life is that autonomy matters as much as interconnectedness."[6]

We're becoming a people who are united not by a professional leaning or an upbringing or an economic class or even a particular religious or political ideology, but by a sober assessment that interdependence leads to human flourishing. Or, in more simple terms: I've got your back; you've got mine.

## "HI, COMMUNITY; I'M HOME!"

The most literal form of this new approach to shared daily life is the cohousing community. According to Cohousing.org, these communities are usually designed as attached or single-family homes, either along one or more pedestrian streets or clustered around a central courtyard. "Cohousing dwellings are arranged like people who want to socialize," writes Bella DePaulo. They face one another like people chatting at a cocktail party.[7]

Such dwellings range from seven to sixty-seven units, the majority of them housing twenty to forty families, however that term is defined. The first distinctive cohousing community, Muir Commons, was built in 1991 in Davis, California, by architects Kathryn McCamant and Charles Durrett, who first discovered cohousing while studying architecture in Copenhagen in the eighties. Europeans have been the pioneers in this particular form of shared living; 700 cohousing communities exist in Denmark alone. In comparison, the U.S. is far from meeting the ever-growing cohousing demand; only 120 such communities are sprinkled across the United States today.

While many are drawn to the concept of communal living, some are palpably wary of something that feels so foreign, potentially even a little invasive. I can understand that cynicism: we've been subjected to decades of rhetoric, misguided city planning, and powerful pop culture—everything from Levittown to *Extreme Makeover: Home Edition*—that vividly depict the autonomous family frolicking in their private, palatial home. Even when you peel back that layer of "a man's home is his castle" propaganda, there are some valid concerns about sharing space. How do you balance neighborliness with privacy? What are the best practices for creating a community with reliable expectations but not too many rules? What happens if you ultimately don't like the people you're living with? Or if you'd like them fine if you saw a little less of them?

These were some of the questions on our minds as we moved from our sixty-unit building in Brooklyn, New York, a few years ago to a cohousing community in Oakland, California. A year earlier, John and I had fallen in love with the idea of the collaboration of a group of neighbors sharing meals, yard work, sometimes prayers, and usually some communal space in addition to their private homes.

We'd considered trying to start a cohousing community with family and friends, but after a few Skype calls and some Internet research we grew weary. What if we screwed it up? What if we ended up hating each other? How were we going to handle all that money-talk in a way that didn't alienate anyone? Safer, we concluded, to explore the possibility at a later date, maybe—and, oddly, among people we didn't already care so much about.

We thought our cohousing dream was dead, or at least in a coma of sorts, until one of my husband's Facebook friends posted that she was selling her home in an intentional living community in Oakland, California, and was looking for someone who might be interested in taking her place.

John was the first to respond. But even as we were enthusiastically pursuing the move, we couldn't help but wonder: was cohousing one of those things that sounded better on paper than it actually felt in real life?

## RADICAL HOSPITALITY

I sit at the kitchen table with Cheryl, a children's pastor, as three of her four teenagers mill about. We've been around for a week or two, so it's time for Cheryl—the head of the board—to start breaking down some of the finer points of cohousing life. I'm a little worried that this is going to be the big reveal—the moment when we realize we've moved into a cult and there are ten million tiny rules that we will inevitably break. We will be the failures of the community.

Temescal Commons, as it's called, was founded in 2000, originally by a group of people who went to church together and craved a way of living their values more actively the other six days a week. Over the years it evolved from being exclusively Christian to being interfaith; today the majority of the twenty-five residents identify as Christian, though they attend a variety of churches, and there is also a Buddhist as well as about a half dozen "nones." The land is a sight to behold: one and a half acres of proud, old trees that drop persimmons and apples in our laps, a prolific blackberry bush along a robust vegetable garden, and grass grown responsibly brown during this worrisome drought—all smack dab in the middle of urban Oakland. And while the nine units vary a fair amount—from a studio apartment to a four-bedroom house—everything was built or rehabbed to be as green as possible; for example, the big, shiny black solar cells on our roof ensure the electricity bill rarely exceeds $5 in an average month.

After touring the shared laundry room, tool shed, bike shed, exercise room, and industrial-sized kitchen and eating area, we've landed at Cheryl's kitchen table, where she outlines the logistics around common meals: the glue that keeps the community together. We have two a week, Thursday and Sunday. Each quarter, you have to be the head chef once and the assistant chef once. If you're the head chef, it's your job to plan, shop for, and cook the meal; if you're the assistant chef, you show up at 4:30 PM and do whatever the head chef needs done. Both chefs cook and clean on their night, which makes these communal dinners easy breezy for everybody else—most of the time, all you have to do is show up, share a meal, and fit your dishes in the dishwasher on your way out.

"There used to be a spending limit on dinner and everyone would submit receipts and get reimbursed," Cheryl explains, "but it all ended up feeling too complicated, so we scrapped it." I'm reminded that we are very lucky to move into a community that's already over a decade old; the founders, most of whom still live here, have learned a lot over the years about what works and what doesn't in the advanced art of creating a functional community. I feel a little guilty that we get to parachute in and benefit from all of their growing pains, but we try to reciprocate by bringing fresh energy (and a very cute, very chubby baby).

"The quality of the food can vary a lot," Cheryl tells us. "There was a time when this really young, single guy lived here and you could tell he was just so nervous for his night. He bought frozen lasagna and we all ate it with the biggest smiles of gratitude on our faces and eventually he graduated to other kinds of meals. We all enjoyed watching him relax around it and learn new things."

"And sometimes people forget that it's their night to cook," Kathryn, Cheryl's oldest daughter, chimes in from the kitchen where she's making a crepe for her younger sister.

"Yes, that's true. There have been plenty of nights where someone ordered pizza and called it a night, which is fine," Cheryl agrees.

Matthew, the quintessential thirteen-year-old boy, shouts from the couch: "Pizza is perfect! You guys should totally order pizza!"

Cheryl smiles, then continues: "Guests are great. Bring guests to common meal anytime. All we ask is that, if you bring more than like three people, you let the chefs know so they can plan accordingly. Otherwise, you can show up with a friend any old time."

I tear up. Which is strange. Why am I so touched that I can bring a friend or two to dinner?

Cheryl leans back in her chair and says, "Really, the underlying philosophy of everything we do is radical hospitality. We want people to feel welcome. Always."

## LIVING INTERTWINED

It's difficult to find reliable statistics about cohousing communities, but they appear to be on the rise. National conferences and other networks are popping up, and people are flocking to find out how they can start or join existing communities. Everyone from a white, corporate sustainability expert in his thirties with two kids to a single, black woman in her seventies has inquired about our own community. And the financing models are being reinvented so that a wider diversity of people can take part. Architects, developers, trainers, and others are specializing in the knowledge required to found communities. In short, we're experiencing a zeitgeist moment. Claire Thompson writes on Grist.org:

> The growth of the sharing economy, a focus on walkable neighborhoods, a preference for smaller, more efficient homes—all these developments reflect central values of cohousing. . . . We're starting to realize that our long-term future won't be built around highways, automobiles, and detached houses with fertilized lawns. As more people seek out a different kind of community, cohousing, or projects like it, will grow in popularity.[8]

It's not just our need for shelter that's being overhauled in favor of greater cooperation: grocery co-ops, collectively owned and operated businesses known for being both affordable and ripe for satire, are also flourishing. As of 2014, the National Co+op Grocers represented 143 independent food cooperatives operating more than 190 stores in 38 states with combined annual sales of over $1.7 billion.[9] On Chowhound.com Diane Mehta describes the infamous Park Slope Food "Coop" as "something between an earthy-crunchy health food haven and a Soviet-style reeducation camp";[10] Alana Joblin Ain countered in *The New York Times*: "The co-op, a place that raises aspirations for society, makes us raise aspirations for ourselves."[11]

And at an even smaller scale, dinner co-ops are increasingly popular. They vary in structure, but the basic form is that a geographically close group of cooks agree to alternate preparing and delivering fresh food on weeknights; the idea is that you just scale up what you would already cook one night in exchange for a few nights of meals cooked by fellow members. The authors of *Dinner at Your Door*, a bible for dinner co-ops, write: "The dinner co-op is an essential lifestyle upgrade that has saved our sanity, challenged our creativity, and elevated our own cooking in ways we never thought possible. Along the way it's become our foundation for a happy life."[12]

Along the same lines, some people have home project co-ops; they pick one person's house each month of the summer and all pitch in on a big project, like repainting the exterior or building a shed. It's a way to spend time together out in the sunshine, get some physical exercise, and save money—all at once.

Similarly, babysitting co-ops are popular among working parents with part-time or flexible schedules, or those who just want to get a date night out every once in a while without breaking the bank. Essentially, it's just a system by which parents trade off taking care of each other's kids. Not rocket science, but a game changer in a country where childcare is unsubsidized and so many don't live in the same town as Grandpa and Grandma.

Arrangements like these don't just make our lives easier—they also make us healthier. Studies confirm that people with social ties have better short-term health prospects, like fewer colds and flus, as well as longer-term benefits, like higher survival rates for serious diseases.[13] Judith Shulevitz sums up the explosion in recent science on just how lethal loneliness really is: "Psychobiologists can now show that loneliness sends misleading hormonal signals, rejiggers the molecules on genes that govern behavior, and wrenches a slew of other systems out of whack. They have proved that long-lasting loneliness not only makes you sick; it can kill you. Emotional isolation is ranked as high a risk factor for mortality as smoking."[14]

When you live in a community, domestic labor is spread out among more people—the cooking, the weeding, the repairing. But even the emotional work gets shared. Rather than relying on the idealized family unit for getting all your emotional needs met—likely two heterosexual parents and a couple of kids—you have a couple of dozen people to hold your hand when you cry, laugh with you when you fall, and celebrate when you succeed. Now, this isn't to say that cohousing is for everyone; obviously it's not. But there are still elements of the communal lifestyle that can ease our burdens, brighten our days, and make life feel less solitary. A network of neighbors can decide to do a rotating potluck once a week, or spend one Saturday each month teaming up on repairing each other's homes. Or intergenerational friends can simply pledge to look out for one another—the younger one bringing medicine or going on grocery runs, the older one offering wisdom and perspective.

As it happens, there's a freedom in admitting our limitations. In *The Samaritan's Dilemma: Should Government Help Your Neighbor?*, sociologist Deborah Stone writes:

*We need to untwist our notion of personal freedom by acknowledg-
ing that dependence is the human condition. Genuine freedom can't
be had by denying our individual limitations. Freedom comes from
understanding them and working around them, and from building a
community where bonds of loyalty compensate for the things we can't
do ourselves."*[15]

Without cooperation, without community, our potential is defined in strictly individual terms. And for much of contemporary America, this is still the case. It's why we obsessively talk about work/ life balance as if it were a problem best solved in 82.5 million different ways—that is, one solution for each mother in the U.S. It's why the vast majority of us commute alone in our own cars, an average of twenty-five minutes each way—it's too tricky to fit in errands with carpooling, ridesharing, or public transportation. It's why almost half of us eat fast food at least once a week (wealthy Americans are actually more likely to eat fast food than poor Americans, by the way);[16] the faster we eat those packaged calorie-bombs, the faster we can get on with our busy days.

But when our lives become rooted in communities—whether because we've intentionally sought them out, bucking against the conditioning of our privileged class, or because it's what we've always known out of our economic necessity—our potential expands beyond our individual limitations. We focus less on our own failures and more on structural failures, such as more family-friendly work policies, more public transportation options, more healthy, whole foods available in a wider variety of neighborhoods. We put less energy into figuring out how to hack it solo and more into all the creative ways a group of people could make life easier, healthier, more fun. We become individually less important and collectively more powerful.

# THE TANGLES OF COMMUNAL LIVING

Thera and I move in tandem, trimming the tangled bougainvillea bush that lines the driveway with pairs of slightly rusted but perfectly effective hedge clippers. It's my first monthly workday, where the whole community wakes up early, discusses what needs to be done over a simple, shared breakfast, and then gets to it before the air has lost its morning bite.

I'm feeling hardy—here I am, early on a Saturday morning, wearing dirt-encrusted garden gloves, doing real work next to a neighbor. If I were still in Brooklyn, I would have been fast asleep or, at most, hunting for an egg sandwich in my food desert of a neighborhood. The only words exchanged would be with the guy behind the deli: "Saltpepperketchup?"

Thera and I, in contrast, are talking about our overlapping pasts. I had studied abroad in South Africa, and recently returned from a reporting trip to Malawi and Rwanda; Thera was in the Peace Corps in eastern Africa for many years. And while I struggled with the most basic of expressions in Xhosa, the dominant language in Cape Town's Langa township where I stayed, Thera mastered multiple languages.

To be fair, she's a linguist—though an awfully quiet one. She's introverted, the kind of person who is shy in large groups but who comes alive as we work side by side on a shared project. I'm excited about the prospect of getting to know her better—she's in her thirties and pregnant, just like me. She works at UC Berkeley in the linguistics department; her husband, also named John, is a musician and a janitor in a local church.

Since they live in a tiny studio apartment on the property, we offer to store some of John's musical equipment and Thera's books in the attic of our home. Having lived in New York, we're used to small spaces, but, even so, we're in awe of their determination to raise a baby in such tight quarters. "We'll just make it work," Thera says with a trusting grin. "We don't need much."

The hedge is aggressive. Its little tendrils, tougher than they look, reach up and wrap themselves tightly around the branches of the trees spaced intermittently along the driveway. We have to tear them off and give the bush a close haircut along the top. It's satisfying work—as if we're restoring the proud little trees' autonomy.

The hedge grows beautiful purple flowers near some of its ends. "What should we do with these?" I shout to Tom, the resident wise dad of the community, as he marches by on his way to another project in the process.

"Just toss 'em," he says unsentimentally.

"I don't know if I can," I admit to Thera. "They're so pretty."

"Let's gather them and put them in vases in the common room," Thera suggests. So we do. They wilt quickly, as Tom probably knew they would, but it's worth it for the brief reminder it offers of our newly intermingled lives.

On the next community workday, John and I volunteer to declutter the common house. Okay, *I* volunteer that John and I declutter the common house. I've been eyeing the bookshelf, in particular, for a variety of reasons. I love books. Duh. But also, I can see the potential in it: what a rich resource it could be if we pared down and curated a bona fide library. As is, it looks like a hodgepodge of stuff that was left behind over the many years of writing groups and mothers' teas and Bible studies and game nights. The members of the community who are present seem game to let us try.

We blast a playlist from our housewarming party and get to sorting. Unsurprisingly, there are a lot of Christian books, titles like *Decision Making and the Will of God* and *Listening Prayer*. I try to think like a lost or wondering soul. *What kind of answers might I be looking for on these shelves? What kinds of questions might I be asking?* For this reason some of the many Christian books should stay; they've earned their spot on the shelf because they seem to have sprung from good and genuine questions, or contain comforting and complicated answers. Other books have to go, as they are too redundant or outdated to be useful. We also find cookbooks from the eighties, a couple of self-help titles about healthy marriage, a history or two of Oakland, and a few young adult novels—clearly school assignments long ago completed or avoided and abandoned.

There is also a shoebox full of pictures. Some of them are shots that would have been deleted long ago were they digital—misfires, overexposures, and the backs of people's heads. Some of them are revelatory—the community sitting around, a decade younger, plotting what they'd develop on this little plot of land. The teenagers who now blast through the common house to survey the edibility of the meal were just pudgy, indiscriminate toddlers then. Their parents, now wise and cautious, in the photos look animated and earnest. They sit cross-legged on the floor, the architectural plans fanning out around them like a picnic of their dreams.

John and I sort everything into three piles—the stuff we assume people might be willing to let go of, the stuff we are pretty sure is Goodwill-bound, and the stuff we'll reshelve (pictures included, of course). We spread the word to the community: take a look at the piles, and rescue anything you don't want to part with. We'll cart the rest off to Goodwill in the afternoon.

After what we determine to be sufficient time for the community to browse the piles and pluck their little darlings, we load a couple of boxes into our trunk and run them to the Goodwill on College Avenue. We feel lighter. Accomplished.

And then just an hour or so later, we get a text from the other John: "Hey, do you know where the extra books, etc., are from the common house?"

A wave of panic washes over me. Shit, now we've done it. Here I thought I'd finally figured out a way to channel my own expertise in service of the community, and instead I've just thrown someone's treasure into the black hole that is the Berkeley Goodwill.

We exchange a flurry of text messages: Should I go try to get the boxes back? No, that's okay. It's probably too late. Can I replace whatever it was that was lost? No, it was old stuff; not the kind of thing you can easily find on Amazon. How about eBay? Forget it. I'm sorry. I'm sorry. I'm sorry . . .

When we pull into the driveway, John and Thera are out in the yard. I sheepishly approach and offer my apologies in person. "Not a big deal," Thera says cheerfully, though I can detect the sadness underneath. I sulk the rest of the night—alternating between feeling slightly indignant (why would they keep personal stuff they really cared about in the common house, anyway?! Who listens to audio tapes—it's 2014?!) and terribly guilty. Mostly guilty.

I also feel like we've opened a door that we can't unopen. It was inevitable, but it's daunting all the same. Behind that door are the complex realities of communal living. It's not all trimming the bougainvillea bush in the sunshine, talking about our future children, or laughing over lasagna at common meal. Sometimes it's stepping on one another's toes, throwing away one another's stuff, misunderstanding one another's values. Behind that door is the hard stuff: asking one another for what we need, even when we'd rather appear stalwart; listening to one another even when we're frustrated; telling one another when we've been hurt, apologizing, moving on, staying together.

## SHARING THE EMOTIONAL LABOR

In that way, cohousing is not unlike an extended family. Some configurations of community members get on like gangbusters. Others don't relate much, but still manage to support one another in small, respectful ways. Navigating conflicts is made both harder and easier by the understanding that we're in it for the long haul. There is no way out but through.

Sounds a bit like a marriage, no? In contrast to the small army it takes to actually make a person feel supported, the so-called peer marriage has been cast as the magic bullet of emotional arrangements. In part, peer marriages are a good thing; people increasingly expect more from their partners than a paycheck or a clean house, and thank God for that. But there's a dark side to our remaking of marriage. It's newly equal, but also buckling under the outsized expectations we've added onto it. We make a huge diversity of emotional and practical demands of one person and then wonder why we end up disappointed. As psychologist Esther Perel writes, "Today, we turn to one person to provide what an entire village once did: a sense of grounding, meaning, and continuity."[17]

A comparable letdown is experienced in parenting. Mothers, in particular, are expected to be everything to all people. We suffer from a wide variety of binds born of idealized notions about modern motherhood: we're supposed to be accessible, but still exude the appropriate amount of authority; we're to be passionate about our careers, but never put work above our children; and of course we should be sexy to our partners but sexless to just about everyone else, particularly our children. We can't possibly win.

With these "alternative" living scenarios—cohousing, multigenerational households, shared housing among single moms—we don't have to. Partners can get some needs met by people outside their marriages—whether it's talking about a hard day at work or running to the store for medicine. And kids can get needs—oh so many needs— met by adults who aren't their parents.

This theme surfaced in a big way as I was helping Rachel, a senior in high school, with her college application essay one Sunday evening before common meal. Rachel, who has lived in cohousing her entire life, had a period in middle school when she really struggled with a cruel music teacher. The school she was attending was arts-based, so her entire curriculum drew from her commitment to piano. (She was on her way to becoming a very accomplished pianist.) After slogging through the spring of that school year, she decided to try out homeschooling for the next year.

The trouble was that her dad, a nurse, and her mom, a children's pastor, couldn't be with her all day, every day. So, where they couldn't provide, the community stepped in. "Uncle Tom," as Rachel calls him, a literacy specialist, brought her young adult fiction books that he discussed with her. Mae, another community member, owns a children's clothing store. She employed Rachel informally during the week so she could learn some practical skills and have more social time. From this period Mae and Rachel's relationship grew very strong: "Basically Mae and my mom are similar in a lot of ways. They definitely have similar values," explains Rachel. "So I can ask Mae stuff that I want my mom's answer to, but don't really want to bring up with her."

It's such a subtle emotional calculation, but it's one I understood immediately. Even though Rachel is unusually close to her mom, Cheryl, there are things she just doesn't feel like she can say to her. I had the same experience growing up—my mom was my hero, my best friend in some ways, but she was also, well, my mom. There were times I could have really used someone like her to test things out on. And Rachel's relationship with Mae is a tribute to Cheryl as well: that she recognizes how her daughter can be fed and supported by other adults, that she's secure enough in her bond with Rachel to encourage that kind of relationship.

There's a similar pattern, though less overtly articulated, among the men in our community. I witness the way the three high school boys look around the community and "try on" the versions of masculinity they see. There's supersmart and kind Brian, who knows a lot about economics, has a stalwart belief in God, and has the best laugh in the universe. There's Nathan, who loves to backpack, bake, and do parkour over the courtyard fence. There's John, my husband, who's obsessed with design, vintage banana seat bicycles, and taking photos of his daughter. There's Revy, who loves mountain biking, shoes, and bags, and is always good for an unconditional loving hug. As there are another seven men in the community, the list goes on and on . . .

For most young men in traditional households, there may or may not be the presence of a dad, there might be an uncle or two, but otherwise boys are left with few versions of manhood to either emulate or reject. Teaching is, unfortunately, a female-dominated profession, so teenaged boys aren't likely to get a lot of male role models in school. If they play sports they may look up to their coaches, but not all guys are into sports. What often happens when young guys don't have older men to witness, study, reject, or integrate is that they look to one another—and the loudest, sometimes leastwise influence usually wins out.

And fatherless families are on the rise. A recent study by Johns Hopkins University found that 64 percent of the oldest cohort of millennial mothers (those who turned eighteen between 1999 and 2003) gave birth at least once outside the context of marriage, and almost one-half had all of their children without ever exchanging vows.[18]

As a result, we should be doing more to expand access to shared housing arrangements. "Revolutionary parenting" could actually be the norm in many demographic groups in America—and that would be a good thing. The more adults there are, the more sources of wisdom, food, courage, knowledge, and love there are. Despite all the hand-wringing about the loss of the nuclear family, this is just good, apolitical sense.

Despite the fact that our very public narrative continues to privilege the nuclear family, between the years 2006 and 2010, among the 61.8 million women of childbearing age (fifteen to forty-four), 43 percent didn't have children; for the men in that age range 55 percent didn't.[19] Many of these could-be parents anticipate having them someday, while others have made a conscious and contented choice to remain child-free. And whether we realize it or not, we're all buoyed by the investment the people without children make in our communities and our institutions. Some single folks have more time and energy to devote to serving on boards, volunteering, and creating arts and cultural events. "In the stories we tell each other about the workings of society, it is . . . the traditional families who are holding us all together," Bella DePaulo writes, but "studies . . . show that it is the single people . . . who are creating and sustaining the ties that bind us."[20]

Sometimes it's the little things rather than the big things that really keep us all afloat. I was recently working in the garden with my delightful, exhausting toddler. It had been a long day, and I was feeling that familiar parenting fatigue that creeps up as the sun wanes. I'd run into the house to grab something; when I came out I found Deborah, a perpetually upbeat sculptor in our community who doesn't have kids of her own, washing my daughter's feet: Maya had poured a big shovelful of dirt on her feet and then, of course, freaked out. And here was Deborah, with my little girl's grubby little feet in her hands and a big, uncomplicated smile on her face.

It was a small moment, the kind that mostly gets overlooked in our community as perfectly normal, and yet, it's an example of something essential to our humanity that's been lost in the white picket fence era. The power of our daily example, our instincts for service, our small and profound tenderness, need not be confined to the four walls of our homes or our small families. We are more needy than that, and, as it turns out, we are more expansive than that, too.

For too long we've struggled under what Mia Birdsong and Nicole Rodgers, cofounders of the project Family Story, refer to as "nuclear family privilege."[21] We've built just about all of our infrastructure—our schools, our healthcare system, our workplaces, our dwellings—around the outdated idea that everyone is part of a family unit with two adults and a couple of kids. No more, no less. But that's not how people's families are taking shape any longer, and it's time that the way we learn, work, heal, and live catch up. There is such rich opportunity in this wise departure—with more of us taking care of each other, more of us to parent and partner and befriend, we are all better off.

## A SORT OF LARGER GRACE

It's not all kumbaya. For a few weeks we turn into a real-life version of the movie *Neighbors* when Cheryl's oldest son moves back home and starts blasting his music, vibrating our house, and waking our baby from her naps. Until then, we'd been amazed at how solid the construction was of our house—compared to our Brooklyn apartments, where we could hear every footfall of our upstairs neighbors. After a lot of back-and-forth in which I try my hardest not to sound like the cranky old lady next door to an eighteen-year-old who just wants to play his damn music, two of Cheryl's kids switch rooms—and the bass haunts us no more.

Then Cheryl's eldest daughter hits our car. A few months later, I hit our other neighbor's car. Then the grill, apparently never cleaned well enough, explodes into a ball of fire one Saturday when Randy's trying to cook up a few burgers. Meetings always go too long. The space between our nights to cook never seems long enough. The washers and dryers break down. Or are full. There's dog shit on the lawn. There are rats in the barn.

But all that shadow is cast in the context of so much light. A sort of larger grace. I keep hearing Cheryl's word in my head: "radical hospitality." It's a word that's mostly been co-opted by the hospitality industry—hotel chains that promise beds that feel like clouds and airlines that try to convince you that three extra inches of leg room will entirely change your experience of being crammed into a smelly metal container with three hundred other strangers for five hours.

But what did it mean before? What does it mean apart from that industry—which, it seems to me, would be more accurately called the "escape industry"? The word "hospitality" derives from the Latin word "*hospes*": host, guest, or stranger. That's it: the tenderness I feel concerns the stranger—or who would have otherwise been a stranger.

We were almost perfect strangers to the motley crew of people who welcomed us to Temescal Commons. While the previous owner had vouched for our kindness, the only official barriers to entry were that we show up to a Sunday night common meal and write a letter about our approach to community. We had been nervous on that Sunday: *What should we wear? What should we bring? What should we talk about so they could be sure we'd be good members?* But from the minute we walked in the door, it was crystal clear this was neither a performance nor an interview.

Instead, we just wandered through the buffet line and landed wherever and chatted about whatever with whomever. No one seemed to be tallying our zingers or faux pas. No one seemed to be trying to figure out if we were religious enough or generous enough or hardworking enough or really enough of anything. We just were. And therefore, we were deserving of and capable of community.

Upon reflection, I realized that I had teared up as Cheryl described the guest policy because it was of a piece with this welcoming spirit. This policy, this spirit, feels antithetical to almost every other part of modern life, where the status quo is that you must prove yourself, earn entry, overcome distrust to become someone worthy of trust. We are—it seems—in a constant state of application. We apply to get into schools. We apply to get jobs. We apply to get state or federal assistance, scholarships, insurance, mortgages.

The social worlds that so many of us inhabit are also steeped in statusizing. You meet someone at a conference only to catch his or her eyes dart to your nametag to assess whether you're worth talking to. Or there's that moment at a dinner party when you feel your conversation partner's energy aching to get across the room because you've been deemed not hip/interesting/beautiful enough to spend time with. The truth is, in transactional settings like this, your humanity can't win: you feel humiliated if you're passed over, or gross if you attract people for seemingly shallow reasons.

The constant state of application and social statusizing goes hand in hand with a constant state of self-doubt and social comparison. Every little bubble I've ever filled in, every time I've lost or won someone's interest based on bullshit, has separated me further from my sense that I am worthy. Full stop—end of sentence.

In Temescal Commons, the terms are reversed—you are assumed to be worthy of trust and care until and unless you prove otherwise (and, truth be told, I'm not sure how you'd even go about doing that). You are not asked to perform your value, or submit it via some elaborate calculation of worthiness, or wear a nametag signaling it in big, bold letters. Instead, you are asked to show up, and you are asked to behave as if everyone else is worthy too.

This, it seems to me, is at the heart of one of the most lost and increasingly reclaimed necessities of the good life: that the people you live among share a commitment to radical hospitality. We spend so much time talking about our most intimate relationships—how to build and maintain a good marriage, how to be a decent parent, or accountable employee, or effective manager. But there is this whole other social world that we almost neglect to mention. It's the world that grows up right around us. It's the world we inherit, not painstakingly choose. It's the world that for too long has been seen as quaint or even optional—when really it is critical.

Neighbors. It couldn't sound more milquetoast, and yet a community of neighbors who know and look out for one another can often serve as a safety net in the face of some of life's most cruel and common challenges. When Louise, our eldest community member, suffered from a heart attack, it was Lynne, the former inhabitant of our house, who rushed her to the hospital. Louise, now seventy-seven, lives happily alone in a studio apartment filled with beautifully flawed clay bowls and her fading zazen meditation cushion and lots of silence to accompany her writing. But in her hour of need, she needed people—and they were there.

Life on the other, mundane end of the spectrum is also made substantially easier with the generosity of those who live nearby. I can't tell you how many times a simple "that's normal" from my neighbor Kate, a real-talking mother of two teenage boys, has meant the difference between a day spent fretting and one spent enjoying the always-shape-shifting nature of mothering a baby. Once I ran into beautiful, fiery Kate after a particularly long day and she scooped up Maya and sent me off to take a shower. Fifteen minutes later, I was a new human.

Kate didn't do that for me because I earned it or because I charmed her in some way. She didn't do it for me because she thought I had access to powerful people whom I might one day introduce her to. She did it because I am human, a mother—like her, someone struggling to get through a particularly long day. She did it for me because I needed it, and because she, too, has needed the equivalent.

That's part of what's so restorative about relationships with community members like these. These seemingly mundane collisions allow us to get cared for without a lot of calculation. I never would have called Kate, or even one of my oldest, dearest friends for that matter, to ask for help while I showered. It would feel like much ado about nothing. I so often don't even know what I need in order to ask for it. But when I run into Kate, and she reaches out those long arms and looks positively delighted to interact with a clingy toddler instead of an individuating teenage boy, it feels so easy to be cared for.

When a faucet is leaky, we don't call a plumber—we ask Randy if he'll stop by after dinner and take a look. When someone is locked out, we simply knock at the door of a house with the lights on or the shades up. And Louise sends out epic emails about the bounty to be found in the garden, with very specific instructions about how each vegetable should be lovingly plucked—guardian of our own little farmers' market without the eye-popping prices.

This kind of reciprocity isn't tit for tat. It isn't operated like a business. It manifests spontaneously, over slow time, like a highly intricate and profoundly organic ecosystem. I once expressed to Tom that I felt bad that I didn't have more practical skills to contribute to the community; shockingly, there isn't a lot of demand among our crew for snappy hashtags or vintage clothing expertise. But he reassured me that it takes all kinds: "We all contribute our skills at some point. A monoculture wouldn't work."

And it's true: I may be hopeless at repairing broken gates, and need no end of instruction about what to plant where, but when Nathan—who is going back to school so he can transition from being a window washer to being a nurse—needed help on his English paper, I popped over and we talked about Gwendolyn Brooks's poetry. He got a 97 percent on his assignment, and we both felt like a million bucks. And when Louise's computer got stolen and she needed to get her new one up and running, John became her "genius" for an evening, and was glad to do it.

So many of us have suffered from social monoculture for too long. It's not working. It hasn't been working for decades, and people are finally realizing it. We want to find partners to share the most intimate and ongoing highs and lows of life with. We want to be surrounded by dear friends who get us in textured, time-tested ways, people who speak our language of life stage and culture. But we are also reviving the lost art of nurturing and being nurtured by neighbors. We are delighting in the surprises of spontaneous reciprocity. We are remembering the power of intergenerational interaction. We are colliding and reassuring and repairing and planting and, along the way, turning into imperfect, edifying communities.

# regrowing our roots

## THE POWER AND COMPLEXITY
## OF INVESTING IN YOUR
## LOCAL COMMUNITY

"Think global, act local."

It's a ubiquitous phrase, popularized among leading American environmentalists in the 1970s, a time when globalization was still just a glimmer in the eyes of CEOs and development experts. Its first utterances in the U.S. were largely focused on the environmental impacts of going big. The message was: it's okay, even necessary, to have a worldview that spans the globe; but as for action, stick to your own backyard.

As the seventies turned into the eighties and nineties, global travel and the daily consumption of news about all seven continents became hallmarks of a worldly, successful person. I got this message loud and clear when I was growing up, even though—or maybe because—I'd lived my whole life up to that point in the same house on Tejon Street in Colorado Springs, Colorado. While the consistency was protective, it also planted a seed of longing in me. I wanted to see things, meet people, discover the world. I decorated my walls with pictures of New York City skyscrapers and put little gold stars on the world map in my bathroom. To me the most worthwhile life was one defined not by familiarity but by curiosity.

Not all adventures are made alike. As George Clooney demonstrated with his devastating portrayal of professional asshole Ryan Bingham in the 2009 film *Up in the Air*, road warriors can become hollow men. He says:

> *Make no mistake—your relationships are the heaviest components in your life. Do you feel the straps cutting into your shoulders? All those negotiations and arguments, and secrets and compromises. You don't need to carry all that weight. Why don't you set that bag down? Some animals were meant to carry each other, to live symbiotically for a lifetime—star-crossed lovers, monogamous swans. We are not those animals. The slower we move, the faster we die. We are not swans. We're sharks.*[1]

For the past few decades, success has been increasingly conflated with being a shark—which by some definitions means not being encumbered by even an indifferent, mostly self-sufficient cat at home. "Where is home, really?" say the global elite as they bump into each other at major hub airports or annual conferences. While generations past might have constructed an admirable life within a fifty-mile radius, the modern go-getter has become a "citizen of the world," someone who has friends in Berlin and Bangkok and Boston, someone whose suitcases get far more use than her silverware.

Such is the strange landscape of connection that characterizes the world we live in now. We've been thoroughly globalized, not just economically, but socially, too; the tangled tubes of the Internet and immigration patterns here, there, and everywhere make for a much smaller world. Whereas we used to know a lot about a little, today we're exposed to news happening far beyond our zip code whether or not we choose to step outside it.

And yet, for all the talk of globalization's power, the pull of the local remains an undeniable counterweight. People may know about wars and cuisine and pop bands a million miles away, but when the dog sneaks out the backdoor without a collar, you need to know your neighbors well enough to ask for help finding her. Many of us have tired of the glamorized worldliness of previous decades; today I hear a rumbling of people trying to replant their roots.

The term du jour is "social capital," meaning that people get real, measurable benefits from the relationships they invest in. In practice it's nothing new, but since the 1990s the theory has taken off significantly in academic and policy circles. "Social capital" names a form of power previously overlooked in more bottom line–focused conversations; it also legitimizes the fact that many of us mourn the loss of neighborliness as an essential thread in our social fabric. It's not just that we wish we could borrow a cup of sugar as our grandmothers did; it's that we're finally accurately valuing that cup of sugar—not as a free nickel of sweetness, but as a symbol of our commitment to lend a hand to one another.

We only have so much time in a day, and only so much relational energy. My husband realized this after seeing *Up in the Air*, calling me in tears saying, "I never want to be 1K again."

John had flown 100,000 miles the year previous, which earned him one of United Airlines' top frequent-flyer designations and lots of first-class upgrades. While some might see this milestone as indicating he'd become a wild success, for John—as for so many who practically know their home airport TSA officers by name—the glamour was just the surface story.

Underneath is a far less fabulous reality: arriving home to a fridge with only ketchup and moldy cheese, knowing your friends are having dinner together somewhere but they didn't think to invite you since you're never home; wondering if all your temporary, far-flung encounters actually add up to something close to your goal. You might feel "important," sure, but likely also kind of lost.

The thing is, when we're forced to rip out our roots, or we rip them ourselves in pursuit of some promised transcendence, we suffer. As it turns out, curiosity is not a matter of geography, but generosity. Laying your eyes on new horizons can be thrilling, but having new eyes for old horizons can also be exciting in a completely different way.

There's something edifying in realizing you're someone people you live near can count on to show up, to contribute, to—as insignificant as it sounds—be present in order to be kind. In his 2013 commencement address at Syracuse University, short story writer George Saunders told students: "What I regret most in my life are failures of kindness. Those moments when another human being was there, in front of me, suffering, and I responded . . . sensibly. Reservedly. Mildly."[2]

When we "step over" the suffering in front of us, we betray who we really are—place-based creatures who notice, who care. But when we instead work to make our communities better, more equal, more safe, more beautiful, when we take the risk of knocking on doors, asking questions, listening as long as it takes,we can access a sort of euphoria. In the context of local connections, we remember what it is to be human.

## UNLEASHING LOCAL POWER

While living in a cohousing community in Berkeley for six years, Janelle Orsi fell in love with the virtues of sharing. "The sense of community that I felt was so palpable," she remembers. "Just sharing meals and a garden space increased my happiness exponentially."

Then she started volunteering in West Oakland at People's Grocery, an organization that strives to improve the health and sustainability of low-income people of color through everything from cooking classes to business-development workshops. She'd spent much of her early twenties working with marginalized youth in Los Angeles—teaching in after-school programs, organizing for antiracist policies, trying to help young immigrants navigate educational and legal barriers. The work had been deeply rewarding for her—but often equally disappointing.

The youth involved in People's Grocery seemed to be thriving in a completely different way. "They were growing food in community gardens, and learning how to stay healthy, and getting work opportunities," Janelle recalls. "It felt so solutions-oriented in comparison to a lot of what I'd been doing previously, like it actually prevented some of the problems that I'd been fighting back in L.A."

Witnessing kids with their hands in the dirt planted a seed in Janelle: "What if I could become a lawyer that helps people share? Share businesses, share houses, share cars—anything where people use the resources they have to meet more people's needs."

So that's what she did. After Janelle graduated from UC Berkeley School of Law in 2008, she introduced herself at events around Oakland and Berkeley saying: "I'm a lawyer and my goal is to help people share."

"People would give me very funny looks," she admits. "A lot of them actually thought I was joking."

But soon the economic realities of 2008 started to set in, and the sharing economy continued to grow. Six months later, the American Bar Association asked Janelle to write the first book on the legal complexities associated with this expanding economic sector: *Practicing Law in the Sharing Economy: Helping People Build Cooperatives, Social Enterprise, and Local Sustainable Economies.* Over time, Janelle's goal didn't sound so crazy after all.

At first she thought it would be as straightforward as simply establishing entities and drafting agreements between people who wanted to share. But she quickly realized that small-scale and cooperative businesses are often so hamstrung by health and safety laws and other regulatory red tape that they struggle to survive—even before getting a chance to do business. "The very structure of our legal system is designed to keep people from each other, and privilege large-scale commercial enterprises," Janelle explains.

So Janelle's version of the sharing economy is less Uber and more City CarShare, less Instacart and more People's Grocery. The organizations she's trying to encourage and support are not designed to serve the masses, but to serve particular communities. The target isn't scale, but sufficiency; the geography isn't global, but unapologetically and fiercely local.

Janelle is part of a movement that's gained huge momentum since the Great Recession. While it's called by a lot of different names—"localism," the "new economy," "community wealth building"—at its core it's about creating an economy that works more fairly for everyday people because it's rooted in real relationships. Sharing, for these folks, is not about something as soft as caring (though that's a nice by-product); sharing creates a more balanced economy and more resilient communities in times of disaster.

In many ways, Janelle and her widespread collaborators—the New Economy Coalition, the Business Alliance for Local Living Economies, the National Center for Employee Ownership, the Democracy at Work Institute, etc.—are beating an old drum. In E.F. Schumacher's *Small Is Beautiful: Economics as If People Mattered*, published in 1973, he argues that smaller, localized economies are not only environmentally superior, they're also socially and morally superior. He writes:

*If human vices such as greed and envy are systematically cultivated, the inevitable result is nothing less than a collapse of intelligence. A man driven by greed or envy loses the power of seeing things as they really are, of seeing things in their roundness and wholeness, and his very successes become failures. If whole societies become infected by these vices, they may indeed achieve astonishing things but they become increasingly incapable of solving the most elementary problems of everyday existence.*

As we worship at the altar of scale—big companies, big ideas, big solutions—we conflate bigness with worthiness. We begin to see every problem, even the most personal, as something that can be solved by a large market, an abstract idea, a person we will never meet. In this way, we grow dumb about the power of the people in our own backyard, dumb about how to make things—basic, meaningful things like food and shelter. We grow dumb about small.

When in 2008, banks got a $700 billion government bailout, even Americans who'd never considered macroeconomics became familiar with the adage "too big to fail." It's the idea that some corporations get so big and so intertwined with every aspect of our lives that their failure would be disastrous—and, therefore, that the government must shore them up to save us all from destruction.

Opponents believe that bailouts like this encourage moral corruption, meaning that, since companies can count on the government to save them from total destruction, they can take big, some would say irresponsible, risks without suffering the consequences. Whereas the risk-taking individuals who default often end up bankrupt.

In response, many communities have begun to regrow their grassroots. Buying locally, as an example, is a pretty straightforward prospect. If you're interested in a book you found at your delightful little neighborhood bookstore, buy it there; don't go home and order it from Amazon. And if you can choose between a national chain grocery store and a locally owned one, shop at the latter. Keeping profits and sales tax in the state benefits your entire community, yourself included.

But when it comes to investing locally, that's a fairly problematic process. Let's say a friend is opening up a children's clothing store in your neighborhood and needs some additional start-up funds. You've got some extra cash and think the idea is a no-brainer; the proliferation of strollers on the sidewalk lately, plus a good, hard look at her business plan, has you convinced this thing is going to thrive. But it's not that simple. It's unfortunately exceedingly difficult for the vast majority of the public, considered "nonaccredited," to invest locally. (Accreditation requires that an individual have a net worth of at least $1 million [excluding property value] or annual income of $200,000 for the previous two years—a very elite club indeed.)[3]

What started in the 1930s as beneficent securities laws to protect people from fraud has created what Michael Shuman, author of *The Local Economy Solution: How Innovative, Self-Financing "Pollinator" Enterprises Can Grow Jobs and Prosperity*, calls an "investment apartheid"—two completely different classes of investors in the American public. He explains, "The vast majority of us are systematically overinvesting in companies we distrust and underinvesting in businesses we care about."[4]

Americans currently have nearly $30 trillion in investments, but only a fraction of 1 percent of that is invested locally. So, in the case of our above example, when you can't figure out how to legally invest $1,000 in your friend's business, you'll likely send that check to Vanguard or another management company. Consider the fact that, in terms of both jobs and output, half of any economy is local; Shuman argues that in an efficient capital market half of that $30 trillion would be circulating locally.[5]

In 2012, a political coalition of unlikely bedfellows—largely "localist" progressives, techies, and tea party conservatives—pushed Congress to pass a major reform of securities law: the Jumpstart Our Business Startups (JOBS) Act. But while some of the barriers to local investment have been felled, many remain, especially since commissioners at the Securities and Exchange Commission (SEC) have dragged their feet in getting specific language pinned down for various aspects of the legislative shift promised through the act.

A number of the laws that Janelle and her coworkers oppose are at the state level. Many were originally created to protect consumers from big companies, but now they prove to be onerous for people who, for example, make granola or bread in their home kitchens to sell at farmers' markets.

For the most part, reform is a state-by-state effort. For example, in 2012 the Sustainable Economies Law Center (SELC) was able to get a law passed in California that allows people to have home-based food businesses ("cottage food operations") for food that's not seen as high risk (typically that doesn't require refrigeration) as long as they make less than $50,000 a year.[6] "It's the kind of bill that Republicans loved because it's pro-business and a little bit anti-regulation," Janelle explains. "But Democrats also are into it because it expands economic opportunities for people who have been marginalized in our current economy."

Now the SELC is focused on training people in other states to advocate for similar and related reforms like removing legal barriers to seed sharing. Legislation intended to protect the consumer from commercial farming abuses is also preventing grassroots gardens and farms from sharing seeds, which is a life-sustaining practice for everyone. At the city level, the SELC is helping people agitate for worker cooperative ordinances to streamline the process of both starting new co-ops and converting more traditional businesses into co-ops.

In many ways, what Janelle and a growing network are doing is redrawing what a successful, safe economy looks like. They're using the power of the Internet to educate and organize to make it possible to legally practice some of the most ancient values: cooking for others, sharing homes, starting businesses with friends and neighbors. Over four decades ago, E.F. Schumacher wrote: "It takes a certain flair of real insight to make things simple again. And this insight does not come easily to people who have allowed themselves to become alienated from real, productive work and from the self-balancing system of nature, which never fails to recognize measure and limitation."

Our most secure future is not "too big to fail," but small enough to thrive.

## THE LOST ART OF NEIGHBORLINESS

Localism is not just an economic opportunity—it's a social and spiritual one too. All the securities law reform in the world won't automatically reweave local connections. As Duane Elgin, founder of the Great Transition Stories project, puts it: "If an economy is alive, it has a story—one that includes both the joys and the sorrows, the good times and the difficult times. When local communities understand and appreciate their ever-changing story, people are in a much stronger position to build a resilient future by consciously telling new stories that fit a new future."[7]

But too many of us aren't telling new stories so much as performing monologues. As an overeducated, big-hearted transplant living in Brooklyn in my midtwenties, I had serial fantasies about how I'd befriend the neighbors in my hallway. Cookie drop-offs? I've never really been the baking type. Collaborative stoop sale? I didn't have much to sell. Potluck brunch? I could slip the invitations under everyone's doors and see who showed up. But I chickened out. I didn't know them well enough to know if they had to work on Saturdays. Plus, was brunch too bougie? What if it was just me, myself, and my earnestly prepared egg dish?

I meant to take the social risk and just invite people the hell over, but I never did. I did become close to one neighbor, Mary. She was a fortysomething-looking sixtysomething who lived alone, an aide in a nursing home in Brighton Beach. She became a sort of godmother to me. She would feed my cat when I was gone and sometimes bring over big Tupperware containers filled with jerk chicken and delicious rice. On occasion she'd offer unsolicited romantic advice: "Marry the one that loves you more. And get pregnant soon! You're not getting any younger."

I'd check in on her if I hadn't seen her in a while and bring little gifts for her beloved birds. (When she went to work each day, she left the static-filled TV set to NBC so they could watch *The Jerry Springer Show*; she swore they were die-hard fans.) Despite our ethnic and class differences, we became tight. Silly as it might sound, I think part of what allowed us to leap over all those boundaries was our pets; pets and kids often pull otherwise orbiting neighbors together. While this might result from common appreciation—love of animals or of children—it could also just result from the effects of cuteness, even on shy people.

Which is great . . . if you've got a big, drooly dog or a little, drooly baby. But what if you're not in that zone? A quick Google search of "how to meet your neighbors" turns up a ton of blog posts and angsty comments sections on sites like *Apartment Therapy*. People have noted it's "invasive and awkward" to simply knock on a neighbor's door as in the (imagined) good old days. So some recommend getting involved in local activism, striking up conversations at block parties or street fairs, going to game nights at local bars, meeting people through religious institutions, or even creating something called an "introduction card" that you can slip under doors. (Nerd alert! I'm shocked I never resorted to this myself.)

Adolescent fear can resurface at the prospect of meeting our neighbors, particularly among the privileged and out of practice. In the threads that unspool after those upbeat neighborly tips you can easily read the commenters' pimply inner teens between the lines: *Will they like me? Will they think I'm weird? I just want to be seen.*

Let's be real: it's totally worth it to overcome your social anxiety and just knock on a neighbor's door, freshly baked pie in hand. Someone might think you're weird. But someone else might think you're brave, and even be eternally grateful that you did the thing she meant to do instead of just reading the upbeat blog tips and then going about her mildly discontented, slightly isolated day. And yet another someone else might have thought you were weird because you *hadn't* done it yet.

Who your neighbors actually are, and how they would receive your initiative, are a crapshoot, but the benefits are not. Having relationships with people around you—even in a seemingly innocuous, wave-on-the-street, exchange-pleasantries kind of way—makes you physically and mentally healthier. Juliana Breines of the Greater Good Science Center reports that a combination of strong and weak ties makes people heartier. She writes, "Research suggests that people who have a broad range of different kinds of social roles tend to be healthier and more likely to attain professional success. Occupying varying roles across multiple domains can create a psychological safety net that protects us against perceived threats to our sense of self-worth, and in turn we are likely to suffer less stress and stress-related illness."[8]

That should make the initial awkwardness feel well worth it in the long run. But if that doesn't get your butt into the kitchen, consider this: being a good, connected neighbor also makes you safer. Crime rates can decrease when neighbors know one another. Felton

Earls, a professor of human behavior and development at Harvard School of Public Health, explains: "We found that trust and reciprocity among neighbors is a much stronger predictor of violence levels than race or poverty."[9]

Sociologist Eric Klinenberg studies what sets apart the neighborhoods that fare best during natural disasters like heat waves and hurricanes. His findings? The communities that best ride the waves of crisis aren't those with more money or preparedness, per se, but are those that are tightly knit. In a *New Yorker* feature exploring ways cities can adapt to our era of climate crisis, he quotes Nicole Lurie, President Obama's assistant secretary for preparedness and response since 2009: "There's a lot of social-science research showing how much better people do in disasters, how much longer they live, when they have good social networks and connections. And we've had a pretty big evolution in our thinking, so promoting community resilience is now front and center in our approach."[10]

While money may realistically buy some forms of self-sufficiency—from someone to take care of your kid to the spare savings needed when your car gets stolen—you can't buy your way out of all dependence. As someone who lived in New York City during the attacks of September 11, I can tell you that the image of a woman in a tarnished, skirted business suit walking alone past my college campus on 117th and Broadway, high heels in hand, numb expression on her face, will never leave me. Neither her job title nor her salary had the power to transcend suffering. Suffering will touch all of us in life—and one of the only real comforts that can get us through is our connections. What the research around social capital teaches us is that, even if we feel satisfied with many of our friendships and family relationships, not connecting to those who are geographically close is a wasted opportunity for an even more secure, happy, and healthy life. Plus, it's just good, plain sense. We all want to be known.

The scientific term for all this cooperation is "pro-sociality." Essentially, it means "other-oriented behaviors and attitudes that ultimately benefit the giver as much as the receiver." In his book *The Neighborhood Project: Using Evolution to Improve My City, One Block at a Time*, evolutionary biologist David Sloan Wilson, a lifelong researcher on the subject and cofounder of The Evolution Institute, documents how he abandoned the safe confines of his lab in order to test his theories in his hometown of Binghamton, New York. He found that optimum pro-sociality requires a combination of conditions, things like a strong group identity and a sense that everyone experiences both costs and benefits from participating in the community (in other words, no one person does all the work).

Not one of the eight conditions he identifies has anything to do with money. In fact, in an interview with Krista Tippett of On Being he explains that financial security seems to actually repress many people's pro-social behaviors: "In some of the more wealthy neighborhoods, because people have so much money, they don't need to cooperate, and so they don't . . . they're not even in practice."[11]

While privileged people may be good at leveraging professional networks—a form of social capital—they've gotten pretty shitty at creating meaningful networks in their own neighborhood. Chalk it up to the College Industrial Complex, pitting kids (and, by extension, their families) against one another. Chalk it up to the road warrior mentality—people who see their frequent-flier rank and their professional success as one and the same. Chalk it up to bigger houses and home entertainment systems, the delusion of perfect autonomy performed on social media, the messy reality necessarily sealed behind closed doors (a teenager's struggle with drug addiction or a couple's broken marriage . . . the kinds of experiences well-to-do folks don't say out loud). There are so many reasons, all of them very real, all of them very destructive.

In contrast, in low-income neighborhoods, researchers like Sloan Wilson have found, many people cooperate out of necessity—and as a result, they're better at it. It's not an intellectual exercise or an abstract desire; it's a mindset and a muscle. Now, this is not to paint too rosy a picture of the conditions that motivate low-income folks to collaborate in the first place; stagnating wages, unemployment, and inadequate public schools are all structural failures that must be addressed. However, until those root causes of vulnerability are shifted, it's notable that people make a way out of no way . . . together.

Economic dependence necessitates a certain kind of vulnerability: looking a neighbor in the eye and saying you need help. Perhaps your need is somewhat benign: you simply can't find someone to take care of your kid while you're at work. Or perhaps your need goes deeper than that: you simply can't afford as much food as you'll need to get through to the next payday. Of course, if you own a big house in a fancy suburb, you're less likely to be asked for food at your door. But that kind of life too often hinders the real connections that come out of needing your neighbors.

This is a key explanation for all those blog posts with fumbling instructions about how to meet your neighbors. The demographic of people who read *Apartment Therapy* is relatively economically secure twenty- and thirtysomethings, many of whom have grown up in isolated suburbs. They're looking for the kind of social ties that poor people have, by necessity, been building for years. They've been socialized to associate *need* with *purchase*, to believe that it's weird to ask for things from other people, that it's "invasive and awkward" to knock on doors.

Wherever privileged people are emotionally stunted, the Internet rushes in. The twenty-first-century version of the neighborhood listserv is Nextdoor. In addition to Facebook and Meetup groups, Nextdoor is an app increasingly used to link neighbors to one another. Founded in 2010, it boasts over 53,000 "microcommunities" where users, verified by their real names and addresses, sell and buy things, ask for help finding lost pets, organize block parties or community meetings, and report crimes. As of 2015, five million messages are exchanged on the app every single day.[12]

But for all the pets brought home and babysitting jobs found via Nextdoor, all is not hunky-dory. For one thing, the crime reporting aspect of the app often features unchecked racism. Members note "suspicious" (read: black) people walking around the neighborhood, or get into discussions about parenting styles with no consideration for cultural context (not to mention humility). Taken together, there is potential for good with Nextdoor—nodes of real connection between locals who might not otherwise find one another—but there's also potential for stirring up shit and reinforcing already dangerous stereotypes, especially in gentrifying neighborhoods where racial tension is already brewing. Fusion's Pendarvis Harshaw writes: "Let's hope these semi-public, semi-private conversations lead to diverse communities better understanding each other[—] rather than Nextdoor . . . simply becoming yet another place to safely air long-held racial assumptions."[13]

This is at the heart of a lot of this new neighborly anxiety. The word "gentrification" flashes like a neon sign in so many people's minds when they're considering growing the fuck up and just, at long last, knocking on that neighbor's door. I know it did mine. Though part of why I chose my Brooklyn apartment was that it was a mixed-income dwelling, meaning some people had lived there for decades thanks to rent control, no one would know that when they answered the knock at the door. And my good intentions didn't change the facts: I was another white girl who'd been priced right around the southern tip of Prospect Park—from Park Slope to Lefferts Gardens—another "cultural creative," in urbanist Richard Florida's parlance, making another Brooklyn neighborhood unaffordable for the longtime, working-class residents. So, while maybe some would have seen me as just Courtney, and been happy to eat at my brunch table, maybe others would have seen me as representative of a larger force, one that made their lives feel increasingly insecure and their neighborhood increasingly unrecognizable—and conclude they didn't really want to "do brunch." And that would be fair.

We live in a moment when it's never been so important for people of all economic classes to acknowledge their interdependence—both the healthy kind that keeps us safe and the interclass tension that can leave us feeling displaced and misunderstood. In the midst of that, there is no one-size-fits-all way to build community; the privileged among us must move past social anxiety and just reach out to people in real life—IRL, as they say. bell hooks writes, "To build community requires vigilant awareness of the work we must continually do to undermine all the socialization that leads us to behave in ways that perpetuate domination."[14]

The economic strife will remain. But if anything has a chance at making it feel less like a zero-sum game, it's the endlessly regenerating well of social capital that we can build with one another. And while it cannot deny difference, it can be built across it. It can be built slowly, over time, with nods of the head, smiles, greetings, even earnestly baked and anxiously delivered pies.

Having become a hipster cliché of myself, I left New York and found myself in the "Brooklyn of San Francisco": Temescal. Just months after we moved in, Blue Bottle Coffee opened down the street, in a light-filled space where wiry white dudes with rusty beards tinker with espresso machines. Meanwhile, black kids from Oakland Tech in high-waisted jeans and throwback sneakers mingle in front of the regal white columns of their school sipping Monster energy drinks. Google buses with their ominously dark windows lumber in and out of the neighborhood.

One morning we woke to find our car perilously perched atop jacks, all four wheels gone, their lug nuts carefully lined up like an enigmatic message. While we hated the hours spent on the phone with our insurance company, we had to respect the studied silence of those thieves. And in our cohousing community, everyone talks about the skyrocketing housing prices with a mix of awe and disgust. We are baffled by the news of homes going for cash, $100,000 over the asking price; we couldn't compete, which means we couldn't live here if we tried to move in now, just three years after we actually moved in.

In my neighborhood, there are beautiful murals and so much anger and beautiful people everywhere.

I'm here. Again. In the midst of an economic experiment with profound implications for everyone, most importantly for people I don't know who've lived here for generations. And I'm sleep-deprived and busy and trying to make sure my daughter doesn't rip out any-one's planted flowers on walks and loving how the guy at the donut shop calls her "rubber band wrists" and knowing it's not enough to just know the guy at the donut shop. So I read Chinaka Hodge's "The Gentrifier's Guide to Getting Along: An Open Letter from a Child of Oakland," with some exhausted urgency:

> So, you want to fit in, huh? You want to get along? Here's what I'd suggest: get to know your neighbors. Do the basics—the same way you'd act if you moved to Paris or Jakarta. Learn the language. Study the social cues. If that middle-aged black man waves from his stoop on Myrtle Street, he's saying hello. Say hello back. It'll go a long way, I promise. Engage in politics in a respectful way. Make your issues the issues we've been mobilizing around for years: the success of students in our underfunded schools, the benefits of community

*policing, the removal of ecological hazards in our highly industrial-*
*ized neighborhoods. . . .*

*. . . We want to know you. We want to make friends we can*
*trust, whom we can invite into our city in a way that feels respectful*
*and natural. We'll probably never fling wide our doors: let's face it,*
*being Oakland-born and -bred makes us a little more gritty than that.*
*But many of us are descendants of folks who arrived via train during*
*the great migration, via boat or rail as first- or second-generation*
*Americans, or even by BART when we could no longer afford the rent*
*in San Francisco—yeah, just like you.*[15]

In part, our anxiety about whom we live among is also about the histories we live on top of. What Chinaka makes so clear in her wise piece is that neighborhoods are not bricks and mortar—they are flesh and blood. It is in neighborhoods that kids roam the streets as dusk falls, laughing at the stupid jokes of their junior high friends and wishing for just one more hour of light. It is in neighborhoods that adult children watch their parents wither away on porches, hollering at cars to slow the hell down when they blow through stop signs. It is in neighborhoods that people worship, worry, and weather their deferred dreams. It is in neighborhoods that people mourn and celebrate. It is in our neighborhoods that we became whom we have become.

Wendell Berry writes: "There can be no such thing as a 'global village.' No matter how much one may love the world as a whole, one can live fully in it only by living responsibly in some small part of it."[16]

This is our call. Neighborhoods are contested geographies, in part, because they are so powerful. The complexity of the local, how-ever, can never be an excuse for disengagement. If anything, it's an invitation for us to stretch—to become more brave, more humble, more invested, more creative.

How you live responsibly in a given neighborhood isn't something that you can study in school or read about in a self-help book. There's no checklist. It's an ongoing intention to know the people you live among, to honor their histories and gifts, and to make yourself known, too. It's the slow and often joyful work of building relationships—one morning wave, one passing conversation, one tool borrowed, one flyer handed out at a time.

Somehow it all adds up; it always will. But it requires believing that success is measured by social and economic ties right in the place where you live. It requires staying put long enough to pursue an honest accumulation of moments. It requires relationships intricately entangled with one beloved geography.

# ritual remixed

## MAKING MEANING AND
## MARKING MOMENTS AMIDST
## THE CHAOS OF MODERN LIFE

I stood in front of about two hundred expectant people, whose ear-to-ear grins seemed to warm the giant, damp barn. Outside, down came the rain, playing dumb to our big plans. The music began—an instrumental piece composed by Nelson, the groom, for his bride, Katinka. Everyone turned to see them enter. A huge, floppy golden retriever bounded in instead, the official farm dog who'd been chasing babies and eating dropped appetizers all weekend. Laughter echoed off the rafters. And then Katinka, six months pregnant and radiant in a white, silk dress, and Nelson, handsome as ever, strutted from different corners of the barn to meet in the middle. They joined hands and approached me. Katinka and I could have done a belly bump (I was just a couple of months behind her). Instead, we got down to the business of getting these two kind souls married off.

The scene was, in some ways, as old as time. Two young lovers, dressed beautifully, take vows in front of their family and friends. Celebration ensues. Drinks flow. Sublimely bad intergenerational dancing commences. But look a bit closer and this scene is so thoroughly modern. The bride is pregnant, yet no one bats an eyelash. Even weirder, perhaps, the celebrant, ordained by "the Internet," is pregnant. And wearing a turquoise dress. With cowgirl boots.

In the last decade, the wedding ceremony has been thoroughly remade by people who crave ritual but are increasingly unaffiliated with the religious institutions that usually perform them. Pew Research surveys have seen a gradual decline in religious commitment across the U.S., particularly among young people; one-third of millennials are religiously unaffiliated (twice the share of unaffiliated baby boomers and more than three times the share of members of the Silent Generation).[1] When you consider that the average age of marriage is now twenty-seven for women and twenty-nine for men (a historic high),[2] that translates to scores of couples tying the knot who have no logical authority figure to look to for guidance.

The disentangling of religion from the ritual of vowing life partnership is undeniably significant. My parents' wedding was as formal as they come, despite the fact that they were married in 1969, a famous year for social upheaval. They were both twenty years old (the average age of first marriage then was twenty-one for women and twenty-three for men, so they were just slightly ahead of their peers). A priest presided; they recited vows devoid of any personal flare; they walked down the aisle afterward, announced as "Mr. and Mrs. Ron Martin." My mom explains that my rule-abiding grandmother planned the whole thing, down to the colors and the cake.

I find this confounding. My mother, who has rarely met a rule she liked, and my father, who brags about shutting down the student union to ensure Colorado State University diversified the student body, didn't see their wedding as, well, theirs. When I asked them about it, my mom said, "It would have been taken as a slap in the face of [our parents'] religion and their values, a real break with them, not merely a different preference. At that time, kids were seen much more as a reflection of their parents, not as separate, differentiated individuals, especially until they turned twenty-one and were living financially on their own."

Contrast my parents' wedding with mine. I was thirty-three, my husband thirty-five. My parents embraced the ceremony John and I chose, which took place in their backyard. My big brother married us, a friend sang my favorite gospel song, "Oh Happy Day," and another played Sufjan Stevens's "Chicago" as we walked down the aisle. The most traditional we got was the Irish Blessing, an ode to our thoroughly Irish heritage on both sides. We recited vows we wrote ourselves and read one another love letters about our hopes for our life together. I wore a gold dress and a leather coat (it was New Year's Day in chilly Santa Fe, New Mexico). After the ceremony, we processed out to the sounds of an all-female mariachi band. I didn't change my name.

John and I saw our wedding as an opportunity to have our relationship described, celebrated, and witnessed. We saw it as a moment to perform a sacred echo of the celebrations of the parents and grandparents and great-grandparents who had come before us. And though our ceremony may have looked very different from theirs, stripped down to its essence—two people, willingly choosing one another as life partners—we were nonetheless aligning with a lineage of sacred promises. Having in fact been previously resistant to marriage, I was surprised by how profound that felt.

And that's the thing: the reinvention of ritual is not—as it's so often framed—a "fuck you" to tradition. In many ways, it's actually the opposite: a creative reclaiming of the importance of ritual, but on more nuanced, authentic, communal terms. We—unconventional brides, happy singletons, agnostics, intentional parents, and unapologetic mourners alike—are looking to create moments that are both grand enough to make us feel sewn into the fabric of human history *and* specific enough to make us feel our unique strand within that fabric is witnessed and celebrated. It's like the summer's best love song played on a really old record player.

"Authenticity" is such a wildly overused word, but it's really the best fit here. We want to feel like our real selves, even in moments where our place within a larger human story is being performed out loud, in front of an audience of people we love.

The American Dream of the past began with the pageantry of a religious, white wedding deemed official by a religious institution and its authority figure. The couple, heterosexual of course, were then morally free to acquire the house and the white picket fence and start reproducing.

For those who could fit into this paradigm—people like my parents—following this preset course could sometimes feel like acting in a play someone else wrote, one that didn't necessarily reflect one's authentic self. For those who couldn't fit the paradigm—because they were gay, had kids first, were unable to afford it, etc.—the big white wedding may have been alluring because it symbolized a longed-for legitimacy. Lord knows that pundits love to hold up traditional marriage as the magic bullet for all of society's various woes.

It's not just that marriage is being abandoned altogether by many,[3] but that the ritual has been reconstituted. It's no longer just the gateway to legitimacy in the eyes of the state or the church or our parents (though all three have, as a whole, gotten remarkably more flexible). To an increasing number of people, a wedding celebration is a moment to express love and gratitude and to promise something a little preposterous and very brave. It's a chance to pause and talk about what matters most, in public. It's an occasion to gather a network of family and friends, so often only experienced virtually, requesting their witness and support in the long haul of partnership.

Many of us are moving from a model of ritual that was really about social control, authorized by hierarchical institutions, to a model based on social cohesion, authorized by the very people participating. We aren't rejecting tradition; we're rejecting the relative anonymity, discrimination, and dogma inherent in many formal ceremonies of yesteryear. We are drawing on a mix of ancient and modern ingredients, including Corinthians and Cheryl Strayed side by side; we're still walking down the aisle, as has been the custom for hundreds of years, but we feel free to do so in customized Chuck Taylors, not white high heels.

Pew Research polls find that Gen Xers—roughly those born between 1965 and 1980—are "skeptical and self-reliant," neither of which suggests the embracing of ritual.[4] They are the generation of filmmakers like Richard Linklater (*Slacker*) and Kevin Smith (*Clerks*), alternative music like R.E.M.'s "Losing My Religion" and Nirvana's *Nevermind*. While Gen Xers are known for being allergic to authority and covetous of the unscripted experience, millennials, the generation that followed them, actually seem to take comfort in structure. But they want to build that structure, or at the very least tweak it, not inherit it fully formed, with an impersonal set of inviolable instructions.

Part of this shift is surely related to the perfect storm of transitions we're living through. The economic and social upheaval of the last decade has us hungry for the grounding sensation that comes from rituals—both personal and communal. There's nothing like large-scale chaos to drive people back toward the solace of small-scale structure. Ritual provides that—a way to mark and make meaning when the world around you seems unpredictable. As Jeanette Winterson writes, "In the space between chaos and shape there was another chance."[5]

Ritual remixed, but with a deep reverence for our legacies, is that between. It gives us a chance to assert that, despite all the uncertainty and darkness we experience, a sureness, an indistinguishable light, exists in our connections and promises to one another. While yes, there are forces that we can't control—economic, political, social— that are much larger than we are, there is also our sacred will, which is tenacious as hell. It just keeps pushing back against the anomie in a million beautiful, creative ways.

## THE BASIC ANATOMY OF RITUAL

But first things first: what is ritual, really?

"Ritual" has formally been defined as "a sequence of activities involving gestures, words, and objects, performed in a sequestered place, and performed according to a set sequence." But rather than see rituals as defined by place and sequence, a sort of litmus test for whether something has earned the label, we're starting to play around with the boundaries and behaviors that constitute the sacred. Edmund Leach, a social anthropologist, argues that ritual is better understood as existing on a spectrum:

> [A]ctions fall into place on a continuous scale. At one extreme we have actions [that] are entirely profane, entirely functional, technique pure and simple; at the other we have actions [that] are entirely sacred, strictly aesthetic, technically nonfunctional. Between these two extremes we have the great majority of social actions, which partake partly of the one sphere and partly of the other. From this point of view technique and ritual, profane and sacred, do not denote types of action but aspects of almost any kind of action.[6]

214

In other words, even washing the dishes can be a ritual if we treat it as such. It's about pace and intention, the senses and the symbols. It's about the meaning we imbue into an object or an act rather than a script we inherit.

In the first ritual I remember, I climb up onto our tall kitchen chairs. I feel my dad's big, strong fingers separate my fine, curly hair into three equal pieces and begin folding one on top of the other.

We did this every night—after he got home from work and took off his suit, after we ate dinner, after we watched *The Cosby Show* and then I begged to stay up to watch *Cheers* like my big brother, after the lunches were packed and the homework stuffed into the backpacks. After all this, my dad would transform my rat's-nest-waiting-to-happen hair into one solid braid down the center of my back.

The profundity of this seemingly mundane nightly ritual rocks me as I think about it now. My family and I didn't attend any religious services. Though we celebrated Christmas, those traditions mostly revolved around green bean casserole topped with cornflakes and what I consider an obscene amount of gifts. There was no acknowledgment of Jesus' sacrifice. I knew little of Jesus and even less about the Bible. After complaining to my mom of my disadvantage in not being able to detect the biblical references like my classmates, she bought me an illustrated *Child's First Bible*—in my freshman year of college.

As I look back on it now, I realize that I may have been raised without religion, but I wasn't raised without ritual—and that is a critical difference. Religion is the story that we tell ourselves, tell our children, tell our communities, about why we are here on earth and how we should live based on this most important "why." But the daily version of ritual is something less intellectual. Daily ritual, by its very nature—repetitive, precise, often very physical—prompts a turning off of the mind and settling back into the body.

Through daily ritual, we taste the sacred; through rites of passage, we devour it. In ritual we literally step toward one another so we can metaphorically step back, taking in the profound nature of our lives, the ways we are changing and growing, gaining and losing. In the Celtic tradition they call these "thin times" and "thin places"—moments when the barrier that separates the earthly and the divine becomes porous.

As we seek to find new ways of honoring that rare and profound permeability, it's interesting to consider what anthropologists have discovered about what makes a ritual a rite of passage.

The term "rites of passage" was coined by the ethnographer Arnold van Gennep, who wrote *Les Rites de Passage* in 1909 after witnessing and studying hundreds of ceremonies in various cultures. He believed that three important stages characterize most rites of passage: separation, transition, and incorporation. During separation, as when a couple sleeps separately the night before they wed, people experience the gifts of solitude, reflecting on who they are and what they are about to commit to. During transition, as when a couple stands before an officiant (even one whose power is vested in some random website), people shed their old identity and, for a brief liminal moment, are in a sense spiritually naked—neither here nor there, but in an ambiguous, sacred state. Last comes incorporation, when the couple marches back down the aisle to the uproarious whoops and cheers of the people who love them.[7]

Interestingly, many anthropologists consider this critical third step to be missing from some of our most modern interpretations of rites of passage. For example, girls who start menstruating are often handed a box of pads and expected to act as if nothing has changed. Whereas in other cultures and at other times, the significance of menses was right up there with birth and death. We crave to be welcomed back after powerful journeys and ceremonies, however secular; when we aren't, we can be left grasping for how to integrate our changed identities on our own (the enigmatic tattoos my friends got on our last few days studying abroad in South Africa come to mind).

The rite of passage, at its most basic, is about identity and community. As we age, experiencing the highs and lows of this wild world, who we are changes, and many of us crave to have those around us to see and acknowledge that change in some obvious way. Without that acknowledgment, we can be left feeling lost, a little at sea, sometimes even profoundly unseen. Van Gennep writes: "social groups . . . have magico-religious foundations."[8]

"Magico-religious!" What a word, right? Van Gennep is getting at the idea that the people we surround ourselves with and the ways we interact with them, especially in these significant moments, have the magical effect of making us feel less isolated, despite the fact that we are—not to get too dark on you—ultimately alone. We are each as unique as a snowflake—that's one of the miracles of existence. But it's also the source of some of our most profound struggles, existentially speaking. Ritual is like the magic glue, in Van Gennep's framework, that keeps our social worlds together. Without it, our encounters and epiphanies can be too random, too unhinged. We suffer that "unbearable lightness of being" that Milan Kundera wrote so beautifully about.

To me, this analysis opens up a whole world of worthwhile questions as we compose modern lives of meaning here in the U.S. *When and in what ways do we mark the most important transitions in our lives, the changes in consciousness, the accomplishments, the losses, the commitments? How do we borrow from traditions that our parents and grandparents enacted, while also bringing in new symbols, language, values, practices? How much structure and how much spontaneity do we need? Without the prompting of a formal institution, how do we make sure to pay attention to the moments that beg to be marked?*

The average American adolescence doesn't get a lot of training ground for this kind of exploration. For many of us, adolescence was both remarkably free of rites of passage and filled with what we might call "ritual lite"—think proms and football games. The preponderance of ritual lite performances, competitions, and award ceremonies—which nodded toward something deeper but ultimately stopped short of spiritual substance—left many of us feeling empty (recognized, but not in an edifying way) or unanchored (not recognized at all).

To be fair, many parents tried. I vividly remember my mom threatening to have some sort of party for me when I got my period; to this I rolled my eyes as far back into my head as they could go and made it clear that under no circumstances was a "period party" to take place. Luckily, some strides have been made since then in reclaiming what's cool about marking menstruation—tweens can laugh at Bloody Becky comics on *Rookie* and read *Are You There God? It's Me, Margaret* by Judy Blume (many girls' primary such resource back in the day).

College actually follows the classic rite-of-passage formula—separation from home, college itself being the liminal experience, and graduation as a welcome back into the "real" world—and yet it, too, is mostly lacking in intentional ritual. The average American guy is left totally out in the cold when it comes to experiencing some larger ceremony unless it's related to sports, and that often drifts into hazing territory. Drinking copious amounts of tequila may feel "magico-religious" on some level, but I don't think it's what Arnold van Gennep had in mind. Perhaps some of what drives young men to carry out these headline-grabbing, intricate, and often dangerous initiation ceremonies in their sports teams and fraternities is really a form of expressing a good thing—a deep desire to have their changing identities publicly acknowledged—just in the wrong way.

Come to think of it, perhaps the absence of rites of passage in so many of our lives also explains the rise of outrageously expensive weddings—a different kind of danger than binge drinking, to be sure, but one that still threatens our financial health and leaves us feeling remarkably empty when it's all said and done. I'll never forget the moment when I was perched on top of a vinyl stool at a dive bar back home and one of the most stunning girls from my high school class leaned over and said, of her over-the-top wedding, "It's *my* day, you know . . . the first and last time when all eyes will be on me."

While I found that profoundly depressing at the time, now it strikes me as a poignant description of the kind of desperation people feel when they choreograph freakish pseudo-rituals, whether they be life-threatening hazing or debt-accruing wedding. It also may explain some of the cultural appropriation that too often takes place when people decide to invent ritual. Take a walk through your local yoga spot and you'll find plenty of sage wrapped in leather ribbons, mass-produced talking sticks, and other approximations of ancient traditions, often originated by indigenous people. The clientele, white and well-intentioned, miss the point: rituals are enacted in centuries of context, generations and generations and generations who have passed down these rites and sometimes even lost their lives trying to protect them. They're not two-for-one specials in spiritual bookstores.

When we don't get enough of what we need on a very basic level—to be seen for who we are as we change, within community—we force it in weird and risky ways. It's not actually the Greek letters emblazoned across our chest or the white dress that we really want—it's the sense of being a visible, valued part of something larger than ourselves. It's not other people's cultures and traditions that we need; we need an excavation of our own past, our own origin stories and ancestral legacies, however deeply buried they are.

## MAKING RITUALS OUR OWN

For many of us, the absence of ritual in our young lives—or the presence of rituals that didn't feel particularly meaningful—has led us to want to create a richer range of experiences for our kids.

Rikha Sharma Rani of Oakland, California, wanted to create a ritual that would make her two little girls feel loved and safe, something she experienced growing up with the Hindu tradition of "rakhi," when she tied a bracelet around her brother's wrist in exchange for his pledge of love and protection. Though at the time this rite of passage had been meaningful to Rikha's mother, who grew up in, as Rikha put it, "old school India," in retrospect Rikha's mom realized she found the whole protection thing antiquated. So she suggested Rikha put a feminist spin on the tradition and have her girls tie *rakhi* on each other. "I loved the idea!" Rikha shares. "It's an alternative version of the traditional ritual that takes out some of the, let's face it, misogyny."

Karen Boyett of Las Vegas, Nevada, was raised Jewish, and continues to identify that way. But she feels that the traditional approach to bat mitzvah—the ceremony by which Jewish girls become women, at least in terms of Jewish law, at age twelve—doesn't fully encompass the values she wants to pass down to her two girls. As the executive director of the Interfaith Council of Southern Nevada, Karen constantly thinks about the mingling of different faith traditions; she also lives out the cultural complexities and gifts of an interracial family on a daily basis, as her daughters' father is black and she is white. She explains, "I'm designing my daughter's bat mitzvah focusing on Jewish values *and* social justice instead of the process I went through as a child—just reading my assigned Torah portion and reciting prayers and such that I didn't understand."

For too long, coming-of-age moments in particular have been marked by a sort of performance of status for the neighbors. The carefully pressed Confirmation suit becomes less a symbol of "the bond with the church more perfect" and more a symbol of how perfect the family is. This kind of statusizing only reinforces the delusional and unhealthy concept that the nuclear family as a unit can satisfy all the needs of a growing, searching soul, spiritual needs included. The trouble is, when rites of passage become purely performance, instead of "incorporating" (as Arnold van Gennep would phrase it) the individual or family into the community, the rites can reinforce a sense of isolation. So, on the surface, the ceremonies purport that everything is on track and perfect, yet underneath there may be unmet needs, especially a yearning for real talk about big, messy questions.

In the New Better Off worldview, we still want our children to grow up with a sense of our most dearly held values as a family (however that is defined). We can only hope that our values are passed down through the accumulation of the everyday—the way we talk to a homeless woman on the street, the empty coffee cup we pick up on the sidewalk, that we grow some of the food we eat. But we also want them to understand that they are part of larger communities—and we recognize the importance of ritual in translating to our children who we are and who our larger communities are.

Quinn and Kristin Cox of Denver, Colorado, wanted an initiation ceremony for their children but didn't identify with any religion, so no bar mitzvah or baptism felt right. Fortunately, they found that the Geneva Glen Camp that Kristin attended and worked at for a decade of summers offers "nature induction" ceremonies for children of alumni of the camp during which blessings are read by the wider community that loves the child. Part of the ceremony involved Quinn and Kristin curating a collection of small objects that represent the values they want their kids to grow up with—things like compassion for all people and reverence for nature—and burying them in a marked spot; later, the kids can return to that spot and be reminded of those intentions. Kristin explains, "We find spirituality in nature and want to share that with our children. We want them to know that there is something to life beyond what meets the eye, not necessarily God per se."

When Kristin's and my parents were coming of age in the 1950s, fewer than 4 percent of Americans grew up in secular families; in contrast, 11 percent of Americans born after 1970 report having been raised in nonreligious households.[9] So, in a sense, today we are seeing the first critical mass of young people raised without religion becoming adults.

And lo and behold, they're not heathen derelicts! So reports the largest study of religion and family life in the U.S. to date, the Longitudinal Study of Generations, begun in 1971 and led by Vern Bengtson, a University of Southern California professor of gerontology and sociology. When in 2013 Bengtson added secular families into the mix of data, he found high levels of family solidarity and emotional closeness between parents and their nonreligious children, as well as strong ethical standards and clearly articulated moral values.[10]

Bengtson told the *Los Angeles Times*: "Many nonreligious parents were more coherent and passionate about their ethical principles than some of the 'religious' parents in our study. The vast majority appeared to live goal-filled lives characterized by moral direction and a sense of life having a purpose."[11]

The downside of being secular is that you lose the structure that religion provides concerning rites of passage; in a busy, stressful life, it's simply easier to have authorities and communal schedules dictate when and how you mark important moments. Plus, taking part in tradition and ceremony can be quite beautiful and deeply meaningful. Secular families also miss out on the baked-in community—the fellowship, the music making, the community service opportunities—that religious institutions provide.

The upside of being secular is that one can bring more intentionality to rites of passage by virtue of being in a position to invent them. This can mean being vigilant about communicating our values to our kids and being thoughtful about how we mark moments of transition and transformation. The buck, in a sense, stops with us—and that can be both frightening and liberating. But, as our first generation of secularly raised kids is proving, this freedom seems to feed, not starve, the moral imagination.

## THIS IS YOUR TRIBE

So many of our modern rituals are tied to marriage and children—but what becomes of someone who doesn't want either?

Deanna Zandt is a digital strategist with pink-streaked, short, spiky hair. Her social media feed is largely filled with pictures of her dog, Izzy. She is in an open relationship with a "wacky robot artist" and doesn't want children. Over her two decades of living in New York City, she's carefully collected a community of amazing friends, and has stood witness with many of them as they got married or welcomed babies into the world. Despite not being a marriage person herself, let alone monogamous, she's shown up to all the weddings and baby showers and shed lots of genuine tears.

Now, she figured, it was her turn. Ever since she first saw the *Sex and the City* episode where Carrie Bradshaw questions why big parties should be only for getting married, she'd wanted to throw herself a wedding-sized bash for her fortieth birthday. So, almost a year in advance of her big 4-0 she booked a beautiful rooftop venue in Brooklyn; found a caterer, a makeup artist, and a photographer; set up a website; sent out beautiful invitations—the whole nine yards. At a friend's prompting she even registered! As you might imagine, it confused a lot of people. "At every juncture," Deanna says, some "people needed the explanation: 'No, this [won't be] a wedding. Yes, this is as "important" as a wedding.' But that was okay, because it gave me a chance to introduce people to a different way of thinking about what matters most."

The invitations that Deanna sent out read: "THIS IS NOT A DRILL. I AM HAVING A FORTIETH BIRTHDAY PARTY THIS YEAR WHICH WILL SERVE AS MY NON-WEDDING."

With her own friends she didn't have to explain much: "My tribe is super important to me, and they got it immediately. I'm blessed to be in a milieu of people who value friendship as much as romantic and sexual relationships, so to them it was like, 'Well, duh.'"

What her "tribe" may have been surprised by was that there was a ritual at the party by which Deanna, in a sense, married her community. Her friend Brianne Leslie, a clairvoyant with a thick Queens accent, said, "I love the idea for this party. You're going to have a ceremony, right?"

"No, I think that's taking it a little far," Deanna had said, laughing. But Brianne cut her short: "No, stop right there. When people get married, it's a public affirmation of their commitment. You need a ceremony that acknowledges the work you've put into creating this community and asks for their ongoing love and support."

While Deanna had to admit it made sense, it still made her more than a little uncomfortable. She'd come to see ritual as something intimate: her daily meditation, the moments when she marked the new or full moon with a lit candle and an intention or two. "I think that rituals are really useful and powerful as introspective ways to look at your place in the world," Deanna explains. "I think that's part of why the ritual was squeamish for me, because I view it as very private, and this was so public."

Plus, she kept hearing this voice in her head—*who do you think you are?* Deanna is from a low-key, Lutheran family, and she appreciates the version of Christianity she grew up with: "It was lovely. You spent five minutes in the beginning saying, 'Oh, we sinned. Sorry about that,' and the next fifty was, 'Yeah God! Let's go get coffee.'

"I learned activism and community organizing from the church," she continues. "My mom was really active and my dad was a handyman. We're German, that's what you do: you help." But you don't necessarily throw blowout parties for yourself marrying one hundred people on a Brooklyn rooftop. Even for someone who loves the spotlight (the website offered the hashtag #DeannaFest and read: PLEASE POST ON ALL PLATFORMS PUBLICLY. I AM A LEO, AFTER ALL.), it felt like a stretch: "The public affirmation was the final piece that fell into place, and was a little bit squishy and scary."

Another unexpected moment came the night before the big day. Deanna, playing on the elaborate and bizarre customs of the bachelorette tradition, had made herself a skull-and-crossbones sash reading: NEVER THE BRIDE. When her mom, to whom she is super close, read it she stepped back. "Really, never?" she said, her eyes pleading.

Deanna was shocked. "Mom, we've talked about this. We've been having this conversation for twenty years. I'm probably not getting married and I'm definitely not having kids."

"Probably?" her mom said.

"Unlikely, Mom."

And here's the thing about creating your own ritual, as Deanna did: you force answers to potentially hot-button questions. Things that might have remained open questions—*Will she ever get married? Will they christen that baby?*—get resolved when you ritualize an alternative. In some ways, that's nice; it pushes people to own who they are: not just those who can handle nontraditional views, but everyone, no exception. No more shape-shifting with conservative relatives. No more letting people hold out false hopes. In Deanna's case, the open question of whether she may, in fact, get married someday suddenly felt put to rest when her mother saw her in that skull-and-crossbones sash. It was hard, but honest.

And honest is what Deanna has decided forty is all about. "Part of turning forty is that you give way less of a fuck," she explains bluntly, then quickly laughs and lovingly adds, "Yes, there are some members of my extended family who might be totally freaked out by this whole thing. But I'm like, Aunt Helen, you do you; I'm going to do me."

On the big day, Deanna, wearing a long, purple, sequined dress, stood beaming before her people as Brianne made it official:

*Today, Deanna is actually asking each of you, the members of her tribe, to enter into a commitment with her. In light of that, I would like you each to jointly take a vow with me. Do all of you promise to continue to love and support Deanna in her crazy and wonderful life and to laugh with her, celebrate with her, cry with her and be there for her when she needs your counsel, your compassion, or just your silence as you listen to her? If so, let us together say, "I will."*

And they did! Her family, her local tribe members, even people who'd flown in from all over the country. (Deanna had arranged a fund by which friends with frequent-flyer miles to spare could sponsor those who couldn't swing a ticket.) Everyone was directed to wear "whatever makes you feel *fabulous*. Seriously. Show me who you are. PJs to gowns, faerie wings to T-shirts." And they did: they showed up in sequins and high-top sneakers and everything in between.

And just like a wedding, the evening flew by in a blur, like "an episode of that old show *This Is Your Life*." Happily, Deanna closed down a nearby bar at 4:00 AM alongside those she loved most and felt most loved by in return. She'd also talked so much she lost her voice for two days.

She sums it up: "It was a wonderful terrifying mix of seeing all of my worlds talking to each other. It felt dreamlike and magical."

## JOYFUL COMMUNITY BONDED BY LOSS

Sometimes the dreamy state of ritual has its roots in a nightmare scenario. When Lennon Flowers was a senior in high school, her mom was diagnosed with lung cancer. So this spark plug of a young woman with a dark, pixie haircut and big, bright eyes abandoned her dreams to go to NYU and become an actor; instead, she enrolled at the University of North Carolina to be close to home. Shifting away from theater, she dove headfirst into community organizing and activism. But though she was surrounded by a community of friends, she rarely mentioned her mom. "I became good at not talking about what was happening to me," she explains. "I got really, really good at being really, really busy."

When her mother died during her senior year, many of Lennon's friends hadn't even known she was sick. In part, she justified her silence with the belief that it protected other people. Who wants to talk about such sad things? We're ill-equipped to respond, as a society. We say stupid things like "I'm sure she's in a better place." (For the record, Lennon says that's the worst thing you can say to a kid who has lost a parent.)

In part, she avoided talking about her grief because it took a while to hit her. A whole year, in fact. Lennon remembers: "By then, the surge of attention had disappeared. It made me feel like there was something wrong with me for feeling something a year later. It was a deep source of shame."

This is an important acknowledgment as we consider the reinvention of ritual. Too often, we walk through the formal paces—have the funeral, stuff the fridge full of casseroles, and then expect everyone to move on as usual. Much of the energy behind coming up with new ways of honoring transitions is born out of the wisdom that our identities don't unfold according to the Gregorian calendar. The "container" of a funeral can be very comforting—especially in the first few days, which some go through completely numb—but it's ultimately artificial to think we do all of our processing and integrating on schedule.

Three years after her mother died, Lennon moved to Los Angeles for a boy and a job. On her first day there she met Carla, a woman her age with whom she felt an immediate connection. Later, while apartment hunting, Carla admitted that her father had died just six months earlier, so Lennon shared her own story. Though it was only a ten-minute conversation, it kindled something significant.

A couple of months later, Carla organized a dinner party for five women, Lennon among them. Though they were only in their twenties, all of them had lost a parent, and all of them had felt remarkably alone in that loss. Of course there had been funerals, but nothing as profound as the loss of a parent can be contained within just days of death. They'd all been walking around since with a sense that something was missing, and it wasn't just their loved ones—it was a process, a practice, by which they could reflect on their losses.

Lennon remembers feeling visceral trepidation as she walked in to the gathering, but also the disarming attention to detail that was evident everywhere she looked. The back deck was covered in Christmas lights and candles. Carla had cooked her late father's signature paella. The wine and the stories flowed through the evening.

What had been planned as a simple dinner party became more of a rite of passage, and then a ritual. They talked until 2:00 in the morning. On a Sunday. They fell asleep curled around one another in Carla's bed. Lennon was stunned by the experience: "I'd become particularly good at never 'going there.' And then to not want to leave was such an incredible contrast."

The women continued to meet on a fairly regular basis, breaking bread and sharing stories of how their lives were unfolding in relation to their grief. They started inviting other people in their twenties and thirties who had also lost parents. Friends started referring friends. They were not a small minority, but a largely silent critical mass of people hungry for ritual community.

Lennon and Carla eventually created an organization to encourage others to launch their own "tables"—as they now refer to the dinner parties. Though these tables are designed for sharing stories of loss and grief, as groups get to know one another they inevitably realize that their stories are "incredibly unfinished." It so happens that it isn't a big leap from telling the story of how your mother died to asking, in Lennon's words, "Why the fuck are we here?" Many of those who host and become a part of tables are in their twenties and thirties, and as such are navigating their careers and longer-term romantic relationships for the first time *without* the guidance of one of their parents.

"What we've learned is that telling our stories and creating personal rituals create forward movement. A lot of people around our tables make career changes, switching to service work or to a career that has some direct connection to the person that they've lost. A lot of people end up discussing how to talk about their loss with their boyfriends or girlfriends, and that inevitably leads to more general conversations about relationships."

The truth is, so many of the young people gathering for these potluck gatherings don't even identify with the word "grief." It feels too clinical to them. It feels attached to institutions that most of them have avoided because they seem too prescriptive, too determined to show them the ways in which their grief is just like everybody else's, thinking this will make them feel less alone—when really it just makes them feel misunderstood.

"The number one rule of The Dinner Party is that no two stories are ever the same," Lennon says. The potlucks work because they're organic, idiosyncratic, fun, and built on the foundations of friendship. There are now thirty-one hosts across the U.S.

"The bigger thing we're after is normalizing getting together and practicing being vulnerable enough to take the mask off, tell our stories, and create rituals," Lennon explains. "Whatever your scarlet letter is, how can you surface that with people who have a shared experience?"

Rituals abound among the Dinner Partiers, both those invented whole cloth and those adopted and adapted from faith traditions. People decorate sugar skulls and burn joss paper (borrowed from the Mexican Día de los Muertos), sit Shiva (a Jewish tradition), read a new poem every day, and cook and eat specific foods that remind them of their loved one. Amanda from Hoboken, New Jersey, writes:

> *Last March 18, I bought a six-pack of his favorite beer Negra Modelo, drank one, wrote my dad a letter, and sealed up the bottle with an old wine cork. I then went down to the Hudson River, emotionally wished my dad a happy sixty-fourth birthday, and tossed my thoughts into the black turbulent waters. It was freezing, wet, and snowing; I couldn't help but envision my dad chuckling at my misery in the cold, as he never did understand why I liked New York. With any luck, the bottle's made its way out of the tri-state area and moved on down to warmer waters. I like to envision the bottle washed up on a Caribbean shore in the sun, exactly where my dad would want to be enjoying a nice cold Modelo.*

"The key is to find whatever works to keep you connected to those who have passed," Lennon explains. Though conventional wisdom held that healthy mourning requires coming to terms with the definitive and eternal end to your relationship with the deceased, more recent research argues that, in fact, figuring out a way to stay *in* that relationship, albeit at a different level, is actually the healthiest thing one can do.[12]

When asked what her mom would think of the work she's doing now, Lennon pauses and thinks a bit before responding: "My mom was an introvert, a talented photographer, but she was also a fierce lioness, the kind of person who would never stand down from speaking the truth."

It seems that, after all that busy silence, "real talk"—as Lennon puts it—is her treasured inheritance.

## SACRED REINVENTION

Ritual is the container for our confusion. It's the prompt for our reflection. It is the necessary moment when we hold our humanity up to the light and examine it, forgive, give thanks, give up, get witnessed, stand awed, admit confusion, make promises, and love out loud and in front of people in sometimes powerfully embarrassing ways. And more and more, we're doing all this not dictated by tradition but inspired by it, not in obedience to authorities but in organic craving for acknowledgment, not in fear but in love.

It so happens that people who do affiliate with a religion are being influenced by this wave of sacred reinvention—considering how they might innovate within the four walls of their more traditional institutions. In that sense, it's not really about whether you affiliate with an organized religion or not, but what you crave from the rituals you participate in. Some of us are reinventing ritual almost entirely outside of faith traditions, though no doubt drawing on those that speak to us personally; others of us are reinventing ritual within religions that we love enough to push and evolve.

Sacred tinkerers want ritual, first and foremost, to be a fortifying, healing, ongoing part of our lives. Oprah's *Super Soul Sundays* just don't cut it. Neither does SoulCycle or CrossFit, as enjoyable as it may be to get your sweat on in a crowd. On some very deep level, we know that the commercialized version of what we crave will never satisfy. We need spaces and places that don't see our craving for ritual as a market opportunity.

And we need those spaces and places, not just for ourselves individually, but for each other as well. Mary Catherine Bateson writes of a neglected aspect of ritual's importance in our lives:

> We talk in this country often about property rights. We talk more rarely about the shares people have in each other's lives, and about people's rights to participation and pleasure, especially at the moments of passage: the right to throw a handful of earth on a coffin, the right to stand up to catch a tossed bouquet, and dream of one's own future wedding, to kiss the bride or groom, or hold a newborn. Couples today devise new rituals or set up housekeeping together in ways most meaningful to themselves without wondering whether meaning is something they owe to a larger community.[13]

For the witnessed, rituals are crucial ways to feel supported by a community. But for the witnesses, they also play a powerful role. They are, in a sense, "why we are alive" ceremonies for everyone.

There are both audacity and humility in it: the audacity to believe that the rituals you use to mark meaning in your life should feel personal and real; and, at the same time, the humility to acknowledge that you are a tiny part of a vast, unfolding story about human beings—how we gather, how we are born, how we love, how we die.

# the thread of revelation

## CREATING COMMUNITIES THAT HELP US ASK HARD QUESTIONS

How do you know if you're a good person?

It's such a problematic but necessary question. I don't mean good as in pious, or good as in perfect. I just mean good: as in quietly brave and often intentional. Good as in you take stock of your life and—all things being equal—feel proud of the person you're striving to be, even when you fail. Good as in decent. Good as in trying.

Too often we're told that this pursuit is a naïve one. That adulthood is inherently full of contradictions, so we're better off just surrendering to the moral mess and seeking pleasure instead. "Don't waste time trying to be good—it's a fool's errand." "Have fun, just don't be an asshole. End of story."

But to surrender our moral imagination, that childlike part of us that spots contradictions like a heat-seeking missile, is also to surrender to the status quo. It's the part of me that—at five—asked my parents why some people sleep in the streets while others have warm houses and soft beds. It's the part of me that—at fifteen—railed against the idiocy of an abstinence-only education policy in a high school where girls were already walking around with babies. It's the part of me that—at twenty-five—had burning questions about the amount of money that one could earn and even save when there were people dying every single day for lack of it.

That last one really got me. I used to wake up in the middle of the night sweating because of this question. I got in fights with my parents about it (ah, the cruelty of having your child, for whom you'd sacrificed and saved for twenty-five years, turn around and tell you you're immoral for having done so). I developed a slapdash philanthropic style; I would send a check to Oxfam as large as my month's rent because I made an intellectual decision that the kind of lack found in the developing world was the *most* important thing I could use my income for. The next month, I would buy my friends drinks and invest in their Kickstarter projects, convinced that the local was where to start. Plus, it felt good. I wanted the emotional high of supporting people I loved. The next month I would shame myself for succumbing to a philosophy built not on intelligent generosity, but on what made me feel good. I'd go back to the check-writing. My friends could buy their own drinks, make their own damn movies; kids were starving in Ethiopia.

This kind of moral thrashing about is enough to make me intolerable to be around. Faced with a question I couldn't shake in my twenties, I would muster enough energy for some brave experiment— if impulsive and inadequate. I offered able-bodied men my seat on the subway. I looked every homeless person in the eye, even if I didn't give them a dime. I created something called the Secret Society for Creative Philanthropy, through which I gave ten friends $100 and asked them to give it away, then come to a bar to tell the story about it. But ultimately those efforts didn't lead me to any coherent philosophy, and I slowly settled into the status quo.

As for finances, for example, I still give money, but never in a satisfying way. I save more of my income than the twenty-five-year-old part of me (still buried not so deep beneath the surface) would consider ethical in a world of so much suffering; my SEP IRA, however humble, makes her seethe. I rationalize this decision with the fact that I've got a kid now, and a husband with whom I share financial decisions. College is getting more and more expensive; isn't it my duty to save up for my daughter's future?

I'm no longer inclined to fight with my dad about money; his cautious voice has become my own. All those things he said to me that once made me furious, that sounded like capitulation to "the man," now float around in my brain unbidden, just at a higher pitch.

And it's not that I think my parents are entirely wrong. I *do* think I owe Maya something solid, though I'm not sure what it is. For that matter, I owe my parents. If they should ever need my time or my money in order to be okay in the world, I want to make that possible. In a sense, my current excess—however small—could translate into future comfort for people I love. That means a lot to me. Perhaps more than it should.

But the rub is not really in the existence of my little nest egg. The rub is in the numbing of my outrage, the quieting of my questions, the taming of my naïve and urgent heart. Is that what adulthood is? To stop asking moral and philosophical questions because it's the responsible thing to do? Or to stop asking them because they're inconvenient or impractical? Do we trade in our courage for responsibility?

We often accept reality because we don't have the creativity or energy to imagine or enact an alternative. Or because we feel too alone in our quest for something more ethical. But what if we could spot other souls swimming ungracefully upstream? What if we created communities where we *can* ask the hard and naïve questions? Some are grand, like my eternal confusion about money. Some come from a more personal place, but with grand consequences: *Am I living with integrity? Do my values and my actions align? Am I who I believe myself to be?*

Our daily lives are structured to provide us with a million reminders of the small stuff—the overdue parking ticket and the dishes in the sink and the meaning we attach to both that makes them larger than paper and water and ceramics. We sweat it all. We produce. We achieve. We churn. We pass out. We wake up and begin again.

And then, every once in a great while, in the average adult life, there will be this little break in the already scheduled program. You watch a beautiful film and walk out into the moonlight feeling alchemically changed, open, hungry to talk about your *real* life. Or you hear that someone you know, someone just about your age, is on the brink of death. Or you swerve at the last minute and save your life, or wake up from a terrible dream and feel the palpable relief of being in your bed, next to your sweating, snoring partner whom you love so deeply even though you were really mad about the unwashed dishes before you went to sleep. Or you have one of those moments when you look over at your kids and realize that your entire life is built on inexplicable miracles that you mostly don't notice because you're so busy cleaning up around them.

But these profound and life-sustaining pauses are mostly serendipitous. You don't plan for them. (If you could, they would likely end up being one more thing on your to-do list, which is kind of gross to think about.) And they're fleeting, like the smell of baking bread when you're driving past a bakery well over the speed limit. So good. And then so gone.

It seems to me that the only way we can plan for these moments, or at least approximations of them, is by being in community and by creating structure within that community that invites the big questions to come out of the shadowy hiding places in our overscheduled, self-important lives. It's easier to tease out the subtleties of a moral life alongside another. Alone, we catapult ourselves—solo and desperate—from indignation to resignation; together, we're strengthened for the painstaking work of living with our minds and hearts open.

As lovely as the serendipitous moments of existential awareness can be, they are internal and slippery. They are hard to articulate because they're left in a netherworld of our psyche—a place where we notice something, feel something, and then struggle to wrap words around that something. While this is the source of a lot of wonderful art, it's also inherently isolating. We might sit in front of a Kehinde Wiley painting for twenty minutes and have all kinds of brainsplodes about race and pageantry and dignity, or be driving along and lose ourselves completely in the lyrics of Regina Spektor, but before long we're often looking around for someone to share the feeling with. It is lovely to grapple internally, but in order to extend our inquiry—both in time and in space—we have to find a way to ask some of the big questions among others.

This is what religions are supposed to do for people. I've heard from friends who've never felt more alive than after soul-searching for hours in a church community group. And from friends who feel most connected in synagogue, singing a chant that they know has reverberated for more than five thousand years. And from friends who've found Muslim communities where studying the Koran leads them into challenging, gratifying questions. But for all those who've found this kind of connection within such sacred walls, there are so many others running out of religious institutions en masse—and so many young people who never entered in the first place.

So many of us feel as if our moral imaginations are homeless. Perhaps it's why these days we're drawn to television shows with complex moral dramas—*Orange Is the New Black* and *Mad Men* and *Transparent*. At least these are "places" where we see characters, proxies for ourselves, playing along the spectrum of generous and self-protective, courageous and terrified, right and wrong.

So these conversations do have a forum in some television shows. They can also happen in private therapy sessions. It's a rite of passage for many: the moment you sit with a therapist and—for the first time—speak the unspeakable. For most it's not exactly moral wandering that gets them in the door, but a broken heart of one variety or another. But even in the most personal of breakdowns, there are profound ethical quandaries. How do I deserve to be treated? is a personal, microcosmic version of the wider question: How do people deserve to be treated? Similarly, How can I heal? is only a small distance from How can the world heal?

I've had my share of self-reflection on the couch; I've also spent many days (maybe months?!) staring at a computer screen trying to get the words just right all by my lonesome. When in my late twenties I found myself unsatisfied by both art and therapy, I considered going to divinity school. Surely the hallowed halls of Union Theological Seminary were a place where people were discussing the practical implications of power, privilege, money, love. Perhaps. But when I went on the prospective student tour they mostly talked about biblical history and did close readings of texts I felt no visceral connection to. I'm sure there was a classroom where my questions were being explored, but it was a place you could visit only after the foundational courses were taken. But ultimately, I didn't so much want to be a theologian as I wanted to talk about theological stuff with smart, kind, honestly confused people. I can't tell you how many people I've met in recent years who, like me, considered getting a theology degree—not because they wanted to do theological work, but because they had no idea where else to go to think out loud about the examined life. This strikes me as being similar to people going to law school because they have questions about law itself, not because they want to be lawyers per se.

In a report called "How We Gather," Harvard Divinity School students Angie Thurston and Casper ter Kuile profile ten communities—such as Camp Grounded, a summer camp for adults, and Sanctuaries, a DC-based organization for art, social change, and spirituality—that they see as satisfying people's deep need for personal and social transformation, purpose-finding, creativity, and accountability.

They write, "Churches are just one of many institutional casualties of the Internet age in which young people are both more globally connected and more locally isolated than ever before. Against this bleak backdrop, a hopeful landscape is emerging. Millennials are flocking to a host of new organizations that deepen community in ways that are powerful, surprising, and perhaps even religious."[1]

When we are aching into adulthood, as well as in the years thereafter, we need a place to lay down our heaviest mental and intellectual burdens with others. For most of us, most of the time, it still feels lonely to ask big questions about the ethical, adult life. We surrender, sometimes little by little, sometimes all at once, to the status quo—the hypocrisy and cognitive dissonance we once cringed at in parents and teachers, coworkers and friends. We often surrender, eventually, because it feels too hard, too heavy, to do anything else.

And yet, some of us are stubborn. Some of us feed our moral imaginations even when starving them would seem to be far more convenient. Some of us find communities where our questions are safe, even admired. Some of us choose to gather.

## THE HUMAN CONDITION

It was an exquisitely sunny day. Twenty-five-year-old Courtney Baxter, bursting with questions and courage, was lying in the grass in New York City, home to eight million people, and feeling horribly alone.

So she did what she always does when feeling lonely and anxious, two surprisingly common emotions for a social, effective human: she reached out to her motley crew of a community. More specifically, she wrote a letter, right there in the park, and later typed it up and sent it out via email. An excerpt:

> *A year and a few months ago, a young woman named Marina Keegan died in a car accident days after graduating from college. I read about her, her death and consequential legacy, and the powerful essay that she wrote mere weeks before her death for the* Yale Daily News. *Despite her being a stranger, something about her story touched a deeper place in me. Reading about her on the days following the accident, I came across an article that mentioned her preoccupation with "the human condition." I felt the part of my brain that says "YES, tell me more" start to glow.*

Intrigued by Keegan's interests, Courtney had looked up "human condition" and found that it described something she hadn't quite had the name for, an obsession really: "the irreducible part of humanity." Further research on the phrase led her to Hannah Arendt's book *The Human Condition*, which—like a true New York cliché—she found in the enigmatic stacks of the Strand bookstore. "It was very wonky," she admits. "I read it. I reread it. She's talking about the workforce and this is not what I'm expecting. I decided that I really need to talk about this with other people."

And there certainly was a lot to talk about: love, ethics, courage, power, guilt, grief. Courtney was raised Catholic in a suburb of Cincinnati, but she escaped services by volunteering in the preschool room; when she came out to her mom as queer, she was furious that the pope's official position filled her family with fear about the state of her soul. But she didn't lose all affinity for the Catholic Church, or interest in finding a religious home: "Until I find a church that feeds what I really believe, I'm okay with tapping into something else, going to light a candle at the Catholic Church, or hosting the Human Condition. I need places to ask, 'Why do we wake up in the morning?'"

Cut back to the exquisite day and the grass, and that truly human condition of being alone while surrounded by people. "You find people who are creating community out of playing soccer," Courtney explains. "I don't want to just go play soccer. I want to find people who want to talk about these crazy things with me." Then she quickly adds: "While having fun, of course."

She wrote in that letter to her friends:

*The Human Condition that I'm building is a school? lab? society? family? all of it? What I can boil it down to is spending real time with real people. Getting the hell off our smartphones. An intellectual, emotional, community-based space for the kind of people who like to ask the big and small questions.*

As it happens, Courtney's ponderings resonated with her tribe as well, many of whom answered her call. Her idea shaped up like this: each season Courtney hosts a "class," as she calls it, but with a spin. The first one was a philosophy poker night . . . without the poker. "It was too hard to keep track of all those rules and talk about the theme," Courtney admits, so they played the card game Bullshit (a.k.a. Cheat or I Doubt It) instead. About a dozen people participated on that first night.

Another night they talked about technology, specifically: *how do we deal with this growing need to be connected to the Internet?* Courtney chose this topic because she was more than a little frustrated with her own habits, especially being addicted to her iPhone in a way she never thought possible. In advance of this gathering she sent out a TED talk and a few articles to the participants. "The major takeaway from the conversation," Courtney remembers, "was that technology actually has enabled more connection with friends and family across the country. I walked away feeling like there's a gray space between 'iPhones are destructive' and 'being disconnected is best' that I hadn't really allowed myself to acknowledge.

"It was so fun. Exactly everything I imagined," Courtney said. "I found that people do actually want to talk about the big existential questions. Most people don't swig a beer and say, 'Well, what do you think your funeral is going to look like?' But I find they're actually happy when I do just that."

Philosophy "poker" nights in the fall led to "fireside chats" in the winter and then "Sunday chapel" on Courtney's Brooklyn porch come spring. At one particular gathering of Human Condition she requested that her friends wear all white. Everyone ate a hodgepodge of bodega snacks and drank beer. A long-distance bestie Skyped in. But one person who attended that Sunday acted too cool for school, rolling her eyes when Courtney asked everyone to sing, just to loosen up and get in the spirit of things. "She was kind of looking at me like, 'Are you really going to do this right now?'" Courtney recalls. "And I was like, 'Yeah, I am, are you? I am going to sing a song on my deck. Are you going to sing with me?'"

Courtney isn't intimidated by skepticism. She's also not rigid about structure. She's hosting Human Condition events whenever she has a craving and the capacity for one—which seems to be about four times a year given her consuming nonprofit job. She continually tweaks the structure. She doesn't care exactly how the conversation goes, as long as it goes big: "I would have these conversations with myself in my head," she says, "so the fact that anyone else is engaging with them is a gift."

# THE MUTUAL IMPROVEMENT CLUB

Thirty-seven-year-old Ruthie Ackerman picked up Ben Franklin's autobiography on a whim. A self-described "seeker," she'd been reading Gretchen Rubin's best-selling book *The Happiness Project: Or, Why I Spent a Year Trying to Sing in the Morning, Clean My Closets, Fight Right, Read Aristotle, and Generally Have More Fun* when she saw a reference to Franklin, often regarded as the godfather of self-improvement. *What the hell?* she thought. She'd been meaning to read more biographies, and was a little embarrassed by her own lack of knowledge about the most famous of America's founding fathers.

What she discovered would change her life. Franklin created what he called a Mutual Improvement Club, also known as the Junto, in 1727, which met every Friday for forty years. The idea behind the Junto was to bring together individuals with diverse interests and skills to work toward improving themselves and their community.

The Junto was founded on thirteen virtues: temperance, silence, order, resolution, frugality, industry, sincerity, justice, moderation, cleanliness, tranquility, chastity, and humility. Franklin's autobiography includes a framework and specific guidelines for how he created the Junto. His framework explains how he defined each virtue, how he kept track of his progress, and where he fell short—all so that future generations would have a template for developing themselves as active citizens and leaders.

At the time that she discovered this, Ruthie was feeling untethered to the world. She'd transitioned careers, finding that her first love—journalism—wasn't all it was cracked up to be. She enjoyed her consulting work, but she was still piecing it all together, figuring out how to balance a new marriage, a range of demanding clients, a wide variety of curiosities and interests, and financial realities. Sometimes she felt life was wonderful but in pieces, never quite whole. When she read about Franklin's Junto, it was as if a life preserver had been thrown to her from three hundred years earlier. She decided to create her own mutual improvement club.

This Junto is a group of New Yorkers, mostly in their twenties and thirties, who meet once a month for two hours. They split those two hours into thirds: the first is spent discussing the virtue from the month prior, the second is spent discussing the virtue ahead, and the third is spent exploring Franklin's list of questions, which includes things like *What is something you're looking for help on? Is there any advice we can give each other about our work/personal life? Do you know of any deserving young beginners whom the power of the Junto may encourage?*

Ruthie facilitates, but very loosely. Mostly the group guides its own discussion. One meeting on justice got at the tangled knot of modern ethical complexity. Ruthie explains, "At first, when we were talking about justice it seemed straightforward: *am I a just person?* But we really struggled with what that means. Sure, we might not intentionally harm people, but if we really think about it, so many of our smallest choices have unintended consequences. It's very hard to live a just life. We collectively admitted that we didn't even know what that would look like."

One member, a social worker in Harlem who works in homeless services, described her daily struggle to square her own existence—where the basics are always covered—with those of her clients. In one meeting she said aloud for the first time: "Why should I eat when someone else can't?"

"The questions we raised were all so interesting and tough," Ruthie recalls. "But, at the same time, we decided that if we get bogged down, we can't function. The group allows us to talk about these things, go deep, and then pick our heads up and keep going."

Ruthie is an atheist, but she describes the group's religious identity as diverse. Some members identify as Christian but, interestingly, even some who attend church find themselves still hungry for the sort of discussions that the Mutual Improvement Club encourages. Others don't have a religious label per se, but—like Ruthie—want to explore how to be a good person within a community of other seekers.

The conversation veers from the deeply philosophical to the absolutely pragmatic. For example, after they discussed temperance, which Franklin defined as "eating not to dullness and drinking not to elevation," Ruthie decided to stop using any technological device during meals, even when eating solo. "I realized that my iPhone was making my meals duller, in Franklin's parlance," she explains. It was a small shift that made a big difference with her relationship to food, to her husband—even to her own thoughts.

In between meetings, members share insights from their experiments, ask for help with a challenge, and send support using a thread on WhatsApp—a Wi-Fi-enabled instant messaging service. But though the group is adept at online communication, they believe the in-person meetings are foundational. Ruthie admits to being starved for, as she puts it, "IRL interaction" after a life so filled with digital connection.

A couple of years in, the group's exploration of virtues continues to be refreshingly nuanced, and their relationships with each other continue to deepen. "We're much more vulnerable than we were in the beginning," Ruthie explains. "We're having our quarter-life crises. We don't know who we want to be when we grow up. And that's all okay. There's just not a good place in modern life to talk about these things, so we've had to create them."

Talking to Ruthie got me thinking about what it is that allows people like her—the founders, gatherers, party throwers—to take the initiative to create communities like this. After all, so many of us yearn for these spaces, but it's easy to let the rush of modern life or a fear of no one showing up prevent us from building something ourselves.

I wrote Ruthie an email to ask if this go-getter attitude was modeled for her growing up. Her response:

*I laughed out loud reading this because it was the complete opposite. I grew up with divorced parents whose lives were a mess in very different ways and they took no responsibility for it.*

*My framework couldn't be more different than theirs. I believe nothing is given to you. We must seek out the people and situations we can learn from and do our best to extract whatever wisdom and beauty from within. That is the only meaning I have found in life.*

*It has been painful for me to realize that most of our lives are spent superficially interacting with those around us, even our closest friends and family. When I realized earlier this year that I didn't want to live in a world where I couldn't ask the big questions and hear how others are struggling with them as well, I set out to find my tribe.*

For those of us who weren't born into tribes that felt like they fit us, or tribes at all, it's become increasingly important to find, create, and claim our own. In so doing we find a way to weather the overwhelming sensations that are so typical of the daunting modern life, to sort out what matters and what's minutiae, and maybe to even laugh at ourselves a little bit in the midst of all the seriousness. The headlines on morality tend to focus on the loudest voices—the zealots, the pundits, the polarizing figures—but the majority of us aren't debating; we're discerning. We're not gunning for big headlines; we're making a dozen decisions a day that we hope add up to a life well-lived. And as long as we are trying to make considered decisions, it's far easier to decide which ones matter among a Junto of friends.

## MAN ENOUGH TO BE EARNEST

On the other side of the country, Nat Manning, who is twenty-nine, herds his own version of a tribe. "It's a safe space to talk about our emotions," he says with a chuckle. The phrase "safe space" feels self-important, like something that requires air quotes and an eye roll, and that's not really Nat's style. But, of course, he means it. It *is* a space apart, a moment when he and about a dozen other guys in their twenties and thirties gather to explore a variety of themes—promises, dads, sex, conflict, creativity—with the expectation of earnestness and an unspoken but deeply felt commitment to talk about the complexity of their inner lives without the contemporary man's standard armor: humor.

They meet every few weeks at different members' houses in the San Francisco Bay Area. They show up at 6:00 PM to pitch in on cooking and shoot the shit, and the official conversation begins at 7:00. The host sends out a theme in advance. "It's intentionally not academic," Nat explains. "Often it will be something that people are struggling with in that moment. In fact, we have a collective agreement to steer away from abstractions and analogies and really make things concrete, to ask, 'how is this showing up in my life right now?'"

Nat, the COO of a developing world-focused tech company called Ushahidi, started the men's group in 2013 because he was missing a similar crew that he'd been a part of while a student at Brown University seven years earlier. Though Nat is no stranger to organized religion—he went to a Quaker high school and now practices Buddhism—he wasn't finding the kind of conversations he was hungry for in formal institutions. Nor did he feel it was easy to create these connections in purely informal settings: "It's actually not that easy to reach out to people when you need to talk about something and organize a hang," Nat explains. "Truth is, it's not always that easy to know when you need to talk about something. The nice thing about men's group is that there's a consistency and a structure to fall back on."

The structure is up to each gathering's host, but it generally follows a fairly similar pattern. First, everyone sits in a circle and each guy offers a "goods and news": What's good? What's new? Then the theme is introduced and the whole group discusses it for thirty minutes or so. Then people pair up and each person has ten minutes to talk about what's coming up for him related to that theme. Importantly, when it's one guy's turn to talk, the other guy simply listens—no advice, no interjection; if the talker doesn't feel he has anything else to offer but the ten minutes aren't up, the pair sits in silence. Then the whole group gets back together to talk until the conversation finds its natural end.

What might sound like a surprisingly rigid schedule for a Wednesday night of dudes and beers is exactly the point. "Men have a hard time talking about these issues with other men," Nat explains. "The point of the structure is to help facilitate that."

As I listen to Nat describing his men's group, I start thinking about some of my best guy friends and how much they would benefit from an experience like this. You probably know the type: the wickedly smart, good-hearted guys who spend their time together alternating among deconstructing the latest HBO series, busting each other's balls, and coming up with the most ridiculous puns they can think of. They're not bros, but they're also not women's studies majors. They would die for each other, and yet they rarely talk about the stuff that nearly kills them—feeling lost in their professional lives, breakups, family drama, loneliness. Or if they do, it's in this sort of safe, halfhearted way—an elephant acknowledged and then quickly covered up with a thick blanket of humor. Often while drunk.

I ask Nat about this. Though the vulnerability and intention with which he approaches his life feel exceptional, he also seems like someone who could hang, jump in on the banter, volley a few corny puns. "Some of the people in this group are very jokey, but usually it's taking the piss out of ourselves," he explains. "There are four of us who have a whole series of jokes around calling ourselves the 'new newage'—a boy/hip-hop band. We're basically making fun of ourselves."

But when it comes to the structured time within the group, the new age rap jokes stop. "There's still laughter, but it's understood that this isn't a space to deflect using humor," Nat says. "A number of people really visibly shift gears when group starts. It would be inappropriate to try to make things lighter when the whole point is to sit with the big, serious questions in our lives."

And let's be real: it's not just men who tend to use humor to deflect hard conversations. Some cultural critics, most notably Princeton professor Christy Wampole, have very convincingly argued that a whole generation of "hipsters" has mastered the art of not talking about what's really important because it's an emotional risk they're not willing to take. In a highly controversial article published in *The New York Times* in late 2012, Wampole writes that, for those born in the eighties and nineties, "irony is the primary mode with which daily life is dealt."

The typical self-defensive millennial, according to Wampole, dodges "responsibility for his or her choices, aesthetic and otherwise. To live ironically is to hide in public. It is flagrantly indirect, a form of subterfuge, which means etymologically to 'secretly flee' (subter + fuge)."

But lest you think she's another boomer pointing fingers and lamenting the devolution of the newest, most narcissistic generation, think again. Wampole admits her own collusion in the self-protective irony. She writes in the plural first person: "Somehow, directness has become unbearable to us."

So we might be emotionally safe, not to mention ridiculously mustached and expensively caffeinated, but are we happy? Wampole talks about the biggest losses of such subterfuge: "While we have gained some skill sets (multitasking, [being] technological savvy), other skills have suffered: the art of conversation, the art of looking at people, the art of being seen, the art of being present."[2]

In other words, the most important arts there are. Nat's group is an effort to radically refocus on these neglected skills—at least on every third Wednesday.

And the results can be extraordinary. Nat recalls a moment when animosity developed between two members—a self-described "raging socialist" and a business school student. The latter was convinced that the former judged him; he was sick of feeling like his choices were somehow sullied in the eyes of his fellow group member, a purist and a radical. Instead of doing what guys would usually do, what most of us would usually do (i.e., let the tension fester), the group decided to use it as a test case of the kind of healthy, nonviolent conflict resolution they were trying to cultivate in their own lives.

The two guys sat down across from one another and the rest of the group listened as they revealed the tension and talked about it directly. It turned out that the "raging socialist" actually felt far less judgmental about the business school student's choices than the latter had imagined. They were both able to reflect on the power of dominant institutions. For example, *How does one go to business school—theoretically a place built on the idea of profit as an inherent good—and not lose sight of one's true north?* And, likewise, *How does one stay open to the possibility of transformation in unlikely places?*

An emotional muddiness between two guys—the kind that exists in so many neglected places in all of our lives—was bravely recognized for what it really was: an ethical muddiness that we are all ankle deep in if we care about justice. Through brave and direct communication, these guys became unlikely allies, and the group got a rare chance to witness two humans vulnerably asking one another to be seen more generously, and to be interpreted more gently. If that isn't the opposite of subterfuge, I don't know what is.

## ORDINARY ETHICS

I am one of the 11 percent of Americans alive today who grew up in a secular household.[3] Looking back, I realize that all of my family's answers to why we are here on earth were translated through acts rather than scripts, through action rather than language. I watched the way my parents talked to repairmen who showed up at our house to fix the ancient furnace or asked cab drivers about their countries of origin and I learned to be kind to everyone and curious about everything. I watched my mom bang a sign into our front lawn that said No on 2—homophobic local legislation—and learned to trust my own outrage and to take injustice personally, even when it didn't directly affect me.

There were times when I found the subtlety of our family spirituality frustrating, even anxiety-producing. "What are the answers!?" I practically screamed at different moments of existential crisis in my adolescence. My parents would look back at me—the Catholic-turned-Buddhist and the Episcopalian-turned-feminist/naturalist/humanist—with empathic eyes, but they refused to hand me a rule book. Though they never explicitly said this to me, or to one another for that matter, I think they understood that my frustration was born of a genuine acknowledgment of the complexity of the modern, moral life. I think they'd both had their hearts broken enough to know that, while dogma may be comforting—like bumpers on a bowling alley—the teachings of dogma are too easy to be real. Because the truth is that good people do bad things, and if you peel back enough layers you can find good in "bad" people. And we're all just making it up as we go along.

Even from an early age I had a built-in tendency toward righteousness. I wanted to know that I lived in a world of rights and wrongs—and of course I wanted to be right. The older I get, the more I understand that right and wrong are not actually different topographies, but tectonic plates layered on top of one another underneath the surface. You don't climb the mountain of goodness, stand on top, and revel in your moral superiority—or at least you don't if you're really thinking critically and being honest with yourself about all your myriad fuckups (intentional or otherwise). More likely you take one faithful step after another, ever aware that the ground beneath your feet is shifting—sometimes imperceptibly and sometimes in quakes and rumbles.

Too many religions promise the view from the mountaintop at a time when many people are brave and confused enough to resist the self-satisfaction they might feel at that height, as tempting as it might be. But just because you've rejected the rule book doesn't mean you don't crave to be better. It doesn't mean you don't crave to live a life distinguished by an ever-diminishing gap between what you believe and the choices you make every day, how you make other people feel, what you produce, how you consume. Even those of us who don't believe in a god surely believe in spending our time on earth with grace—but that's a daunting prospect, the kind one shouldn't try to define and act on alone.

In the midst of such moral complexity, the groups described in this chapter are a way of pressing the PAUSE button, a way of bringing us back to ourselves, and to each other. What Courtney, Ruthie, and Nat are all doing—on different days, with different approaches, with different questions—is creating a space where they can explore hard questions alongside smart, kind people they trust. They are deliberately building a container for the existential, inconvenient, long-term questions that otherwise slip through the cracks of overfull lives. This is what anthropologist Veena Das calls "ordinary ethics"—"the vulnerability of everyday life to the facts of our being both embodied creatures and beings who have a life in language."[4]

The luckiest of us get the chance to test out our "ordinary ethics" with family over a particularly good Thanksgiving dinner conversation or in the corner of a dark bar over beer and a sudden rush of revelations and exclamations. But sometimes even these memorable moments of connection and acknowledgment feel over before they've even begun. How do we continue the thread? How do we have difficult, sometimes even frightening conversations? When do we know our friends are down for a "what do you want your funeral to be like" kind of hang?

We are seeking out collective settings, frameworks, and chosen families within which we can be accountable to our evolving ethics of everyday life. Angie Thurston and Casper ter Kuile found that the ten communities they profiled in *How We Gather* all "use secular language while mirroring many of the functions fulfilled by religious community. Examples include fellowship, personal reflection, pilgrimage, aesthetic discipline, liturgy, confession, and worship. Together these groups encourage friendship, promote neighborhood welfare, and spread messages for the betterment of individuals and society."[5]

The gathering is the permission for vulnerability, the invitation for unsolvability. It is a moment when you can realize both how terrifically unique you and also how many of your potent struggles are totally universal. This was, of course, the power of the consciousness-raising groups that so many feminists participated in during the 1970s—seeding massive transformation in America regarding gender. Gathering is a time and a space to be seen and heard beyond your job title or your physical appearance—to be known, at the very best, for your inherent worthiness, replete with so many questions and contradictions. It's a setting for revelation. As novelist Eudora Welty has said, "The events in our lives happen in a sequence in time, but in their significance to ourselves they find their own order: the continuous thread of revelation."

We gather to examine what makes us human—both in its most miraculous aspects and at its most messy. We gather so that we don't lose the thread of what is most difficult and dear.

# conclusion

Well here we are, at the end of this story, which is really just the beginning of yours. Did you see yourself in these pages? Did you see a version of yourself that hasn't yet found the courage or companionship to exist, but that wants to? Do you feel even one iota more convinced that we have the collective power to change structures and systems that no longer serve us?

When we began, I warned you: If you feel like a failure, the good news is that you might just be a success based on standards that you've had a hard time articulating, but have been bravely grappling toward. Or, if you feel like a success, the bad news is that you might be a failure by standards you actually—underneath all the hype—strongly believe in.

Of course, none of us is either a success or a failure. We are each an accumulation of decisions about how we spend our energy and the fruits that come from those decisions. Over the course of writing this book I've realized that I've often mislabeled failures and successes in my own life. For example, a work project that made me a nice chunk of change also forced me to compromise my ethics and work with unaccountable collaborators. The fact that I pushed through it, head down, teeth clenched, was something that I've always held as a victory. Now I realize it was a failure: I chose duty, the deliverable, and money over things that are far less measurable but that are very meaningful—my own sense of integrity, joy, and health. The truth is, sometimes bailing is the most New Better Off thing you can do. It signifies that you're willing to swim in the deep waters of *your* life, of what means success to you, not cling to someone else's definition of what success looks like.

Likewise, I've often found myself leaving fancy writers' events, usually in New York City, with this little puddle of shame in my stomach. Despite having a fairy tale bookselling experience when I was twenty-five (my manuscript went to auction after twelve publishing houses expressed interest), I've not been on *The New York Times* best seller list. I've not appeared on *Oprah*. I don't have the magic dust that the fancy writers also invited to fancy writers' events sprinkle onto their books that makes them hit the Amazon heights.

I know now that I've got a different kind of magic dust. I'm damn good at creating community. When so many other writer-hopefuls in that literary borough of Brooklyn were hunched over their laptops, feeling isolated and dispirited, I said, "Everyone, come over to my house and let's read each other's work and eat pizza."

Before writing this book, I'd never fully internalized how important that instinct in me is, how life-giving, and how life-saving it is. I may never have a best seller, but I will always have the capacity to create community around and among the books I write—and, in the end, that makes me a success by my own standards. The congruence of that—of my values and my actions—is as deeply satisfying as my supposed "success" with the sketchy project described above was dispiriting.

That's the thing about success—or, in the context of this book, the American Dream: it's only satisfying if it's defined by you and influenced most deeply by the people you love and trust. Every era will have its dominant narrative about what a successful American does, likely defined by a strange mix of mortgage rates, television shows, political scandals, and educational trends. It's easy to swallow that narrative whole without inspecting it first, inspecting it constantly.

But the good life is not about easy. It's about rigorous discernment. It's about playful dissent. It's about constantly holding your life up to the light and asking, *Where is the potential for connection and creativity? What can I let go of because it's somebody else's idea of what would make me secure/happy/accomplished? Who are my people and how can I build a life where I am with them more of the time in a less distracted way?*

In these pages I've tried to lay out a perhaps idiosyncratic but at least rich breadth of the areas of life you could, if you chose, examine for neglected opportunity. I've tried to honor the history of how things came to be the way that they are, as well as to point toward the future. I've tried to acknowledge the personal power each of us has to shift the way we relate to the most fundamental of elements: love, money, work, home, faith—but also the unfinished cultural and systemic revolutions that we are a part of.

For example, you don't have a work *slash* life; you do work that is interwoven into the larger context of your life. (Increasingly and refreshingly, that's true of both men and women.) That work will change constantly in this new professional climate. You are the common denominator, so the better you understand your own gifts, and the more you build your own crews of ideal collaborators, the better off you will be. And, meanwhile, be encouraged that a lot of creative people are figuring out how the hell you can get health insurance and a 401k in the process.

Money is not an end. It is a beginning, a tool, a resource (among many). Once you have a critical amount of money that allows you to live the kind of life that makes your heart sing (and this is really such a personal thing), you are better off figuring out how to use your time to do things other than make money. Like make beats, and run up mountains, and visit your grandmother, and paint a neighborhood mural. Like come home before dark, and sit on your porch, and have a beer over Skype with the friend whom you never talk to enough. Like write thank you notes.

Like raise little humans, even if you are a member of the male-identified species who has been socialized to underestimate how fascinating and rewarding that might be. Artist Ann Hamilton says that "labor is a way of knowing." If that's true, and I think it is, then American women, who have done a disproportionate amount of the caretaking for little ones and sick ones and aging ones in this country, have disproportionately benefited from the most profound kind of knowing there is—knowing the human condition. But today, now that American men are beginning to share in the most seemingly mundane of actions—changing diapers, wiping faces, holding hands, braiding hair—they are, in a sense, staking their claim to the full range of human experience.

One of your most precious tools is your attention. This, too, is easy to spend in the wrong places at the wrong times ("wrong" as can only be determined by you). Too many of us still are victims to our cell phones, addicted to the small hits of social media "likes" while starving for a much larger, more satiating kind of human interaction. The good news is that your cell phone isn't in charge; the bad news is that you are. It's on all of us to create rules and rituals for ourselves that help us be more present to the people we love and more in tune with the wanderings of our minds. Yes, we can advocate for designers to create less distracting gadgets, but the buck stops with us.

The other vilified group of inanimate objects that we have somehow imbued with evil intentions is our stuff. Here, too, we have it wrong. Your stuff isn't out to get you, to overwhelm you, to disappoint you. Stuff is servant to statusizing. The more sober we get about the time/stuff equation, and how truly draining it can be on an otherwise lovely life, the more we will take part in all the grand experiments in sharing that are afoot.

Even owning a home doesn't mean you've "made it." It just means you own a home, which may or may not be a good thing depending on how you experience ownership. Drowning in debt is perilous, as is living under the delusion that you should get all of your needs—practical and emotional—met by your immediate family. You can live differently. That might mean setting up informal networks of friends who swap meals and tools and support one another through rough spots. Or it might mean creating formal cohousing communities or shared houses with people who also want to live as if villages, not nuclear families, are the safest bet to stay sane and nurtured.

In truth, the village is not defined by architecture, but by mentality. If you want to live like this with other people, you need not move somewhere special; you need only be intentional about asking them to embrace interdependence with you, and then ritualize that commitment. We often fantasize about the village growing up around us spontaneously, as if frequent reciprocity will magically appear in the cracks of our overscheduled lives. But when we move so fast, we don't see one another well enough to know where the needs are, and when. We struggle to ask for help. Rather than wishing for intentional community, we have to doggedly pursue it. Make it concrete. Make a shared Google calendar. Just make it real, even if you feel earnest and vulnerable.

Creating communities like these, creating community at all, requires shared space and time. It requires a genuine commitment to slowing down, to listening to those around you, to listening to yourself even. That's where our rediscovery of the local comes in. We might feel fancy jet-setting, but our encounters with other people on the go can only add up to so much—whereas our encounters with the people who live near us, and our interest and investment in them, can be deeply edifying. It may not earn us frequent-flyer miles, but it earns us the wisdom that comes from struggling to be from a place, of a place, even when it is complicated. (And it is always complicated.)

And, finally, when the blur of life is clarified by a big, life-changing transition—a new partnership, a big birthday, a birth, a death—we are learning how to pause and experience the moment together, in a way that feels both intertwined with generations past and authentic to the one we are just now experiencing. We are realizing that, just because some of the institutions or doctrines that have historically dictated ritual have been flawed, only fools would forgo the vital meaning of witnessing these moments. It's the honoring, not the authority, that matters.

This all requires a tremendous amount of creativity and fortitude, self-examination and coordination. But it's worth it. It's all we've really got, this one chance to live lives that give us pleasure, that make us proud, that connect us to some of those undying questions that humans ask of themselves and each other when they're muddling through: *What am I for? Why are we here? What matters?*

Toni Morrison once wrote, "There is nothing, believe me, more satisfying, more gratifying than true adulthood. . . . Its achievement is a difficult beauty, an intensely hard won glory, which commercial forces and cultural vapidity should not be permitted to deprive you of."

A difficult beauty. An intensely hard won glory. That's what I wish for you. That's what I wish for myself.

In the midst of economic and political dysfunction and widespread uncertainty, we may, indeed, be insecure. But that insecurity can make us either brittle or supple, depending on how we relate to it. We can turn inward, adopt a psychology of deprivation, lose faith in the changeability of institutions, even lose faith in the changeability of ourselves. Or we can turn outward, adopt a psychology of abundance, cultivate faith in the changeability of institutions based on the rich history of this country, where even the most intractable systems have—at different moments—been profoundly remade. We can believe in our ability to change, to adapt, to create.

The bottom line is this: if you're yearning to work, to care, to live, to gather, to witness in a way that doesn't quite go with the gravitational pull of the typical American Dream, listen to that yearning. Don't call it naïve. Don't banish it to a "someday" purgatory—you know, someday when you're older, richer, when the world is less scary, less volatile.

Be brave enough to listen *now* and seek out your fellow travelers, people who also aren't sure that they buy what the American Dream is selling. Together, you'll constitute a new force—small, but mighty.

As more and more of us do this—quit jobs that make us feel less than human, reject the conditioning that says men aren't nurturing, toss our cell phones in a drawer on the weekend and talk with people face-to-face, gather and hold one another accountable to our dreams—the more all of this will seem inevitable.

I believe it is.

It's who we really are.

# acknowledgments

Thank you to the dear friends and colleagues who gave me feedback on chapters of this book, influenced my thinking in huge, important ways, and/or were just faithful champions along the way: Chris Anderson, David Bornstein, Mia Birdsong, Louise Dunlap, Natalie Foster, Trent Gillis, Brian Jones, Kate Madden Yee, Molly May, Dan Pallotta, Parker Palmer, Dena Simmons, Rachel Simmons, Kelly Stoetzel, Krista Tippett, Ethan Todras-Whitehill, and Kate Torgovnick.

I wrote this book for anyone, but I especially wrote it for you, Courtney Baxter. Thank goodness I said yes to that coffee with a stunningly ethical and creative stranger.

Thank you to Tracy Brown, who first trusted that I had something at twenty-five years old to say. You are my agent, but more than that, you are someone whose way of being in the world I respect deeply.

Stephanie Knapp, thank goodness for your conviction that this book deserved to exist. There is nothing sweeter than writing a book for an editor who is also an authentic reader, not someone who has simply done the market analysis. Other than, perhaps, collaborating with an editor *and a publisher* you adore and respect. Thank you,

Krista Lyons. Thank you to Eva Zimmerman for seeing herself in the book and the book in the world.

I discovered that writing a book while mothering a small being is a whole different ball game. Thank goodness my bench is deep. Thank you to Koay Saechao and Betsy Garcia, in particular, who took such loving care of my Maya while I was typing away. Thank you to Christina Zanfagna and Kate Levitt, for sharing our crazy, fantastic lives and a cabin full of ambition and really good vodka. Thank you to Anna Verghese and Vanessa Valenti, who are not only my best collaborators, but my dearest friends. Thank you to my cohousing community, who help me get closer to the person I want to be in so many small and graceful ways. Thank you to Mugs, who has been just a phone call away for a lifetime.

And thank you, always, always, to my family: the whole clan of Carys, whose loyalty and spirit of service are unmatched; Chris and Mary, who teach me about the awake, artistic life; and my parents, who worked damn hard so that I could question all the security they provided. You two modeled the examined life long before I ever read about it in political theory class.

John, my Chief Domestic Officer, how can I possibly summarize my gratitude? You were this book's first and biggest proponent. And you never wavered. You made it emotionally and logistically possible.

Maya, thanks for reminding me that nothing is as important as stomping around the yard and blowing bubbles and watching Chicken TV at Uncle Rick's. You were the best reason to miss a deadline I've ever had. I'm trying to get wiser about how to live, in large part, for you.

# notes

## INTRODUCTION

1. Andrew Kohut, "What Will Become of America's Kids?," Pew Research Center, Washington, DC (May 12, 2014), www.pewresearch.org/fact-tank /2014/05/12/what-will-become-of-americas-kids, accessed February 21, 2016.
2. Tony Kushner, *Thinking About the Longstanding Problems of Virtue and Happiness: Essays, a Play, Two Poems, and a Prayer* (New York: Theatre Communications Group, 1995), 40.
3. Paul Elie, interview by Krista Tippet, On Being, podcast audio, September 28, 2006, www.onbeing.org/program/faith-fired-literature/transcript/912, accessed February 21, 2016.
4. Sandra L. Colby and Jennifer M. Ortman, "Projections of the Size and Composition of the U.S. Population: 2014 to 2060," *Current Population Reports*, P25-1143, U.S. Census Bureau (Washington, DC, 2014), www .census.gov/content/dam/Census/library/publications/2015/demo /p25-1143.pdf, accessed February 22, 2016.
5. "America's Changing Religious Landscape," Pew Research Center, Washington, DC (May 12, 2015), www.pewforum.org/files/2015/05 /RLS-08-26-full-report.pdf, accessed February 21, 2016.

## *HOW* DO YOU WANT TO BE?

1. Gillian Tett, *The Silo Effect: The Peril of Expertise and the Promise of Breaking Down Barriers* (New York: Simon & Schuster, 2015).

2. U.S. Department of Labor, Bureau of Labor Statistics, "Employee Tenure in 2014," September 18, 2014, www.bls.gov/news.release/pdf/tenure.pdf, accessed February 21, 2016.

3. Julie L. Hotchkiss and Christopher J. Macpherson, "Falling Job Tenure: It's Not Just About Millennials," The Federal Reserve Bank of Atlanta, June 8, 2015, http://macroblog.typepad.com/macroblog/2015/06/falling -job-tenure-its-not-just-about-millennials.html, accessed February 21, 2016.

4. Anya Kamenetz, "The Four Year Career," Fast Company, January 12, 2012, www.fastcompany.com/1802731/four-year-career, accessed February 21, 2016.

5. Administration on Aging, Administration for Community Living, U.S. Department of Health and Human Services, "A Profile of Older Americans: 2014," www.aoa.acl.gov/Aging_Statistics/Profile/2014 /docs/2014-Profile.pdf, accessed February 21, 2016.

6. U.S. Department of Labor, Bureau of Labor Statistics, "May 2014 State Occupational Employment and Wage Estimates, California," www.bls .gov/oes/current/oes_ca.htm, accessed February 21, 2016.

7. Michael Greenstone, Adam Looney, Jeremy Patashnik, and Muxin Yu, "Thirteen Economic Facts About Social Mobility and the Role of Education," The Hamilton Project (Washington, DC: The Brookings Institution, June 2013), www.brookings.edu/research/reports/2013/06 /13-facts-higher-education, accessed February 21, 2016.

8. Julia B. Isaacs and Isabel V. Sawhill, "Reaching for the Prize: The Limits On Economic Mobility," *The Milken Institute Review* (Washington, DC: The Brookings Institution, 2008), www.brookings.edu/research /papers/2008/10/winter-economic-mobility-isaacs-sawhill, accessed February 21, 2016.

9. Richard Florida, *The Great Reset: How the Post-Crash Economy Will Change the Way We Live and Work* (New York: Harper Collins, 2010, 22).

10. Lawson Wulsin, Toni Alterman, P. Timothy Bushnell, Jia Li, Rui Shen, "Prevalence Rates for Depression by Industry: A Claims Database Analysis," *Social Psychiatry and Psychiatric Epidemiology* 49, no. 11 (November 2014): 1805–1821, http://dx.doi.org/10.1007/s00127-014-0891-3.

11. Matthew B. Crawford, *Shop Class as Soulcraft: An Inquiry into the Value of Work* (New York: Penguin, 2009), 9.

12. Rebecca Seguin, David M. Buchner, Jingmin Liu, Matthew Allison, Todd Manini, Ching-Yun Wang, JoAnn E. Manson, Catherine R. Messina, Mahesh J. Patel, Larry Moreland, Marcia L. Stefanick, and Andrea Z. LaCroix, The Women's Health Initiative, "Sedentary Behavior and

Mortality in Older Women," *American Journal of Preventative Medicine* 46, no. 2 (February 2014): 122–135, http://dx.doi.org/10.1016 /j.amepre.2013.10.021.

13. Rogelio Saenz and Louwanda Evans, "The Changing Demography of U.S. Flight Attendants," Population Reference Bureau, June 2009, www .prb.org/Publications/Articles/2009/usflightattendants.aspx, accessed February 21, 2016.

14. Mark Hansen, "As Law School Enrollment Drops, Experts Disagree on Whether the Bottom Is In Sight," *ABA Journal*, March 1, 2015, www .abajournal.com/magazine/article/as_law_school_enrollment_drops_ experts_disagree_on_whether_the_bottom, accessed February 21, 2016.

15. Jim Saska, "You Can Do Anything with a Law Degree," *Slate*, May 14, 2014, www.slate.com/articles/life/culturebox/2014/05/you_can_do_ anything_with_a_law_degree_no_no_you_cannot.html, accessed February 21, 2016.

16. "Public Esteem for Military Still High," Pew Research Center, Washington, DC (July 11, 2013), www.pewforum.org/2013/07/11/public-esteem-for-military-still-high, accessed February 21, 2016.

17. American Academy of Arts & Science, Academy Data Forum, "Danger Signs for the Academic Job Market in Humanities?," www.amacad.org/content /research/dataForumEssay.aspx?i=21673, accessed February 21, 2016.

18. Patrick Iber, "(Probably) Refusing to Quit," *Inside Higher Ed*, March 10, 2014, www.insidehighered.com/advice/2014/03/10/essay-about-inability-find-tenure-track-job-academe?utm_source=slate&utm_ medium=referral&utm_term=partner, accessed February 21, 2016.

# WORKING ALONE, TOGETHER

1. Adam Grant, "Friends at Work? Not So Much," *The New York Times*, September 4, 2015, www.nytimes.com/2015/09/06/opinion/sunday /adam-grant-friends-at-work-not-so-much.html?_r=1, accessed February 21, 2016.

2. U.S. Government Accountability Office, "Contingent Workforce: Size, Characteristics, Earnings, and Benefits," April 20, 2015, www.gao.gov /products/GAO-15-168R, accessed February 21, 2016.

3. Sheryl Jean, "Contingent Workers Might Be the 'New Normal' Workforce," *The Dallas Morning News*, August 4, 2012, www.dallasnews.com /business/headlines/20120804-contingent-workers-might-be-the-new-normal-workforce.ece, accessed February 21, 2016.

4. Janet H. Marler and George T. Milkovich, "Determinants of Preference for

Contingent Employment" (CAHRS Working Paper #00-03), Ithaca, NY: Cornell University, School of Industrial and Labor Relations, Center for Advanced Human Resource Studies, January 2000, http://digitalcommons.ilr.cornell.edu/cahrswp/82, accessed February 21, 2016.

5. Edelman Berland, "Freelancing in America: A National Survey of the New Workforce," September 4, 2014, http://fu-web-storage-prod .s3.amazonaws.com/content/filer_public/c2/06/c2065a8a-7f00-46db-915a-2122965df7d9/fu_freelancinginamericareport_v3-rgb.pdf, accessed February 21, 2016.

6. Global Workplace Analytics, "Latest Telecommuting Statistics," September 29, 2015, http://globalworkplaceanalytics.com /telecommuting-statistics, accessed February 21, 2016.

7. Carsten Foertsch, "The Coworking Forecast 2014," *Deskmag*, January 1, 2014, www.deskmag.com/en/the-coworking-market-report-forecast-2014, accessed February 21, 2016.

8. David Gelles, "At WeWork, an Idealistic Start-Up Clashes with Its Cleaners," *The New York Times*, September 10, 2015, www.nytimes .com/2015/09/13/business/at-wework-an-idealistic-startup-clashes-with-its-cleaners.html?_r=0, accessed February 21, 2016.

9. "Coworking Manifesto (Global—For the World)," The Coworking Wiki, last modified October 6, 2015, wiki.coworking.com/w/page/35382594 /Coworking%20Manifesto%20%28global%20-%20for%20the%20 world%29, accessed February 21, 2016.

10. Gretchen Spreitzer, Peter Bacevice, and Lyndon Garrett, "Why People Thrive in Coworking Spaces," *Harvard Business Review*, September 2015, https://hbr.org/2015/05/why-people-thrive-in-coworking-spaces, accessed February 21, 2016.

11. Mark S. Granovetter, "The Strength of Weak Ties," *American Journal of Sociology* 78, no. 6 (May 1973): 1360–1380, www.jstor.org/stable/2776392.

12. Margaret Wheatley, *Turning to One Another: Simple Conversations That Restore Hope in the Future* (San Francisco: Berrett-Koehler, 2002), 145.

13. Ann Friedman, "Shine Theory: Why Powerful Women Make the Greatest Friends," *New York Magazine*, May 31, 2013, http://nymag.com /thecut/2013/05/shine-theory-how-to-stop-female-competition.html, accessed February 21, 2016.

14. Edelman Berland, "Freelancing in America" (see note 5).

# NORMA RAE FOR A NEW CENTURY

1. Erik Ortiz, "Where Did the 40-Hour Workweek Come From?," NBC News, September 1, 2014, www.nbcnews.com/news/us-news/where-did-40-hour-workweek-come-n192276, accessed February 21, 2016.

2. Bella DePaulo, *How We Live Now: Redefining Home and Family in the 21st Century* (New York: Atria, 2015), 9 (ebook).

3. Will Rinehart and Ben Gitis, "Independent Contractors and the Emerging Gig Economy," American Action Forum, July 29, 2015, http://americanactionforum.org/research/independent-contractors-and-the-emerging-gig-economy, accessed February 21, 2016.

4. Intuit, Inc., "Intuit 2020 Report: Twenty Trends That Will Shape the Next Decade," October 2010, http://http-download.intuit.com/http.intuit/CMO/intuit/futureofsmallbusiness/intuit_2020_report.pdf, accessed February 24, 2016.

5. Sarah Kessler, "The Gig Economy Won't Last Because It's Being Sued to Death," *Fast Company*, February 17, 2015, www.fastcompany.com/3042248/the-gig-economy-wont-last-because-its-being-sued-to-death, accessed February 21, 2016.

6. Harold Meyerson, "The Seeds of a New Labor Movement," *The American Prospect*, Fall 2014.

7. Allison Schrager, "The Gig Economy Is Only Good for Some Workers—But It Doesn't Need to Be That Way," Quartz, August 21, 2015, http://qz.com/477270/the-gig-economy-is-only-good-for-some-workers-but-it-doesnt-need-to-be-that-way, accessed February 21, 2016.

8. Coworker.org, "Why Workplace Democracy Matters," http://about.coworker.org/why-workplace-democracy-matters, accessed February 21, 2016.

9. Steven Melendez, "Contratados: A Yelp to Help Migrant Workers Fight Fraud," *Fast Company*, October 9, 2014, www.fastcolabs.com/welcome.html?destination=http://www.fastcolabs.com/3036812/contratados-is-a-yelp-that-fights-fraud-for-migrant-workers, accessed February 21, 2016.

10. George Packer, "Change the World," The New Yorker, May 27, 2013, www.newyorker.com/magazine/2013/05/27/change-the-world, accessed February 21, 2016.

11. Jeremy Heimans and Henry Timms, "Understanding 'New Power,'" *Harvard Business Review*, December 2014, https://hbr.org/2014/12/understanding-new-power, accessed February 21, 2016.

12. Jana Kasperkevic, "Census Data Shows Obamacare and Welfare Kept Millions out of Poverty," *The Guardian*, September 17, 2015, www.the

guardian.com/us-news/2015/sep/17/census-data-obamacare-welfare-poverty, accessed February 21, 2016.

13. Paul Krugman, "Hooray for Obamacare," *The New York Times*, June 25, 2015, www.nytimes.com/2015/06/26/opinion/paul-krugman-hooray-for-the-aca.html, accessed February 21, 2016.

14. Chris Klint and Sean Doogan, "$2,072: 2015 Alaska Permanent Fund Dividend Amount Announced," *Alaska Dispatch News*, September 21, 2015, www.adn.com/article/20150921/2072-2015-alaska-permanent-fund-dividend-amount-announced, accessed February 21, 2016.

15. Danny Vinik, "Everyone's Talking About This Simple Solution to Ending Poverty by Just Giving People Free Money," *Business Insider*, November 12, 2013, www.businessinsider.com/giving-all-americans-a-basic-income-would-end-poverty-2013-11, accessed February 21, 2016.

16. Annie Lowery, "Switzerland's Proposal to Pay People for Being Alive," *The New York Times*, November 12, 2013, www.nytimes.com/2013/11/17/magazine/switzerlands-proposal-to-pay-people-for-being-alive.html?pagewanted=1&ref=annielowrey, accessed February 21, 2016.

17. Douglas MacMillan, "Sharing Economy Workers Need 'Safety Net,' U.S. Senator Says," *The Wall Street Journal*, June 8, 2015, http://blogs.wsj.com/digits/2015/06/08/sharing-economy-workers-need-government-safety-net-u-s-senator-says, accessed February 21, 2016.

18. "Airbnb: How the Sharing Economy Is Redefining the Marketplace and Our Sense of Community," Aspen Ideas Festival 2014, video 1:01:28, www.aspenideas.org/session/airbnb-how-sharing-economy-redefining-marketplace-and-our-sense-of-community, accessed February 21, 2016.

19. Nick Hanauer and David Rolf, "Shared Security, Shared Growth," *Democracy: A Journal of Ideas*, no. 37 (Summer 2015), http://democracyjournal.org/magazine/37/shared-security-shared-growth/?page=all, accessed February 21, 2016.

## THE WISDOM OF ENOUGH

1. Anat Shenker-Osorio, "Why Americans All Believe They Are 'Middle Class,'" *The Atlantic*, August 1, 2013, www.theatlantic.com/politics/archive/2013/08/why-americans-all-believe-they-are-middle-class/278240, accessed February 21, 2016.

2. "Most Say Government Policies Since Recession Have Done Little to Help Middle Class, Poor," Pew Research Center, Washington, DC (March 2015), www.people-press.org/files/2015/03/03-04-15-Economy-release.pdf, accessed February 21, 2016.

3. Patricia Cohen, "Middle Class, but Feeling Economically Insecure," *The New York Times*, April 10, 2015, www.nytimes.com/2015/04/11/business /economy/middle-class-but-feeling-economically-insecure.html, accessed February 21, 2016.

4. Ibid.

5. David U. Himmelstein, Deborah Thorne, Elizabeth Warren, and Steffie Woolhandler, "Medical Bankruptcy in the United States, 2007: Results of a National Study," *American Journal of Medicine*, http://dx.doi.org/10.1016 /j.amjmed.2009.04.012.

6. Carmen DeNavas-Walt and Bernadette D. Proctor, U.S. Census Bureau, Current Population Reports, P60-249, "Income and Poverty in the United States: 2013," U.S. Government Printing Office, Washington, DC, 2014, www.census.gov/content/dam/Census/library/publications/2014/demo /p60-249.pdf, accessed February 21, 2016.

7. The Pew Charitable Trusts, "The Complex Story of American Debt, Liabilities in Family Balance Sheets," July 29, 2015, www.pewtrusts.org /en/research-and-analysis/reports/2015/07/the-complex-story-of-american-debt, accessed February 21, 2016.

8. Erin El Issa, "2015 American Household Credit Card Debt Study," NerdWallet, www.nerdwallet.com/blog/credit-card-data/average-credit-card-debt-household, accessed February 21, 2016.

9. U.S. Department of Labor, Bureau of Labor Statistics, "American Time Use Survey—2013 Results," www.bls.gov/news.release/archives /atus_06182014.pdf, accessed February 21, 2016.

10. Jordan Weissmann, "Americans, Ever Hateful of Leisure, Are More Likely to Work Nights and Weekends," *Slate*, September 11, 2014, www.slate.com/blogs /moneybox/2014/09/11/u_s_work_life_balance_americans_are_more_ likely_to_work_nights_and_weekends.html, accessed February 21, 2016.

11. Joe Lazauskas, "Why We're So Obsessed with Amazon's Work Culture," *Fast Company*, August 21, 2015, www.fastcompany.com/3050125/why-were-so-obsessed-with-amazons-work-culture, accessed February 21, 2016.

12. John Pencavel, "The Productivity of Working Hours," Forschungsinstitut zur Zukunft der Arbeit/Institute for the Study of Labor, April 2014, http:// ftp.iza.org/dp8129.pdf, accessed February 21, 2016.

13. William D. Cohan, "Deaths Draw Attention to Wall Street's Grueling Pace," *The New York Times*, October 3, 2015, www.nytimes.com/2015/10/04 /business/dealbook/tragedies-draw-attention-to-wall-streets-grueling-pace.html, accessed February 21, 2016.

14. Daniel Kahneman and Angus Deaton, "High Income Improves Evaluation of Life but Not Emotional Well-Being," *Proceedings of the National Academy of Sciences in the United States of America* 107, no. 38 (September 21, 2010): 16489–16493, http://dx.doi.org/10.1073/pnas.1011492107.

15. Melanie Pinola, "The 'Perfect' Salary for Happiness by State," Lifehacker, July 15, 2014, http://lifehacker.com/the-perfect-salary-for-happiness-by-state-1605278164, accessed February 21, 2016.

16. DeNavas-Walt and Proctor, "Income and Poverty in the United States: 2013" (see note 6).

## FIGHTING TO BE WHOLE

1. Carmen Solomon-Fears, "Nonmarital Births: An Overview," Congressional Research Service, Prepared for Members and Committees of Congress, July 30, 2014, http://fas.org/sgp/crs/misc/R43667.pdf, accessed February 21, 2016.

2. Gary J. Gates, "LGBT Parenting in the United States," The Williams Institute, February 2013, http://williamsinstitute.law.ucla.edu/wp-content/uploads/LGBT-Parenting.pdf, accessed February 21, 2016.

3. Elizabeth Lesser, "Women/Men: The Next Conversation," Omega Institute's 2014 Women & Power Conference, www.elizabethlesser.org/keynote-speech-at-omega-institutes-2014-women-power-conferencewomenmen-the-next-conversation, accessed February 21, 2016.

4. Tom Stocky, Facebook post, July 7, 2013, www.facebook.com/tstocky/posts/996111776858, accessed February 21, 2016.

5. Kim Parker and Wendy Wang, "Modern Parenthood: Roles of Moms and Dads Converge as They Balance Work and Family," Pew Research Center, Washington, DC (March 14, 2013), www.pewsocialtrends.org/2013/03/14/modern-parenthood-roles-of-moms-and-dads-converge-as-they-balance-work-and-family, accessed February 21, 2016.

6. Peter Mountford, "I'm Not a Hero for Taking Care of My Kids," *Slate*, July 10, 2013, www.slate.com/articles/life/family/2013/07/life_as_a_stay_at_home_dad_everyone_i_meet_calls_me_a_hero_for_taking_care.html, accessed February 21, 2016.

7. James Norton. "I'm a Dad, Not a Hero: Thoughts on Tom Stocky's Facebook Post," *The Christian Science Monitor*, July 12, 2013, www.csmonitor.com/The-Culture/Family/Modern-Parenthood/2013/0712/I-m-a-dad-not-a-hero-Thoughts-on-Tom-Stocky-s-Facebook-post, accessed February 21, 2016.

8. Judith Walzer Leavitt, *Make Room for Daddy: The Journey from Waiting Room*

*to Birthing Room* (Chapel Hill: The University of North Carolina Press, 2009), 285.

9. Clarissa Pinkola Estés, *Women Who Run with the Wolves: Myths and Stories of the Wild Woman Archetype* (New York: Ballantine Books, 1996), 116.

10. Stephen Marche, "Manifesto of the New Fatherhood," *Esquire,* June 13, 2014, www.esquire.com/lifestyle/news/a28987/manifesto-of-the-new -fatherhood-0614, accessed February 21, 2016.

11. Eyal Abrahama, Talma Hendler, Irit Shapira-Lichter, Yaniv Kanat-Maymon, Orna Zagoory-Sharon, and Ruth Feldman, "Father's Brain Is Sensitive to Childcare Experiences," *Proceedings of the National Academy of Sciences* 111, no. 27 (July 8, 2014): 9792–9797, http://dx.doi.org/10.1073/pnas.

12. Robin S. Edelstein and Britney M. Wardecker, "Prenatal Hormones in First-Time Expectant Parents: Longitudinal Changes and Within-Couple Correlations," *American Journal of Human Biology* 27, no. 3 (May/June 2015): 317–325, http://dx.doi.org/10.1002/ajhb.22670.

13. Margaret Talbot, "America's Family-Leave Disgrace," *The New Yorker,* January 22, 2015, www.newyorker.com/news/daily-comment/paid-family- leave-obama-work, accessed February 21, 2016.

14. Alexis C. Madrigal, "On Becoming a Father," *The Atlantic,* September 6, 2013, www.theatlantic.com/technology/archive/2013/09/on-becoming- a-father/279435, accessed February 21, 2016.

15. J.B. Stykes, "Fatherhood in the U.S.: Men's Age at First Birth, 1987–2010 (FP-11-04)," National Center for Family & Marriage Research, 2011, www .bgsu.edu/content/dam/BGSU/college-of-arts-and-sciences/NCFMR/ documents/FP/FP-11-04.pdf, accessed February 21, 2016.

16. "Work-Life Balance and the Economics of Workplace Flexibility," A Report from the Council of Economic Advisers, White House Forum on Workplace Flexibility, March 2010, www.whitehouse.gov/files/documents/100331- cea-economics-workplace-flexibility.pdf, accessed February 21, 2016.

17. Pamela Stone, "Bravo to Sheryl Sandberg for Leaving Work at 5:30," CNN, April 17, 2012, www.cnn.com/2012/04/16/opinion/stone-leave-work-day, accessed February 21, 2016.

18. Max Schireson, "Why I'm Leaving the Best Job I Ever Had," Max Schierson's Blog, August 5, 2014, http://maxschireson.com/2014/08/05 /1137, accessed February 21, 2016.

19. Andrew Moravcsik, "Why I Put My Wife's Career First," *The Atlantic,* October 2015, www.theatlantic.com/magazine/archive/2015/10/why-i- put-my-wifes-career-first/403240, accessed February 21, 2016.

20. Gretchen Livingston, "Growing Number of Dads at Home with the Kids,"

Pew Research Center, Washington, DC (June 5, 2014), www.pewsocial
trends.org/2014/06/05/growing-number-of-dads-home-with-the-kids,
accessed February 21, 2016.

21. Emily Alpert Reyes, "Survey Finds Dads Defy Stereotypes About Black
Fatherhood," *The Los Angeles Times*, December 20, 2013, http://articles
.latimes.com/2013/dec/20/local/la-me-black-dads-20131221, accessed
February 21, 2016.

22. Susie Armitage, "Tech Companies Offer Workers Most Paid Parental
Leave," BuzzFeed, August 25, 2014, http://www.buzzfeed.com/
susiearmitage/tech-companies-offer-workers-the-most-paid-parental-
leave%23.es6NVY4o6#.gxngaYaNo, accessed February 21, 2016.

23. Gretchen Gavett, "Brave Men Take Paternity Leave," *Harvard Business
Review*, July 7, 2014, accessed February 21, 2016.

24. "Bain & Company Named 100 Best Company by Working Mother," Bain
& Company, September 22, 2011, www.bain.com/about/press/press-
releases/bain-and-company-named-100-best-company-by-working-
mother.aspx, accessed February 21, 2016.

25. "Morningstar Benefits for U.S. Employees," Morningstar, Inc., http://cor
porate1.morningstar.com/us/Careers/Benefits, accessed February 21, 2016.

26. Robert W. Van Giezen, "Paid Leave in Private Industry over the Past
20 Years," *Beyond the Numbers: Pay & Benefits* 2, no. 18 (U.S. Department
of Labor, Bureau of Labor Statistics, August 2013), www.bls.gov/opub/
btn/volume-2/paid-leave-in-private-industry-over-the-past-20-years.htm,
accessed February 21, 2016.

27. Brigid Schulte, "Voters Want Paid Leave, Paid Sick Days, Poll Shows.
Obama, Too. Will Congress Oblige?," *The Washington Post*, January 21,
2015, www.washingtonpost.com/news/local/wp/2015/01/21/voters-want-
paid-leave-paid-sick-days-poll-shows-obama-too-will-congress-oblige,
accessed February 21, 2016.

28. Natalie Angier, "The Changing American Family," *The New York Times*,
November 25, 2013, www.nytimes.com/2013/11/26/health/families
.html?pagewanted=all&_r=0, accessed February 21, 2016.

29. Nicole Sussner Rodgers, "Marriage Is Not Safeguard Against Poverty,"
*The Washington Post*, March 20, 2015, www.washingtonpost.com/opinions/
seeking-a-broader-vision-of-family/2015/03/20/e343bcf2-c906-11e4-
aa1a-86135599fb0f_story.html, accessed February 21, 2016.

# HARNESSING THE WIND

1. Daniel J. Levitin, *The Organized Mind: Thinking Straight in the Age of Information Overload* (New York: Dutton, 2014), 6, ebook.

2. Virginia Heffernan, "Should We Stay or Should We Go?," *The New York Times Magazine*, February 18, 2015, www.nytimes.com/2015/02/22/magazine/should-we-stay-or-should-we-go.html?_r=0, accessed February 21, 2016.

3. William James, *The Principles of Psychology* (New York: Henry Holt and Company, 1890), chapter 11: "Attention," 403–404.

4. Levitin, *The Organized Mind* (see note 1).

5. Edward M. Hallowell, *CrazyBusy: Overstretched, Overbooked, and About to Snap! Strategies for Coping in a World Gone ADD* (New York: Ballantine, 2007), 18.

6. Levitin, *The Organized Mind* (see note 1).

7. Ibid.

8. Allison Daminger, Jonathan Hayes, Anthony Barrows, and Josh Wright, "Poverty Interrupted: Combatting Intergenerational Poverty with Behavioral Economics," Ideas42, May 2015, www.ideas42.org/wp-content/uploads/2015/05/I42_PovertyWhitePaper_Digital_FINAL-1.pdf, accessed February 21, 2016.

9. Sendhil Mullainathan and Eldar Shafir, *Scarcity: The New Science of Having Less and How It Defines Our Lives* (New York: Picador, 2014), 29.

10. Ibid., 41.

11. "Cell Phone Ownership Hits 91% of Adults," Pew Research Center, Internet & American Life Project, Washington, DC (June 6, 2013), www.pewresearch.org/fact-tank/2013/06/06/cell-phone-ownership-hits-91-of-adults, accessed February 21, 2016.

12. Mary Meeker and Liang Wu, "2013 Internet Trends," Kleiner Perkins Caufield Byers, May 29, 2013, www.kpcb.com/blog/2013-internet-trends, accessed February 21, 2016.

13. Sherry Turkle, *Alone Together: Why We Expect More from Technology and Less from Each Other* (New York: Basic Books, 2012).

14. Andy Isaacson, "Learning to Let Go: First, Turn Off the Phone," *The New York Times*, December 14, 2012, www.nytimes.com/2012/12/16/fashion/teaching-people-to-live-without-digital-devices.html?pagewanted=all&_r=0, accessed February 21, 2016.

15. Tiffany Shlain & The Moxie Institute Films, *Yelp: With Apologies to Allen Ginsberg's "Howl,"* YouTube video, 2:50, February 17, 2011, www.youtube.com/watch?v=UowVsL3dXjM, accessed February 21, 2016.

16. Andreas Elpidorou, "The Bright Side of Boredom," *Frontiers in Psychology* 5 (November 3, 2014): 1245, http://dx.doi.org/10.3389/fpsyg.2014.01245.

17. "The Case for Boredom," *Note to Self*, WNYC, podcast audio, January 12, 2015, www.wnyc.org/story/bored-brilliant-project-part-1, accessed February 21, 2016.

18. Shaunacy Ferro, Twitter post, February 4, 2015, 10:10 AM, https://twitter.com/shaunacysays/status/563036898739126272, accessed February 21, 2016.

19. Charlotte Donlon, Twitter post, February 4, 2015, 12:24 PM, https://twitter.com/charlottedonlon/status/563070731719041025, accessed February 21, 2016.

20. Nate Bennett, Twitter post, February 4, 2015, 6:48 AM, https://twitter.com/itsnatebennett/status/562986122322907136?ref_src=twsrc%5Etfw, accessed February 21, 2016.

21. Daniel J. Levitin, *The Organized Mind* (see note 1).

## THE END OF "MINE"

1. Burt Helm, "Airbnb Is Inc.'s 2014 Company of the Year," Inc., December 2014/January 2015, www.inc.com/magazine/201412/burt-helm/airbnb-company-of-the-year-2014.html, accessed February 21, 2016.

2. Lisa Gansky, *The Mesh: Why the Future of Business Is Sharing* (New York: Portfolio), 2010.

3. Lawrence D. Burns, William C. Jordan, and Bonnie A. Scarborough, "Transforming Personal Mobility," The Earth Institute, Columbia University, January 27, 2013, http://sustainablemobility.ei.columbia.edu/files/2012/12/Transforming-Personal-Mobility-Jan-27-20132.pdf, accessed February 21, 2016.

4. Lisa Gansky, *The Future of Business Is the 'Mesh,'* filmed January 2011, TED video, 14:47, www.ted.com/talks/lisa_gansky_the_future_of_business_is_the_mesh?language=en, accessed February 21, 2016.

5. Ariel Schwartz, "The Collaborative Economy Is Exploding, and Brands That Ignore It Are Out of Luck," FastCo.Exist, March 3, 2014, www.fastcoexist.com/3027062/the-collaborative-economy-is-exploding-and-brands-that-ignore-it-are-out-of-luck, accessed February 21, 2016.

6. Nielsen, "Is Sharing the New Buying?," May 28, 2014, www.nielsen.com/us/en/insights/news/2014/is-sharing-the-new-buying.html, accessed February 21, 2016.

7. Jon Mooallem, "The Self-Storage Self," *The New York Times Magazine*, September 2, 2009, www.nytimes.com/2009/09/06/

magazine/06self-storage-t.html?_r=1&scp=1&sq=the%2520self-storage%2520self&st=cse, accessed February 21, 2016.

8. Amitai Etzioni, "The Socio-Economics of Property," *Journal of Social Behavior and Personality* 1 (1986): 475–482, www.gwu.edu/~ccps/etzioni/A208.pdf, accessed February 21, 2016.

9. Dacher Keltner, *Born to Be Good: The Science of a Meaningful Life* (New York: Norton, 2009), 54.

10. Mukhisa Kituyi, *Becoming Kenyans: Socio-Economic Transformation of the Pastoral Maasai*, Drylands Research Series (Nairobi: Acts Press, 1990).

11. Jon L. Pierce, Tatiana Kostova, and Kurt T. Dirks, "The State of Psychological Ownership: Integrating and Extending a Century of Research," *Review of General Psychology* 7, no. 1 (March 2003): 84–107, http://dx.doi.org/10.1037/1089-2680.7.1.84. Also http://apps.olin.wustl.edu/faculty/dirks/Psychological%20Ownership%20-%20RGP.pdf, accessed February 21, 2016.

12. Jean-Paul Sartre, *Being and Nothingness: An Essay on Phenomenological Ontology* (Paris: Gallimard, 1943).

13. Kate Abnett, "Do Fashion Trends Still Exist?" The Business of Fashion, January 9, 2015, www.businessoffashion.com/articles/intelligence/fashion-trends-still-exist, accessed February 22, 2016.

14. Elisabeth Rosenthal, "The End of Car Culture," *The New York Times*, June 29, 2013, www.nytimes.com/2013/06/30/sunday-review/the-end-of-car-culture.html, accessed February 22, 2016.

15. Michael Sivak, "Has Motorization in the U.S. Peaked? Part 3: Fuel Consumed by Light-Duty Vehicles," The University of Michigan Transportation Research Institute, Report No. UMTRI-2013-40, November 2013, http://deepblue.lib.umich.edu/bitstream/handle/2027.42/100360/102974.pdf, accessed February 23, 2016.

16. Joe Cortright, "Young People Are Buying Fewer Cars," CityCommentary, April 22, 2015, http://cityobservatory.org/young-people-are-buying-fewer-cars, accessed February 22, 2016.

17. "Auto Bailout Now Backed, Stimulus Divisive," Pew Research Center, Washington, DC (February 23, 2012), www.people-press.org/2012/02/23/auto-bailout-now-backed-stimulus-divisive/?src=prc-headline, accessed February 22, 2016.

18. Brandon Schoettle and Michael Sivak, "The Reasons for the Recent Decline in Young Driver Licensing in the U.S.," The University of Michigan Transportation Research Institute, Report No. UMTRI-2013-22, August 2013,

http://deepblue.lib.umich.edu/bitstream/handle/2027.42/99124/102951
.pdf?sequence=1, accessed February 23, 2016.

19. James Hamblin, "A Brewing Problem," *The Atlantic*, March 2, 2015, www
.theatlantic.com/technology/archive/2015/03/the-abominable-k-cup-
coffee-pod-environment-problem/386501/?utm_source=nextdraft&
utm_medium=email, accessed February 22, 2016.

20. Graham Hill, "Living with Less. A Lot Less.," *The New York Times*, March 9,
2013, www.nytimes.com/2013/03/10/opinion/sunday/living-with-less-a-lot-
less.html?pagewanted=all&_r=2&, accessed February 22, 2016.

21. Jeanne E. Arnold, Anthony P. Graesch, Enzo Ragazzini, and Elinor Ochs,
*Life at Home in the Twenty-First Century: 32 Families Open Their Doors* (Los
Angeles: Cotsen Institute of Archaeology Press, 2012).

22. Ibid.

23. See, for example, D. Marcinko and D. Karlovi, "Oniomania—Successful
Treatment with Fluvoxamine and Cognitive-Behavioral Psychotherapy,"
*Psychiatria Danubina*, June 17 2015 (1–2): 97–100.

24. U.S. Department of Labor, Bureau of Labor Statistics, BLS Reports,
Report 1053, "Consumer Expenditures in 2013" (February 2015), www.bls
.gov/cex/csxann13.pdf, accessed February 22, 2016.

25. Blake Morgan, "NOwnership, No Problem: Why Millennials Value
Experiences over Owning Things," *Forbes*, June 1, 2015, www.forbes.com/
sites/blakemorgan/2015/06/01/nownershipnoproblem-nowners-
millennials-value-experiences-over-ownership/#18076a151759, accessed
February 22, 2016.

26. James Hamblin, "Buy Experiences, Not Things," *The Atlantic*, October 7,
2014, www.theatlantic.com/business/archive/2014/10/buy-experiences
/381132, accessed February 22, 2016.

27. Thomas J. Sugrue, "The New American Dream: Renting," *The Wall Street
Journal*, August 14, 2009, www.wsj.com/articles/SB1000142405297020440
9904574350432677038184, accessed February 22, 2016.

28. Ibid.

29. Dalton Conley, "Race: The Power of an Illusion," California Newsreel,
PBS, www.pbs.org/race/000_About/002_04-background-03-03.htm,
accessed February 22, 2016.

30. "The End of the Affair: America's Return to Thrift Presages a Long and
Deep Recession," *The Economist*, November 20, 2008, www.economist
.com/node/12637090, accessed February 22, 2016.

31. U.S. Census Bureau, "Residential Vacancies and Homeownership in
the Third Quarter 2015," U.S. Department of Commerce, U.S. Census

Bureau News, CB15-170, October 27, 2015, www.census.gov/housing/hvs/data/q315ind.html.

32. Gillian B. White, "Millennials Who Are Thriving Financially Have One Thing in Common . . . Rich Parents," *The Atlantic*, July 15, 2015, www.theatlantic.com/business/archive/2015/07/millennials-with-rich-parents/398501, accessed February 22, 2016.

33. Jacob Davidson, "What Everyone Gets Wrong About Millennials and Home Buying," *Money*, November 12, 2014, http://time.com/money/3551773/millennials-home-buying-marriage, accessed February 22, 2016.

34. Freddie Mac Multifamily, Multifamily Research Perspectives, "Perceptions of Renting and Homeownership," December 8, 2014, www.freddiemac.com/multifamily/pdf/mf_renter_profile.pdf, accessed February 22, 2016.

## TEARING DOWN THE WHITE PICKET FENCE

1. DePaulo, *How We Live Now*, 28 (see Norma Rae for a New Century, note 2).

2. bell hooks, "Revolutionary Parenting," in *Feminist Theory: From Margin to Center* (Boston: South End Press, 1984).

3. Ibid., 123.

4. Danielle Braff, "Is Communal Living Making a Comeback?," *Crain's*, March 20, 2015, www.chicagobusiness.com/article/20150320/ISSUE03/150329991/is-communal-living-making-a-comeback, accessed February 22, 2016.

5. Constance Rosenblum, "Sun City It's Not," *The New York Times*, February 15, 2013, www.nytimes.com/2013/02/17/realestate/sun-city-its-not-upper-west-side-retirement.html, accessed February 22, 2016.

6. DePaulo, *How We Live Now*, xi (see Norma Rae for a New Century, note 2).

7. Ibid., 88.

8. Claire Thompson, "Cohousing: The Secret to Sustainable Urban Living?," Grist, July 11, 2012, http://grist.org/cities/cohousing-the-secret-to-sustainable-urban-living, accessed February 22, 2016.

9. National Co+op Grocers, "NCG Signs Primary Distribution Agreement with UNFI," August 19, 2015, www.ncg.coop/newsroom/ncg-signs-primary-distribution-agreement-unfi, accessed February 22, 2016.

10. Diane Mehta, "Won't Work for Food," Chowhound, September 28, 2006, www.chowhound.com/food-news/53529/wont-work-for-food, accessed February 22, 2016.

11. Alana Joblin Ain, "Flunking Out at the Food Co-Op," *The New York Times*,

October 23, 2009, www.nytimes.com/2009/10/25/nyregion/25coop
.html?pagewanted=all&_r=0, accessed February 22, 2016.

12. Alex Davis, Andy Remeis, and Diana Ellis, *Dinner at Your Door: Tips and Recipes for Starting a Neighborhood Cooking Co-op* (Layton, UT: Gibbs Smith, 2008), 9.

13. Julie Croteau, "Social Ties Are Good for Your Health," BeWell@Stanford, Stanford University, https://bewell.stanford.edu/features/social-ties-good-health, accessed February 22, 2016.

14. Judith Shulevitz, "The Lethality of Loneliness," *New Republic*, May 12, 2013, accessed February 22, 2016.

15. Deborah Stone, *The Samaritan's Dilemma: Should Government Help Your Neighbor?* (New York: Nation Books, 2008), 29.

16. Andrew Dugan, "Fast Food Still Major Part of U.S. Diet," Gallup, August 6, 2013, www.gallup.com/poll/163868/fast-food-major-part-diet.aspx, accessed February 22, 2016.

17. Esther Perel, *Mating in Captivity: Reconciling the Erotic and the Domestic* (New York: HarperCollins, 2006).

18. Andrew J. Cherlin, Elizabeth Talbert, and Suzumi Yasutake, "Changing Fertility Regimes and the Transition to Adulthood: Evidence from a Recent Cohort," Johns Hopkins University, February 28, 2012, http://krieger.jhu.edu/sociology/wp-content/uploads/sites/28/2012/02/Read-Online.pdf, accessed February 22, 2016.

19. Brady E. Hamilton, Joyce A. Martin, and Stephanie J. Ventura, "Births: Preliminary Data for 2011," *National Vital Statistics Reports* 61, no. 5 (October 3, 2012), National Center for Health Statistics, accessed February 22, 2016.

20. DePaulo, *How We Live Now* (see Norma Rae for a New Century, note 2).

21. Mia Birdsong and Nicole Rodgers, "Another 1 Percent White Privilege: The Invisible Advantage We Need to Discuss Now," Salon, September 23, 2015, www.salon.com/2015/09/23/another_1_percent_white_privilege_the_invisible_advantage_we_need_to_discuss_now, accessed February 22, 2016.

## REGROWING OUR ROOTS

1. Jason Reitman and Sheldon Turner, *Up in the Air*, directed by Jason Reitman (Los Angeles: Paramount Pictures, 2009).

2. George Saunders, *Congratulations, by the Way: Some Thoughts on Kindness* (New York: Random House, 2014).

3. U.S. Securities and Exchange Commission, "Accredited Investors," http://edgar.sec.gov/answers/accred.htm, accessed February 23, 2016.

4. "Moving Your Money," *The Laura Flanders Show*, YouTube video, 25:00, January 27, 2015, www.youtube.com/watch?v=UTqu5BJE6S8, accessed February 23, 2016.

5. Ibid.

6. California Department of Public Health, "Cottage Food Operations: New State Law Effective January 1, 2013," www.cdph.ca.gov/programs/Pages/fdbCottageFood.aspx, accessed February 23, 2016.

7. Duane Elgin, "The Power of Compassion and Story for Building Resilience in Local Living Economies," BALLE, https://bealocalist.org/power-compassion-and-story-building-resilience-local-living-economies, accessed February 23, 2016.

8. Juliana Breines, "Are Some Social Ties Better Than Others?," Greater Good Science Center, University of California, Berkeley, March 11, 2014, http://greatergood.berkeley.edu/article/item/are_some_ties_better_than_others, accessed February 23, 2016.

9. William J. Cromie, "Neighborliness Reduces Violence, Study Finds," *Harvard Gazette*, September 11, 1997, http://news.harvard.edu/gazette/1997/09.11/NeighborlinessR.html, accessed February 23, 2016.

10. Eric Klinenberg, "Adaptation: How Can Cities Be Climate-Proofed?," *The New Yorker*, January 7, 2013, www.newyorker.com/magazine/2013/01/07/adaptation-2, accessed February 23, 2016.

11. David Sloan Wilson, interview by Krista Tippet, "Evolving a City," On Being, podcast audio, October 17, 2013, www.onbeing.org/program/transcript/4726, accessed February 23, 2016.

12. Mike Isaac, "Nextdoor Social Network Digs Deep into Neighborhoods," *The New York Times*, March 3, 2015, http://mobile.nytimes.com/2015/03/04/technology/nextdoor-a-start-up-social-network-digs-deep-into-neighborhoods.html?_r=3&referrer, accessed February 23, 2016.

13. Pendarvis Harshaw, "Nextdoor, the Social Network for Neighbors, Is Becoming a Home for Racial Profiling," *Fusion*, March 24, 2015, www.fusion.net/story/106341/nextdoor-the-social-network-for-neighbors-is-becoming-a-home-for-racial-profiling, accessed February 23, 2016.

14. bell hooks, *Teaching Community: A Pedagogy of Hope* (London: Routledge, 2003), 36.

15. Chinaka Hodge, "The Gentrifier's Guide to Getting Along: An Open Letter from a Child of Oakland," *San Francisco Magazine*, May 30, 2014, www.modernluxury.com/san-francisco/story/the-gentrifiers-guide-getting-along, Reprinted with permission from San Francisco magazine, DM Luxury LLC originally appearing in the June 2014 issue.

16. Wendell Berry, *The Art of the Commonplace: The Agrarian Essays* (Berkeley: Counterpoint, 2003), 189.

# RITUAL REMIXED

1. Michael Lipka, "Millennials Increasingly Are Driving Growth of 'Nones.'" Pew Research Center, Washington, DC (May 12, 2015), www.pewresearch .org/fact-tank/2015/05/12/millennials-increasingly-are-driving-growth-of-nones, accessed February 23, 2016.

2. U.S. Census Bureau, U.S. Department of Commerce, "Median Age at First Marriage: 1890 to Present," U.S. Census Bureau, Decennial Censuses, 1890 to 1940, and Current Population Survey, Annual Social and Economic Supplements, 1947 to 2015, http://www.census.gov/hhes/families/files/graphics/MS-2.pdf, accessed February 23, 2016.

3. Cherlin et al., "Changing Fertility Regimes," (see Tearing Down the White Picket Fence, note 18).

4. Paul Taylor and George Gao, "Generation X: America's Neglected 'Middle Child,'" Pew Research Center, Washington, DC (June 5, 2014), www .pewresearch.org/fact-tank/2014/06/05/generation-x-americas-neglected-middle-child, accessed February 23, 2016.

5. Jeanette Winterson, *The World and Other Places: Stories* (New York: Vintage Books, 1998).

6. Edmund Ronald Leach, *The Essential Edmund Leach:* Volume 1: *Anthropology and Society*, ed. Stephen Hugh-Jones and James Laidlaw (New Haven, CT: Yale University Press, 2000), 154.

7. Arnold van Gennep, *The Rites of Passage*, trans. Monika B. Vizedom and Gabrielle L. Caffee (Chicago: The University of Chicago Press, 1960).

8. Ibid., 2.

9. Phil Zuckerman, "How Secular Family Values Stack Up," *Los Angeles Times*, January 14, 2015, www.latimes.com/opinion/op-ed/la-oe-0115-zuckerman-secular-parenting-20150115-story.html, accessed February 23, 2016.

10. Ibid.

11. Ibid.

12. George Bonanno, *The Other Side of Sadness: What the New Science of Bereavement Tells Us About Life After Loss* (New York: Basic Books, 2010).

13. Mary Catherine Bateson, *With a Daughter's Eye: A Memoir of Margaret Mead and Gregory Bateson* (New York: Washington Square Press, 1985), 281.

# THE THREAD OF REVELATION

1. Angie Thurston and Casper ter Kuile, "How We Gather," Harvard Divinity School, April 2015, http://howwegather.org, accessed February 23, 2016.

2. Christy Wampole, "How to Live Without Irony," *The New York Times*, November 17, 2012, http://opinionator.blogs.nytimes.com/2012/11/17/how-to-live-without-irony/?_r=0, accessed February 23, 2016.

3. "America's Changing Religious Landscape," Pew Research Center, Washington, DC (May 12, 2015), www.pewforum.org/2015/05/12/americas-changing-religious-landscape, accessed February 23, 2016.

4. Veena Das, "Ordinary Ethics: The Perils and Pleasures of Everyday Life," in *A Companion to Moral Anthropology* ed. Didier Fassin (New York: Wiley-Blackwell, 2012), 133.

5. Thurston and ter Kuile, "How We Gather," (see note 1).

# discussion guide

## FOR THE NEW BETTER OFF

1. Are you "better off" than your parents? How do you define and/ or measure "better off"? Is it about job title or salary? Home ownership? Security? Freedom? Joy?

2. Do you believe the next generation will be "better off" than you are? Why or why not?

3. What did you want to be when you were 8-years-old? Is there any connection between that and what you do now?

4. Have you ever felt like someone—a teacher, a parent, a friend— really saw you and understood what you were best at in the world? Tell the story.

5. What's the best collaboration you've ever had or team you've ever worked on? What made it so enjoyable and effective?

6. Do you feel that you have job security? What does that mean to you?

7. What did you learn about money's value while you were growing up, either from what the adults around you explicitly said or how they interacted with it?

8. What is the minimum amount of money that you believe you need to earn to feel safe? Abundant?

9. Who are the leaders in your own life that you admire most? What

is their relationship like with their families, friends, and neighbors, and how does this factor into your admiration, if at all?

10. For parents, how does your approach to your children differ from what you witnessed and/or experienced from your parents' generation? What is most challenging about parenting? The most rewarding?

11. Are you happy with your relationship to technology, particularly your cell phone? Do you feel "in control" of when you focus on incoming messages and when you focus on the present moment?

12. What is the longest period that you've disconnected in the recent past? What was that like?

13. If your house were on fire and you had time to grab just a few precious things, what would those be and why?

14. What was the happiest, healthiest living arrangement you've ever experienced?

15. How well do you know your neighbors? How well do you wish you knew them? How much do you know about the history of your neighborhood?

16. Was your transition from childhood to adolescence, or adolescence to adulthood, marked by any kind of ritual? Describe it. What affect do you think that ritual had on you?

17. If you are married or have been in the past: if you were to get married today, how might your wedding be different?

18. What is the most meaningful ritual you've ever experienced or witnessed? What made it so meaningful?

19. Where or with whom do you ask the "deeper questions" on a regular basis?

20. After reading *The New Better Off,* do you think of yourself as a success? In what ways do you feel like you are achieving the "new better off" and in what ways do you have room for improvement?

# SELECTED TITLES FROM SEAL PRESS

*The New I Do: Reshaping Marriage for Skeptics, Realists, and Rebels,* by Susan Pease Gadoua & Vicki Larson. $17, 978-1-58005-5451. *The New I Do* takes a groundbreaking look at the modern shape of marriage. Offering actual models of less-traditional marriages, including everything from a parenting marriage to a comfort or safety marriage, the book covers unique options for couples interested in forging their own paths.

*My So-Called Freelance Life: How to Survive and Thrive as a Creative Professional for Hire,* by Michelle Goodman. $15.95, 978-1-58005-2597. *My So-Called Freelance Life* is a how-to guidebook for women who want to avoid the daily grind and turn their freelance dreams into reality. Michelle Goodman, author of *The Anti 9-to-5 Guide* and self-proclaimed former "wage slave," offers tips, advice, how-to's, and everything else a woman needs to pursue a freelance career.

*Not Buying It: Stop Overspending and Start Raising Happier, Healthier, More Successful Kids,* by Brett Graff. $16, 978-1-58005-5918. In *Not Buying It,* Brett Graff, the "Home Economist," separates the truth about what parents need for their kids to succeed from the fiction perpetuated by ads, peer pressure, and internal fear.

*The Anti 9-to-5 Guide: Career Advice for Women Who Think Outside the Cube,* by Michelle Goodman. $14.95, 978-1-58005-186-6. Many women would love to integrate their passion with their career and are seeking advice on how to do just that. Michelle Goodman has written a fun, reassuring, girlfriend-to-girlfriend guide on identifying your passion, transitioning out of that unfulfilling job, and doing it all in a smart, practical way.

*Brokenomics: 50 Ways to Live the Dream on a Dime,* by Dina Gachman. $16, 978-1-58005-5673. Through stories both painfully honest and laugh-out-loud funny that anyone can relate to, Dina Gachman shares the lessons she's learned about how to live large in the cheap seats.

*Maxed Out: American Moms on the Brink,* by Katrina Alcorn. $16, 978-1-58005-5239. Weaving in surprising research about the dysfunction between the careers and home lives of working mothers, as well as the consequences to women's health, Katrina Alcorn tells a deeply personal story about trying to "have it all," and what comes after.

**Find Seal Press Online:**
sealpress.com, @sealpress
Facebook | Twitter | Instagram | Tumblr | Pinterest